D1244404

Churchill:
Retreat from Empire

Churchill: Retreat from Empire

by Raymond A. Callahan

SR Scholarly Resources Inc.
Wilmington, Delaware

© 1984 by Raymond A. Callahan
All rights reserved
First published 1984
Printed and bound in the United States of America

Scholarly Resources Inc.
104 Greenhill Avenue
Wilmington, Delaware 19805

Library of Congress Cataloging in Publication Data
Callahan, Raymond.
  Churchill: retreat from Empire.

  Bibliography: p.
  Includes index.
  1. Churchill, Winston, Sir, 1874–1965.   2. Prime
ministers—Great Britain—Biography.   3. Great Britain—
Politics and government—1936–1945.   4. Great Britain—
Politics and government—1945–1964.   I. Title.
DA566.9.C5C23   1984   941.082′092′4 [B]   83-20285
ISBN 0-8420-2210-4

To Mary Helen

I went to bed . . . conscious of a profound sense of relief . . . I felt as if I were walking with destiny, and that all my past life had been a preparation for this hour and for this trial . . . I was sure I should not fail.

—WINSTON CHURCHILL, recalling
the moment in 1940 when he
became prime minister

Contents

Preface

Some years ago A. J. P. Taylor wrote a clever essay entitled "Daddy, What Was Winston Churchill?" The title captures the difficulty of getting Churchill properly into focus. Was he the greatest war leader of modern times, a popular view still powerful, or the petulant, nagging nuisance so many generals and their biographers have depicted? Professional historians, swamped by the documentary deluge of the last decade, have produced numerous monographs on Britain's role during the Second World War in which the prime minister appears like a Greek deity, irrupting into the story for reasons not always clear to further or thwart some individual, institution, or policy. It is difficult to form a complete and balanced picture of the man and his effect on the course of events. In a sense Churchill has defeated the historians, for it seems very doubtful that any of them will ever write the final word on his remarkable life. His longevity, the variety of incident that filled his years, and the truly staggering volume of evidence to be mastered are only the beginning of the problems. The most daunting obstacle is the quasi-mythic stature he has assumed. The critical evaluation of a national monument is a tricky business, particularly when the nation in question is not the writer's own. In the face of all these difficulties, I have set myself the task of trying to synthesize in a book of moderate size the mass of material now available on Churchill's role at the climactic moment in British history when victory in war led to the death of an empire. Because this is my purpose I have concentrated on the years from 1940 to 1955. Churchill not only led Britain through its greatest war but also lingered on at the center of the national consciousness to cushion, with his massive prestige, the pain as Britain's world position slowly disintegrated. This last service may have been a distinctly ambiguous bequest to his beloved Island Race.

To write a book is to amass obligations. My greatest is to those students, colleagues, and friends who, over the years, have listened to me discuss Churchill's career and, with their questions, sharpened my own perceptions. I began writing this book while on a sabbatical leave from the University of Delaware and finished it during a year spent at the Combat Studies Institute of the U.S. Army's Command and General Staff College as John F. Morrison Professor of Military History. I would particularly like to acknowledge the support I received from the institute's director, Colonel William Stofft, and from Genevieve Hart, who typed, and retyped, with efficiency and good humor. The dedication expresses my greatest debt.

Raymond A. Callahan
University of Delaware

Abbreviations

CCS   Robert Rhodes James, ed., *Winston S. Churchill: His Complete Speeches, 1897–1963*, 8 vols. (New York, 1974).

CR   Winston S. Churchill, *Closing the Ring* (Boston, 1951).

CV2   Randolph S. Churchill, ed., *Winston S. Churchill: Companion Volume II*, 3 parts (Boston, 1969).

CV3   Martin Gilbert, ed., *Winston S. Churchill: Companion Volume III*, 2 parts (Boston, 1973).

CV4   ———, *Winston S. Churchill: Companion Volume IV*, 3 parts (Boston, 1977).

FH   Winston S. Churchill, *Their Finest Hour* (Boston, 1949).

GA   ———, *The Grand Alliance* (Boston, 1950).

GS   ———, *The Gathering Storm* (Boston, 1948).

HF   ———, *The Hinge of Fate* (Boston, 1950).

OB, 2   Randolph S. Churchill, *Winston S. Churchill*, vol. 2, *Young Statesman 1901–1914* (Boston, 1967).

OB, 3   Martin Gilbert, *Winston S. Churchill*, vol. 3, *The Challenge of War, 1914–1916* (Boston, 1971).

OB, 4   ———, *Winston S. Churchill*, vol. 4, *The Stricken World 1916–1922* (Boston, 1975).

OB, 5   ———, *Winston S. Churchill*, vol. 5, *1922–1939* (Boston, 1977).

OB, 6   ———, *Winston S. Churchill*, vol. 6, *Finest Hour, 1939–1941* (London, 1983).

TT   Winston S. Churchill, *Triumph and Tragedy* (Boston, 1953).

For if the trumpet give an uncertain sound,
who shall prepare himself to the battle?
—1 CORINTHIANS, 14:8.

Prologue

London, 26–28 May 1940

Why write *another* book about Winston Churchill? The simplest answer is that his career is a colorful, fascinating story. Another answer is that without Churchill the story of 1940 and the years that followed might have been very different, and that would have meant a much-altered world. Is this too extreme a claim? Consider, as a way of answering that question, three days in London in late May 1940.

Churchill by then had been prime minister for a little more than two weeks, during which an avalanche of military disaster had crashed down on the Anglo-French alliance. German armor reached the channel coast on 19 May, and the Naval Staff at the Admiralty did not think that more than a fraction of the British Expeditionary Force (BEF), cut off together with the cream of the French army in Belgium, could be saved. The French government's morale crumbled as the panzers surged forward. After a twenty-four-hour visit to Paris on 16–17 May, Churchill ordered studies of how Britain could carry on alone against Germany and probably Italy as well. Now, on Saturday, 25 May the French premier, Paul Reynaud, no faint heart but burdened with a divided and increasingly defeatist cabinet, had asked to come over to London for an afternoon conference the following day. Churchill thought it more than likely that Reynaud was coming to inform him that France could not go on.

Such a declaration would mean a crisis for the alliance, but it also would raise a political danger for Churchill. He had become prime minister on a wave of feeling that he alone would fight Adolf Hitler in the way the führer had to be fought. But the House of Commons, the seat of power, was still controlled by those he had defeated. The Conservatives remained the largest party, and the two leading Conservatives sat with Churchill in his newly formed war cabinet. Neville Chamberlain, now lord president of the council and in the grip of the cancer that would kill him within six months, remained potent politically, commanding the fervent loyalty of most of the Conservative rank and file.

When Churchill first entered the Commons chamber as prime minister, a chilly silence greeted him from the Conservative benches, an attitude that persisted for two months. Their cheers were still for Chamberlain. Edward Wood, Viscount Halifax, foreign secretary since 1938, a tall, gaunt former viceroy of India, a devout churchman, and an instinctive appeaser, had been the establishment's candidate to succeed Chamberlain and had almost done so. Chamberlain, and even more Halifax, had never believed in total war against Germany. There was a large, if rather diffuse, body of opinion in favor of a negotiated peace that looked to Halifax as the man who might prevent what it feared most: "Are we really content to bring our own civilization to ruin in order that the Hammer and Sickle shall fly from the North Sea to the Pacific?"[1] The evening before Reynaud arrived, Halifax told the Italian ambassador in London, Giuseppe Bastianini, that Britain did not rule out a "general European settlement," a euphemism for a negotiated peace. If France faltered, might Halifax not push for just such a peace, and if he did, might he not find a base of support in the House, and the country?

A service of intercession and prayer was held in Westminster Abbey on Sunday morning the 26th. Attending it, Churchill sensed a "fear . . . not of death or wounds or material loss, but of defeat and the final ruin of Britain." That fear of impending catastrophe loomed over the war cabinet when it met at Ten Downing Street before Reynaud's arrival. Churchill, Chamberlain, Halifax, and the Labour party leaders, Clement R. Attlee and Arthur Greenwood, were, as Churchill later wrote, "the only ones who had the right to have their heads cut off on Tower Hill if we did not win."[2] At that moment Churchill must have felt rather isolated. Halifax and Chamberlain were uneasy allies, while the depth of Labour support for him was still highly uncertain. Labour had long had reservations about him, and the Labour leadership would have accepted Halifax as prime minister.

Halifax promptly raised the question of negotiations. Churchill brushed it aside, remarking that peace could certainly be had at the price of a German-dominated Europe, a price Britain would not pay. The Labour ministers were silent. The issue of whether to fight on or to get out was now on the table. Churchill then broke off to lunch with Reynaud. The French premier made it clear that his high command had lost all hope. In consequence his position was rapidly weakening. The French cabinet wanted to approach Italy, satisfy Benito Mussolini's Mediterranean ambitions (a decision, incidentally, that would seriously damage British power there), and hope for Italian mediation with Hitler. Reynaud himself had little confidence that such an approach would work and told Churchill he would never sign any terms with the Germans. It was clear, however, that Reynaud's tenure of office might be drawing to a close. Churchill's attempt to put an optimistic gloss on the military situation was brushed aside by the Frenchman, with the remark that nothing would now divert the Germans from realizing their cherished national dream of marching into Paris.

After lunch Churchill met with the war cabinet again at Number Ten and outlined Reynaud's proposal. Halifax was then sent to confer with him about the suggested demarche to Italy and, in fact, reduced the vague French ideas to the proper form for a diplomatic note. Churchill, Attlee, and Chamberlain followed for a brief session with Reynaud, who received the impression that only Halifax was eager to approach Mussolini. He was right—Halifax had adopted the French scheme and told his colleagues that Mussolini surely did not want a German-dominated Europe and therefore would try to persuade Hitler to be reasonable.

The war cabinet convened for the third session that day, this time informally after Reynaud's departure. Halifax argued strenuously for an approach to Hitler via Mussolini. He was sure, he insisted, that it was not in Hitler's interest to demand too much while it was in Mussolini's interest to maintain the European balance, and that the British would be foolish not to make peace on any terms that preserved their independence. Churchill tried to dismiss the issue, arguing that they should see what could be saved by "Operation Dynamo," the Dunkirk evacuation, before making a decision. Urged on by Halifax, he agreed to discuss it further the next day. At no point during the day had he flatly refused to consider negotiations under any circumstances. That same evening at 6:57 the Admiralty officially ordered Dynamo to begin. During the night Churchill cabled Reynaud that the French proposal would be taken up the following day by the war cabinet. His true feelings about the pending discussions are expressed in that cable: ultimate safety for Britain and France lay only in continuing the fight.

Throughout Monday, 27 May, Halifax strenuously pushed the idea of a compromise peace. Churchill, realizing the critical nature of that day's war cabinet meeting, had added Sir Archibald

Sinclair, secretary of state for air, to those attending. Sinclair was the leader of a tiny remnant of the Liberal party, a partner in the national coalition, and his presence thus could be justified for a discussion of peace negotiations. More to the point, perhaps, he had been Lieutenant Colonel Churchill's adjutant in the trenches of Flanders a quarter century before. Sinclair could be counted on to support Churchill's views. The chiefs of staff also had provided him with timely reinforcement. Asked some days earlier to weigh the impact of a French collapse, their brief had subsequently been made more specific by the prime minister. Could Britain fight on alone? Their answer was in fact not so much a reasoned assessment as an act of faith and, for Churchill, an opportune one: "*prima facie* Germany has most of the cards; but the real test is whether the morale of our fighting personnel and civil population will counter-balance the numerical and material advantage which Germany enjoys. We believe it will."[3] Thus fortified Churchill was prepared to deal more vigorously with Halifax.

It was an emotionally charged meeting. Halifax again argued for the French proposal, which by now was as much his as theirs. Mussolini, Churchill asserted—correctly as it turned out—would treat an Anglo-French approach with contempt. The prime minister's determination rings through even the carefully bland minutes kept by the cabinet secretary Sir Edward Bridges: an approach to Mussolini

> would involve us in a deadly danger by ruining the integrity of our fighting position in Great Britain. Even if we mentioned no details in our approach, everyone would know what we had in mind. If the French were not prepared to go on with the struggle, let them give up. . . . Our best help to M. Reynaud was to let him feel that, whatever happened to France, we were going to fight to the end. Our prestige in Europe was now low. The only way we could get it back was by showing the world that Germany had not beaten us. If, after two or three months, we could show that we were still unbeaten, our prestige would return. Even if we were beaten we were no worse off than if we were now to abandon the struggle. Let us therefore avoid being dragged down the slippery slope with France. The whole of the proposed manoeuvre was intended to get us so deeply involved in negotiations that we should be unable to turn back.[4]

Sinclair spoke strongly against Halifax's position, as did Attlee and Greenwood, while Chamberlain contributed little. Halifax became petulant, complaining that Churchill's position had changed from the previous day, and he proceeded to outline a convoluted, hypothetical scenario in which Hitler, although victorious against France, wished to end the war because of "internal weakness in Germany." Would the prime minister still refuse to talk? Churchill, reasonably enough, treated this as a mere debating point, "an issue which was unreal and unlikely to arise." The war cabinet finally agreed to tell Reynaud that they thought an appeal to Mussolini was inopportune. The technical reason was that Franklin D. Roosevelt, in response to an earlier French appeal, was approaching the Italian government to persuade it to remain neutral. Two simultaneous demarches would be confusing, the British claimed. Halifax was deeply angered by the decision. According to his diary, he told Churchill and Greenwood they were talking rot— the idea of fighting to the end particularly offended him—and then apparently threatened resignation. Still in high dudgeon after the meeting, he told his senior civil servant, Sir Alexander Cadogan, the permanent undersecretary at the Foreign Office, "I can't work with Winston any longer." Cadogan warned him not to do anything silly. Halifax then had a conversation with Churchill, who, he reported to Cadogan later over tea, was "very affectionate."[5]* The prime minister could afford to be affectionate. He had won another round.

The victory over Halifax was the only bright note on that terrible Monday. That evening the Belgian army capitulated after two weeks of ceaseless hammering in a mobile war for which it was utterly unprepared. This opened a gaping hole on the left flank of the BEF and jeopardized further its retreat to the Dunkirk perimeter. On the southern flank of the perimeter, the British garrison of Calais had been ordered by Churchill to fight to the last to gain time, a decision he later admitted made him feel physically sick. The end came for Brigadier Claude Nicolson's troops on Monday evening. Both flanks of the retreating BEF were menaced, and during the first full day of Dynamo, only 7,669 men had been evacuated.

Tuesday the 28th saw both the climax of Halifax's drive for negotiations to end what he saw as a lost war, and Churchill's discomfiture of his foreign secretary by some extremely deft political footwork. With the chances of a successful evacuation from Dunkirk

---

*Cadogan was much tougher than his chief. He had confided to his diary on 19 May: "We must fight on whatever happens. I should count it a privilege to be dead if Hitler rules England."[6]

apparently so slender, the prime minister warned the House of Commons to "prepare itself for hard and heavy tidings." At four o'clock that afternoon the war cabinet met, with Sinclair again in attendance. Halifax once again pressed hard for an attempt, using Mussolini as an intermediary, to discover Hitler's terms. Provided those terms safeguarded Britain's independence, the foreign secretary announced he was prepared to make concessions. What, he did not specify, but Chamberlain did. As part of a general peace settlement, Chamberlain declared, he would be willing to make concessions to Italy in Gibraltar or Malta. (Such "concessions" could only have meant Italian control of those cardinal points on Britain's lifeline to India. Realizing this, a Foreign Office official had told a member of the Italian embassy staff on the 25th that only total defeat in war would wrest them from Britain.) Churchill, supported as before by Sinclair, Attlee, and Greenwood, refused to entertain the idea. Halifax, reverting to a remark made the day before by the prime minister, pointed out that in three months' time France might be out of the war and Britain's aircraft factories bombed out of production. The terms offered to Britain might then be far worse. At this point Churchill read a prepared statement that summarized his objections:

> If we once got to the table, we should then find that the terms offered us touched on our independence and integrity. And when, at this point, we got up to leave the Conference Table, we should find that all the forces of resolution which were now at our disposal would have vanished.[7]

Chamberlain refused to drop the issue, drawing from Churchill the flashing observation that "nations which went down fighting rose again but those who surrendered tamely were finished." Greenwood added that the time had not yet come for a final surrender. Stung, Halifax fired back that nothing he had said could be interpreted that way. In this increasingly testy atmosphere, Attlee made his most significant contribution to the debate, characteristically short and pithy. He underlined what Churchill already had said and did so with the authority of the leader of a party that might be in a three-to-one minority in the House, but nonetheless spoke for nearly half the electorate.* When the public realized the true gravity of the situation, Attlee pointed out, "they

---

*In the 1935 general election, the last before the war, the Conservatives had polled 11.8 million votes to 8.3 million for Labour.

would sustain a severe shock. They would have to make a great effort to maintain their morale and there was a great danger that if we did what France wanted, we should find it impossible to rally the morale of the people." By this time it was after six o'clock and the meeting adjourned for one hour.

During the interval Churchill played his trump card. He assembled about twenty-five cabinet rank ministers in his room at the House of Commons, explained to them the gravity of the military situation, "then . . . said, quite casually, and not treating it as a point of special significance: 'Of course, whatever happens at Dunkirk, we shall fight on.'"

> Then occurred a demonstration which, considering the character of the gathering—twenty-five experienced politicians and Parliament men, who represented all the different points of view, whether right or wrong before the war—surprised me. Quite a number seemed to jump up from the table and come running to my chair, shouting and patting me on the back.[8]

When the war cabinet resumed its sitting, Churchill had this to flourish at Chamberlain and Halifax, stating that the cabinet rank ministers had expressed

> great satisfaction when he had told them there was no chance of our giving up the struggle. He did not remember having ever before heard a gathering of persons occupying high places in public life express themselves so emphatically.[9]

The argument was over. Churchill had mobilized again the mood that had swept him into office on 10 May to beat down the last and most momentous effort by the appeasers. Later that night the prime minister sent Reynaud a telegram, turning down finally the French proposal for an approach to Mussolini.*

---

*Establishing what happened in the war cabinet during the "peace crisis" throws interesting light on Churchill's memoirs as a historical source. In *Their Finest Hour*, published nine years after the events it describes, the entire episode is ignored. Churchill mentions the meeting of cabinet rank ministers on 28 May (99–100) and in another place Reynaud's visit and the French proposal for an approach to Mussolini (126–28). The two are not linked and Halifax's role is never mentioned. When the first volume of the history of British foreign policy during the war was published in 1970, followed by the opening of the British records in 1971, it became possible to piece the story together. Why did Churchill distort the record as he did? There are probably not one but several reasons. He was not a vindictive man. He had beaten Halifax. That was enough. Moreover, by 1949 Churchill was himself Conservative party leader and hoped to return to office at the next general election. His party's chances would not be improved by reminding the electorate how defeatist its leadership had been in 1940. If he got back into office, he would have to keep up Britain's end in an

That same evening in Rome, on instructions from Halifax, the British ambassador had a conversation with Mussolini's son-in-law and foreign minister, Count Galeazzo Ciano. Was there, Sir Percy Loraine inquired, any response to the suggestion of Italian diplomatic mediation that had emerged from the Halifax-Bastianini conversation on the 25th? No, said Ciano, because Mussolini had forbidden any further discussion with the allies. (The speed of the German advance in France had spurred *Il Duce* to accelerate his plans for joining the war lest he forfeit his place at the head table of the "victor's banquet.")

At some point on that crowded Tuesday, Churchill dictated a minute that is an apt commentary on the events of the day. A "strictly confidential" document for ministers and senior civil servants, it stated:

> In these dark days the Prime Minister would be grateful if all his colleagues in the Government, as well as important officials, would maintain a high morale in their circles; not minimising the gravity of events, but showing confidence in our ability and inflexible resolve to continue the war till we have broken the will of the enemy to bring all Europe under his domination . . . whatever may happen on the Continent, we cannot doubt our duty, and we shall certainly use all our power to defend the Island, the Empire, and our Cause.[13]

One week later Churchill stood before the House of Commons. The "miracle of Dunkirk" had snatched the BEF back from the brink of annihilation; the emotional impact on a nation that had always believed in its special destiny was enormous. Churchill capitalized

---

Anglo-American alliance, now heavily weighted toward Washington. His memoirs were intended to remind the English-speaking world of how much the victory over Hitler was owed to Britain, and thus provide postwar Britain with moral leverage. Finally, and perhaps most important, was Churchill's artistic intention of giving 1940 a generous and romantic image before history: "These books are *my* story," he snapped at his long-time South African associate, Field Marshal Jan Christiaan Smuts, who ventured some criticism of his memoirs. "If someone else likes to write *his* story, let him."[10]

Churchill wanted his story to depict an heroic England, united in grim determination to destroy the evil Hitler represented or to perish in the attempt. That was the mood of many, perhaps of most, but certainly not of all the British in 1940. Churchill the romantic artist would make no concessions on this point, however, to Churchill the historian. It is obviously rather important when reading Churchill's war memoirs to bear in mind his own warning about them: "I do not describe it as history, for that belongs to another generation. But I claim with confidence that it is a contribution to history. . . ."[11] Or, as his close associate in 1940, Sir Edward Spears, put it: "Churchill in his books always tones down unpleasant incidents . . . the very great should be kind and sometimes forgetful. He has been both."[12]

on and heightened that mood of irrational exultation with the greatest of his speeches:

> . . . we shall fight on the beaches, we shall fight on the landing grounds, we shall fight in the fields and in the streets, we shall fight in the hills; we shall never surrender. . . .

Harold Nicolson wrote in his diary that "even repeated by the announcer it sent shivers . . . down my spine."[14] A young subaltern, just back from Dunkirk, recalled years later:

> I was . . . at Dunkirk and the Nazis kicked my unit to death. We left everything behind when we got out; some of my men didn't even have boots. They dumped us along the roads near Dover, and all of us were scared and dazed, and the memory of the Panzers could set us screaming at night. Then he got on the wireless and said that we'd never surrender. And I cried when I heard him. . . . And I thought to hell with the Panzers, WE'RE GOING TO WIN.[15]*

Of all the men who sat around the cabinet table on those fateful days in late May 1940, only one could have evoked those responses.

Notes

1. Richard Stokes to David Lloyd George, 4 October 1939, quoted by Paul Addison, "Lloyd George and Compromise Peace in the Second World War," in *Lloyd George: Twelve Essays*, ed. A. J. P. Taylor (London, 1971), p. 371. Stokes was a Labour member of Parliament and Lloyd George the great war leader of 1916–18, an indication of the breadth of the compromise peace movement.
2. *FH*, 13. The mood in Westminster Abbey is described in ibid., 99.
3. Quoted in J. R. M. Butler, *Grand Strategy*, vol. 2, *September 1939–June 1941* (London, 1957), 211.
4. The minutes of this meeting are summarized in Sir Llewellyn

---

*Nicolson, writing at the time, correctly noted that Churchill himself had not broadcast his famous defiance. It was delivered in the House of Commons, whose sessions were neither broadcast nor recorded. It was read over the BBC home service by an announcer. For overseas broadcast, a BBC repertory actor, Norman Shelley, imitated Churchill's voice, with the prime minister's approval. The subaltern's recollection of having heard Churchill reflects the widespread belief that he himself went on the air, a warning of the pitfalls of oral history and a testimony to Churchill's grip on the imagination of a generation of his countrymen.

Woodward, *British Foreign Policy in the Second World War* (London, 1970), 1:202–03. The originals are in the Public Record Office (PRO), CAB 65/13, Kew, London.

5. David Dilks, ed., *The Diaries of Sir Alexander Cadogan 1938–1945* (London, 1971), 291, entry for 27 May 1940.

6. Ibid., 287.

7. Minutes of the 28 May 1940 war cabinet meeting are from PRO, CAB 65/13 and have been printed in Patrick Cosgrove, *Churchill at War: Alone 1939–40* (London, 1974), 219.

8. *FH*, 100.

9. Minutes of 28 May 1940 war cabinet meeting, Cosgrove, *Churchill at War*, 220.

10. Lord Tedder tells this story in the preface to his memoirs, *With Prejudice* (Boston, 1966).

11. *GS*, iv.

12. Edward L. Spears, *Assignment to Catastrophe*, vol. 1, *Prelude to Dunkirk* (London, 1954), 100.

13. *FH*, 91–92.

14. Letter from Harold Nicolson to Victoria Sackville-West, 5 June 1940, in Nigel Nicolson, ed., *The Diaries and Letters of Harold Nicolson*, vol. 2, *The War Years 1939–1945* (New York, 1967), 93.

15. Howard LeFay, "Be Ye Men of Valour," *National Geographic* 128 (1965): 159.

He is a man who leads forlorn hopes, and
when the hopes of England become forlorn,
he will once again be summoned to leadership.
—HAROLD NICOLSON, 1931

Chapter One

The Long Preparation

When Harold Nicolson published this remarkable prophecy
in the society magazine *Vanity Fair,* few could have been found to
agree that either part of it was likely to be fulfilled. Britain, although
depression battered, seemed secure (the British spent less on
defense in 1931 than at any time since 1918). As for Churchill, he
was clearly finished: fifty-seven years old, undeniably talented, but
simply not to be trusted. A judgment passed on him fifteen years
before by Herbert H. Asquith, prime minister from 1908 to 1916,
would have commanded far more widespread assent than would
Nicolson's:

> It is a pity . . . that Winston hasn't a better sense of proportion,
> and also a larger endowment of the instinct of loyalty. . . . I
> am really fond of him; but I regard his future with many
> misgivings. . . . He will never get to the top in English politics,
> with all his wonderful gifts; to speak with the tongue of men
> and angels, and to spend laborious days and nights in admin-
> istration, is no good, if a man does not inspire trust. . . .[1]

That sense of distrust had mounted steadily from the moment
Churchill first came to public notice. Grandson of a duke, son of a
brilliant but flawed Conservative demagogue and a beautiful but
negligent American, he had displayed an aggressiveness and naked
ambition that many found distasteful and frightening. After an
adventurous and controversial five-year career as a soldier and war
correspondent, he entered Parliament in 1900 at age twenty-six and
immediately engaged in a quarrel with his party leadership. By
1931 he was regarded with distrust by most of the political world.
Churchill had had three political careers by then, and each had

ended in failure. He had begun the first by switching parties. Elected as a Conservative, Churchill "crossed the floor" of the House of Commons and joined the opposition Liberals in 1904. That the issue on which he did so—whether Britain should remain free trade or go protectionist—was one that deeply divided the Conservative party, did not prevent many Tories from suspecting that personal advantage rather than principle lay behind Churchill's defection.

This suspicion hardened into certainty when, after the Liberals won the 1905 general election, their glittering recruit was made a junior minister (undersecretary of state for the colonies), the first step in a rapid climb that took him to the cabinet as president of the Board of Trade (1908) and then quickly on to the senior cabinet posts of home secretary (1910) and first lord of the Admiralty (1911). The Conservative party detested him as a turncoat, even more so as he made himself one of their most formidable antagonists on the two most emotionally charged political issues of the day: Should the power of the House of Lords be curbed, which it was, and should Home Rule—that is, limited self-government—at last be given to Ireland? He also angered the small but steadily growing Labour party by the enthusiasm with which he deployed 50,000 troops with twenty rounds of live ammunition per man during a major railway strike in August 1911, while suffragettes and their supporters had no more vehement opponent than Churchill. All this overshadowed much of his constructive work. Churchill, although his performance drew mixed reviews, was effective at the Colonial Office, responsible for important social legislation at both the Board of Trade and Home Office, and surprisingly open-minded about prison reform when he served as home secretary (he briefly had been a prisoner of war in South Africa during the Boer War, an experience he never forgot). Civil servants found him unwilling to defer to their judgment—the criteria by which bureaucracy judges ministers—while his colleagues complained that he interfered with the business of other departments.

Churchill could be maddeningly impulsive, oratorical, and prolix, yet his record of solid achievement was already considerable when he went to the Admiralty. There, during the next four years, his first career reached its peak and crashed. He forced on a reluctant body of admirals a long overdue reorganization that gave the Royal Navy a staff system indispensable to the waging of modern war. He improved the conditions of the navy's common seamen, fostered the infant Royal Naval Air Service, and worked indefatigably to prepare the navy, intellectually and materially, for the struggle with Germany he sensed drawing steadily closer. The admirals, like the civil servants, disliked Churchill's habit of ignoring or overriding their professional judgment, institutional wisdom, and established procedures. Often he was wrong in doing so, but the general effect was stimulating and undeniably effective. A verdict on his four years as first lord, delivered on 25 May 1915 by the secretary of state for war, Field Marshal Lord Kitchener (by no means an admirer), has well stood the test of time and critical scholarship: ". . . there is one thing at any rate they cannot take from you. The Fleet was ready."[2]

Kitchener's brusque tribute was a valedictory to Churchill since the office of first lord, into which he had poured all his tremendous energies for four years, had just been abruptly taken from him. That shattering dismissal was the result of Churchill's passionate espousal of "the one imaginative strategic idea of the war on the Allied side . . . one of the most poignant might-have-beens of the First World War."[3] "The Dardanelles" or "Gallipoli" is the customary short designation for this attempt to break the entrenched deadlock on the western front by methods other than those Churchill so aptly christened "sending our armies to chew barbed wire in Flanders." He had been among that small number of perceptive observers who quickly saw that the late autumn stalemate would not be broken by the frontal assaults upon which, with unimaginative obstinacy, British and French generals relied. "I think it quite possible that neither side will have the strength to penetrate the other's line in the Western Theatre although no doubt several hundred thousand men will be spent to satisfy the military mind on this point," he wrote bitterly in late December 1914.[4] Unlike others upon whom this realization also dawned, Churchill was in a position to try to break the stalemate, both by fostering new tactical devices and by looking for strategic alternatives. The former contributed powerfully to the birth of the tank; the latter led to the Dardanelles project.

"There was no novelty about the idea of an armoured vehicle to travel across country and pass over trenches and other natural obstacles while carrying guns and fighting men. Mr. H. G. Wells, in an article written some years ago, practically exhausted the possibilities of imagination in this sphere," Churchill wrote in 1919.[5] In September 1914, when hastily dug German trenches began to interfere with the operations of the armored cars screening the Royal Naval Air Service advanced bases in France, Churchill immediately gave orders for the construction of an armored fighting vehicle capable of crossing trenches. Then a paper was circulated to the cabinet's War Council on 28 December 1914 by its secretary, Colonel Maurice Hankey, which suggested, among many possibilities, the use of armored machine-gun carrying "heavy rollers" to break the deadlock in France. Hankey, in turn, had gotten the idea from Colonel Ernest Swinton, then serving at British headquarters in France, thus proving Churchill's subsequent assertion that "there never was a person about whom it could be said, 'this man invented the tank.'"[6]

Churchill promptly supported Hankey's paper with one of his own to the prime minister in which he urged action. Then on 17 February 1915, Churchill attended a dinner at the duke of Westminster's London home. Several officers who had served with armored cars in France were present. One of them, Major Thomas Hetherington, so fired Churchill's imagination with his vision of "land battleships" that the first lord "went home determined that I would give imperative orders without delay to secure the carrying forward in one form or another of the project in which I had so long believed."[7] This event led directly to a meeting on 20 February—held in Churchill's bedroom because he had influenza—which set up the "Landships Committee" of the Admiralty chaired by Henry Tennyson-d'Encourt, director of Naval Construction. Churchill funded the committee's work with £70,000 of Admiralty money, committed on his own responsibility and outside of normal channels.

From this point on progress, although at times confused, was continuous. Even after Churchill left the Admiralty the project was carried on, saved from departmental hostility at this irregular use of naval resources by Churchill's personal appeal to his successor, Arthur J. Balfour. Six months later on 29 January 1916, the prototype tank, "Big Willie," was successfully tested on Lord Salisbury's private golf course at Hatfield Park north of London. "There are plenty of good ideas," Churchill wrote to Arthur Conan Doyle in October 1916, "if only they can be backed with power and brought into reality."[8] Churchill had described quite well his role in the birth of the tank.

Long before "Big Willie" performed at Hatfield, however, Churchill's search for a different strategy had ruined him, many hoped finally. With the same enthusiasm he displayed in his search for a tactical method that would avoid the slaughter of frontal attacks in France, he threw himself into the search for an amphibious strategy that would turn one of Germany's flanks either by penetrating the Baltic or by striking at Germany's weakest ally, the ramshackle Turkish state. Baltic possibilities first engaged his attention because the Admiralty had looked in this direction since about 1905. By year's end, however, attention in Whitehall began to swing toward the eastern Mediterranean. A stroke against Turkey seemed the opportune strategy: it would bring relief to hard-pressed Serbia and open a channel for resupplying the badly battered Russian armies, preempt a Turkish attack on the Suez Canal, and rally Balkan neutrals to the Entente. The latter would threaten Germany's Austro-Hungarian ally, already hammered by the Russians, and if Austria-Hungary seemed likely to go down, neutral Italy would want to be in on the kill.

The possibilities seemed endless and were the subject of two lengthy papers circulated at the end of December by David Lloyd George, chancellor of the exchequer and second-ranking figure in the government, and Hankey, rapidly moving into the position of bureaucratic grey eminence that would be his for the next quarter century. (Churchill, by contrast, was still arguing at this point for the Baltic offensive that Admiralty opinion favored.) When to these powerful appeals was added a Russian request for a diversion to reduce Turkish pressure in the Caucasus, War Council opinion veered toward action against Turkey. There was no orderly consideration of the project and no careful weighing of operational possibilities. Neither Asquith's temperament nor the governmental machinery available was capable of that. It was clear though that whatever was done would have to be accomplished by the navy. The Turkish capital was accessible by sea, the navy had ships available, the first lord was eager to try, and the War Council was ready for action. At the end of a long, rambling discussion on 13 January 1915, Hankey recorded the remarkably muddled conclusion "that the Admiralty should prepare a naval expedition in February to bombard and take the Gallipoli peninsula, with Constantinople as its objective."[9] From this point on Churchill became the most visible protagonist of the Gallipoli expedition and consequently its principal victim.

The core of the case against Churchill is that he ignored the obvious fact that a navy cannot "take" a land objective like Gallipoli, much less a huge urban area like Constantinople; that in his impetuous enthusiasm he therefore committed the navy to an impossible task; and that, in Alan Morehead's trenchant phrase, he "bamboozled the Admirals."[10] Once Churchill's vivid imagination fastened onto the possibilities, he became the operation's most determined and forceful advocate. In his eagerness he seems never to have grasped that many of the admirals were less enthusiastic than he thought. However, the decision to mount a naval expedition was not his alone but the War Council's. When Churchill began to recognize the need for troops, which he and everyone studying the problem quickly did, the War Office refused to provide any, and the council refused either to override Kitchener or to call off the all-naval attempt to force a way through the Dardanelles. At this point, Churchill could have declined to press the operation further and found ample professional support in the Admiralty, but so convinced was he of both the need and the possibility of victory, that he pressed on, thereby assuring that if failure occurred he would be the obvious scapegoat. On 18 March 1915 the naval assault on the shore batteries and minefields that blocked the passage of the Dardanelles failed. The margin that separated this failure from success was narrow. After a lifetime's study of the Royal Navy, Arthur J. Marder has argued that better management by the local naval commanders before 18 March, or a determined attempt in April after the minesweeping force (whose failure was crucial on 18 March) had been completely reorganized, might very well have carried the fleet through the Dardanelles and on to Constantinople with incalculable consequences.[11]

The mishandling of the first attempt and the failure to make a second were not attributable to Churchill but to the misjudgments and poor staff work of the naval officers concerned. The obvious fact, however, was that the navy had failed. Troops were now belatedly made available, and on 25 April the Gallipoli peninsula was assaulted to open the way for the fleet. Poorly handled, the army's operations were soon stalemated. Inside the two expensively purchased bridgeheads, the deadlock on the western front was reproduced in miniature. As the entire alternative strategy became bogged down in bloody futility on the Gallipoli peninsula, a political crisis, long simmering, erupted in London and buried Churchill.

The upheaval of May 1915 was not simply the result of the Dardanelles failure. Disquiet over both the progress of the war and the Asquith government's willingness to do everything necessary to win had been spreading in both parties. The Conservatives, excluded from office since 1905, ached to regain power. The potential for an explosion was therefore great, but it was a completely unexpected result of the stalemate at the Dardanelles which provided the needed spark. The first sea lord, the professional head of the navy, had been since October 1914 Admiral Lord Fisher, whom Churchill had brought out of retirement when an ugly public outcry forced the German-born Prince Louis of Battenberg to resign. Fisher was seventy-four. A fiery, dynamic man who had accomplished great work in modernizing the navy during his first tenure as first sea lord (1904–10), he was past his best. Fisher "brought such fire and vigor into the production of ships," Churchill later said.[12] But the strains of war and of working with the equally dynamic, opinionated, and younger Churchill were too much for him. Fisher began almost routinely to threaten resignation. Finally, nearly beside himself with anxiety over the drain on British naval resources that a much-prolonged Dardanelles campaign might become, he sent in a resignation that he really meant early on 15 May. Fisher's departure, which he took good care to see that the Conservative leadership learned about immediately, opened the floodgates.

Asquith preserved both his position and Liberal dominance in the cabinet but at the price of coalition with the Conservatives and at the sacrifice of several Liberal ministers particularly obnoxious to them. Among the proscribed, Churchill stood first. He fell easily because his political base was more fragile than he had ever imagined. Many Liberals had never been convinced that his conversion was genuine. As for the Conservatives, they had a long score to settle with the renegade. A well-informed eyewitness, Lord Beaverbrook, a Canadian millionaire turned British newspaper proprietor and Conservative political fixer, later perceptively analyzed Churchill's position and fate:

> His attitude from August 1914 onwards was a noble one, too noble to be wise. He cared for the success of the British arms, especially in so far as they could be achieved by the Admiralty, and for nothing else. His passion for this aim was pure, self-devoted, and all-devouring. He failed to remember he was a politician and as such treading a slippery path; he forgot his political tactics. . . . He thought of himself . . . as a National Minister secure of support from all men of goodwill . . . it was the error of a big-minded, though self-willed, man . . . the Tory opposition did not regard him as a National Minister at all, but cherished against him a resentment born of pre-war political differences . . . belief in the naval and military experts and intense opposition to Churchill were dominant articles in their creed.[13]

Churchill himself later expressed it differently, ignoring his own political mistakes and concentrating on the flaws in the central direction of the war: "I was ruined for the time being in 1915 over the Dardanelles and a supreme enterprise cast away, through my trying to carry out a major and cardinal operation of war from a subordinate position. Men are ill advised to try such ventures."[14]

So ended Churchill's first meteoric political career. He had established himself as formidable, both in prose and oratory, with a great appetite for work and a matching capacity to handle it, and as a man of great courage, moral and physical. But he was too ambitious, too insensitive to his impact on others, too aggressive, and, above all, too poor a politician to survive his first major setback. It is only necessary to compare Lloyd George's surefooted advance in 1914–15 toward ever greater power (and Lloyd George was perhaps the only Liberal hated more than Churchill by the Tories) with Churchill's increasing isolation to determine what qualities at this stage of his career Churchill lacked. The final word, however, belongs to the highly political admiral who destroyed him. Writing to the chairman of the Royal Commission that investigated the Dardanelles failure, Fisher declared: "I backed him up till I resigned. *I would do the same again!* He had courage and imagination! *He was a war man!*"[15]

All his life Churchill suffered from bouts of serious depression, "black dog" he called it. The result, it has been suggested, of hereditary factors compounded by an unhappy childhood, it swept over him when he was deprived by personal defeat of the stimulus of work he loved.[16] The weeks after his departure from the Admiralty were such a time. "I thought he would never get over the Dardanelles," his wife said later. "I thought he would die of grief."[17] In this mood of despair, he discovered painting, at first a therapy and then a life-long relaxation for a man who permitted himself few.[18] It was fortunate that he had an interest to distract him from the continuous downward movement of his fortunes.

Asquith, unwilling to sacrifice Churchill completely, had made him chancellor of the duchy of Lancaster. The curious medieval title was, in fact, a sinecure, an appointment virtually without duties and therefore offering no opportunity even for parliamentary speeches. Churchill continued to sit in the War Council, now renamed the Dardanelles Committee, but his voice counted for little, especially with the skeptical and unfriendly Tories led by Andrew Bonar Law who had a deep aversion to him. Churchill tried to keep alive the vision of a strategic alternative in the east, but when an attempt, initially promising, to break the deadlock on Gallipoli in August was turned into a fiasco under General Sir Ian Hamilton's hesitant direction, opinion in London swung toward getting out. Churchill fought hard against this trend. He was convinced not only that his future turned on vindicating the expedition but also that the eastern Mediterranean offered an alternative, and perhaps the only one, to bloody futility in France, where a British attack at Loos in the early autumn cost 50,000 casualties and gained no ground. By mid-October, however, he was clearly losing and becoming desperate, writing frantically in a memorandum for the cabinet that "no more terrible decision than the evacuation of the Gallipoli peninsula and the abandonment of the attempt to take Constantinople has been wrung from a British Government since the loss of the American colonies."[19] Early in November, with evacuation inevitable, the Dardanelles Committee metamorphosed itself into the War Committee, and Churchill was dropped from its membership. He immediately resigned from the government and left for army service in France, a forty-year-old reserve lieutenant colonel and back-bench member of Parliament.

For the next six months Churchill served at the front, most of the time effectively commanding the Sixth Battalion of the Royal Scots Fusiliers. Active service gave him an outlet for his energies and helped shake off depression, but it certainly did not reconcile him to his fate. He was haunted by the great lost opportunity and bitter at his exclusion from the direction of the war. "He suffered tortures when he thought lesser men were mismanaging the business," Beaverbrook observed.[20] But if he could no longer hope to shape strategy, he could at least try to encourage more rational tactics. In "Variants of the Offensive," written after a few weeks in France, Lieutenant Colonel Churchill tried to convince British headquarters of the merits of the tank as well as the lavish use of shields, trench mortars, and siege techniques resembling those of the seventeenth century. "Any operation on the Western Front is justified if we take at least a life for a life."[21] A cold-blooded statement perhaps, until it is remembered that at Loos the ratio was 2.5 to 1 in favor of the Germans.

However exhilarating Churchill found frontline command ("It is one long holiday for me," he wrote to his wife[22]), there was never any doubt that he would return to the political arena. In May 1916, when his battalion was amalgamated with another, he seized the occasion to return to London, although the following months were as depressing as those immediately after his dismissal from the Admiralty the previous year. He sat for a portrait by Sir William Orpen. "I had nothing whatever to do . . . almost my only occupation was to sit to the artist," he recalled.[23] Orpen's portrait catches

Churchill's mood of despair. "Orpen . . . used to speak of the misery in his face," Churchill's close friend Brendan Bracken later remarked. "He called him the man of misery. Winston was so sure then that he would take no further part in public life."[24] His unhappiness was deepened by the continual necessity of defending his role in the Dardanelles expedition, which he did so obstinately and obsessively that he confirmed the prevalent idea that he alone had been the responsible party. A less driven man would have realized the virtual impossibility of setting the record straight under wartime conditions. "I am learning to hate," he wrote to his brother after learning that Asquith would not allow him to develop a full defense in public before Parliament.[25]

Gradually events came to Churchill's rescue, and he began to lay the foundation for a new career. The war dragged on, exposing the inadequacies of Asquith's leadership. The failure of the Dardanelles expedition (the evacuation of the Gallipoli peninsula, completed on 8 January 1916, had been the only flawless military operation in the whole enterprise) had confirmed the grip of western front generals and their political backers on British strategy. The apotheosis of the "westerners" was the terrible Somme offensive, launched by BEF Commander Sir Douglas Haig on 1 July 1916. Sixty thousand casualties made that day the costliest not only in British army history but also in the entire war. Haig, undaunted, pushed on toward the 420,000 casualties he would pay by November for a few square miles of ground. At this obstinate persistence, Churchill leveled a powerful critique early in August, circulated to the cabinet by one of his few friends in the Conservative party, Sir Frederick Smith, the attorney general. The British plan had ignored the value of surprise, and the attack had not forced a substantial commitment of German reserves, while Haig had lost, and was continuing to lose, between two and three times as many men as the Germans, Churchill insisted. Moreover, "we have not conquered in a month's fighting as much ground as we expected to gain in the first two hours . . . nor are we making for any point of strategic or political consequence."[26]

Churchill hoped his paper would lead the cabinet to reconsider its support for the offensive, but it was the weather that finally closed down operations over three months later. Churchill marked its close with another memorandum, this one brought before the cabinet by a Liberal colleague, Edwin Montagu. "Mechanical Power in the Offensive" argued that the Somme proved the Allies had to find either "another theatre or another method." Accepting that the Dardanelles failure foreclosed the former, Churchill concentrated on arguing for the latter and sketched an offensive that would open with a night attack, spearheaded by tanks and mechanized artillery and followed by infantry whose mobility would be sustained by supplies carried in tracked vehicles.[27] This attempt to apply imagination and common sense to the tactical dilemma of the western front was what Sir Abe Bailey, the South African mining magnate, had in mind when he wrote to Lloyd George in early December: "I shall be awfully sorry if Winston's brain and push have to be left on the shelf for I know and so do you that he is full of ideas, and good ones too."[28] Lloyd George was well aware of Churchill's gifts, but he was conscious as well that he was deeply hated by the Conservatives, and it was with Tory support that Lloyd George became prime minister on 6 December 1916. In his coalition government there was initially no place for Churchill.

Churchill's abilities, however, were too great to be ignored completely. Moreover, Lloyd George realized the danger of leaving an ambitious and talented figure to sulk in a state of dissatisfaction where he could easily become the focus and spokesman for the government's enemies. By July 1917, Lloyd George felt strong enough to brave Conservative wrath by bringing Churchill back into the government as minister of munitions. And wrath there certainly was. "I am seriously afraid that such an appointment would strain to breaking point the Unionist Party's loyalty to you," Sir George Younger, the Conservative party chairman, wrote to the prime minister.[29] Conscious of the degree of Tory hostility toward him and of the belief voiced by another Tory grandee, Lord Derby, that he could not "occupy a comparatively minor position and do his own work without interfering with other people's," Churchill walked warily, conscious that he had received a chance, not likely to recur, to rebuild his career.[30] A remarkable memorandum of July 1917, written ten days before Churchill entered the government, which urged an offensive naval strategy aimed at seizing an island off the north German coast and discussed tank landing craft and the creation of an artificial harbor similar to the "Mulberries" of 1944, was the last of its kind for the balance of the war.[31] Bearing in mind the *Times* editorial on the morrow of his appointment, which thundered that the country was "in no mood to tolerate even a forlorn attempt to resuscitate amateur strategy," Churchill carefully minded his own shop for the next fifteen months.[32]

The Ministry of Munitions had been established in 1915.

Lloyd George had been the first incumbent, and by the time Churchill took over it was a going concern, although Churchill made significant improvements in its management. The administrative burden was heavy, but the ministry had no voice in making strategic policy, confining itself to supply what the service departments ordered. This doubtless was difficult for Churchill to bear, but in his chastened mood he was more cautious than ever before or afterward about venturing beyond his area of departmental responsibility. His ministry's work in certain areas, however, gave him an opportunity to address themes dear to him. In late October 1917, as Haig's terrible Passchendaele offensive ground to an end (July–November: British casualties 324,000, German 202,000; British advance, four miles), Churchill wrote a massive paper for the war cabinet. Ostensibly simply a request for guidance in shaping the 1918 munitions program, it reprised some of Churchill's favorite themes: a more flexible tactical approach and the untapped capabilities of the tank. A new note was his stress on the possibility of isolating a battlefield by concentrated use of tactical air power, which would finally be done at Normandy in 1944.

Tank production brought Churchill back into continuous contact with the revolutionary weapon whose early development he had fostered, and by the end of 1917, he was already arguing that the cavalry, up to this time useless in France, should discard the obsolete horse and mechanize wholesale.[33] In September 1918 he pointed out to Lloyd George how relatively bloodless tank-supported advances were: "The moral appears to be training and tanks. . . ."[34] From his days at the Admiralty he had been an enthusiast for air power, an enthusiasm reinforced by his belief that it could help break the trench deadlock. But he was careful to qualify his support for air power as a road to victory: "It is not reasonable to speak of an air offensive as if it were going to finish the war by itself. It is improbable that any terrorisation of the civil population which could be achieved by air attack would compel the government of a great nation to surrender. . . ."[35] Such comments on tanks and air power, however intrinsically interesting, were a far cry from the wide-ranging memoranda on a variety of issues he had produced as first lord. This careful self-denial had its reward. By war's end he had gone a considerable distance toward reestablishing himself in the political world.

His rehabilitation was sealed when Lloyd George made him secretary of state for war and air in January 1919. The general election following the armistice had left the prime minister completely dependent on Conservative support, and the promotion of a "coalition Liberal" like Churchill was a defensive measure as well as a recognition of Churchill's abilities. The new war secretary could never become, lacking any political base of his own, a rival to Lloyd George. Churchill was in a lonely position, as dependent on Lloyd George as he had been on Asquith in May 1915. It was not a happy situation and one from which Churchill was resolved to escape. Over the next five years he moved steadily to the Right until he found himself back in the Conservative party, not entirely a welcome prodigal son.

This rightward movement was not totally a matter of opportunism. The years immediately after the war were a time of reorientation in British politics. A new force, the Labour party, was displacing the riven and fading Liberals, while new challenges abroad—revolutionary Russia and an upsurge of nationalism in the empire—replaced Germany. On these issues Churchill took essentially conservative positions which altered little for the remainder of his life. Given to brooding over history, he sensed dark times coming for those causes he cared about deeply: "present civilisation," the traditional social order, and British world power. He gave voice to these fears on 19 November 1918 in a cabinet memorandum entitled "The Unfinished Task," in which he argued that "it is ridiculous to suppose that the war is over because the fighting between the main armies has stopped. . . . We have got to make as great an effort in the next six months as we should have made if the war had been going on at full blast: indeed in some ways we have got to make a greater effort."[36] This argument for consolidating the fruits of victory was out of joint with the mood of postarmistice Britain, but Churchill never accepted that. On the fourth anniversary of the armistice he was still calling for "intense, concerted and prolonged efforts among all nations" to avert "further and perhaps even greater calamities."[37]

Foremost among those calamities was the spread of bolshevism—"the poison peril from the east," he dubbed it. Closely bound with this was Churchill's reaction to the emergence of the Labour party as a serious contender for office. As was the case with the Dardanelles expedition, intervention in the Russian civil war did not originate with Churchill. It began with a desperate search by the Allies in 1917–18 for a way to keep an eastern front in existence and a million German troops away from France. The Russians, willing to oblige them, in fact really wanted to fight their domestic opponents. What began as a strategic expedient turned, after the armistice, into an "obligation of honour" to the "Whites." A large body of British opinion, especially in the Conservative party, was strongly favorable to crushing bolshevism. Churchill, throwing himself into the crusade against the revolution with his customary energy and rhetoric colorful even for him, became the most visible spokesman for this point of view.

As secretary of state for war, Churchill was also in a good position to give reality to the sentiment for intervention. It rapidly became clear that British troops could not be used. Public opinion— and the troops themselves—would not tolerate it, and Churchill recommended early in 1919 that all British troops be brought out of Russia. He fought throughout 1919 and into 1920, however, to give the Whites all they needed, whether in funds, supplies, war surplus equipment, or volunteers to help with specialist advice. His activities and his ferocious oratory marked him as the most prominent interventionist and target of all who disliked the policy. But there can be no doubt that what he did and said followed from one of the most strongly held convictions of his life: "I regard the Bolshevik danger as the most formidable which has ever threatened civilisation," he wrote in January 1920. "It is a movement which will deluge in blood every country to which it spreads, and if it triumphed it would extinguish, perhaps for long centuries, the whole prosperity and genius of mankind." Several months later he added: "I do not believe there will be any real peace in the world so long as the Bolshevik tyranny endures. . . ."[38] Lloyd George, whose respect and affection for Churchill did not exclude an occasional malicious dig, once explained Churchill's antibolshevism by remarking that the ducal blood in Churchill rebelled at the liquidation of the Russian imperial family.

The shock of the revolution, however, fell not only on Churchill the aristocrat but also on a passionate believer in the gradualism of parliamentary democracy: "These men did not overthrow the Tsar. . . . What they overthrew was the Russian Republic. What they destroyed was the Russian Parliament."[39] The European in him feared the spread of communism westward; the British patriot was alarmed over its infiltration into an already restive empire. If Churchill's forebodings about the long-term consequences of the Russian Revolution were accurate enough, his belief that the heterogeneous collection of White armies and fragile, newly born states on Russia's borders could be forged into a weapon able to smash the revolution was badly mistaken, wishful thinking in fact. Furthermore, if Churchill regarded bolshevism with a sincere horror, others, equally sincere, looked upon the Russian Revolution with an interest and sympathy similar to that with which British reformers had initially greeted the 1789 revolution in

France. The most important of these "others" was the Labour party.

Churchill's attitude toward the British working class, the trade union movement, and the Labour party was complex. His upbringing and education taught him little about the life of the majority of Britons. When he began to learn, it was with a genuine sense of shock and pity. A newly elected Tory, he dined at the Athenaeum in December 1901 with the Liberal elder statesman, Lord Morley, who advised him to read Seebohm Rowntree's work on urban degradation, *Poverty: A Study of Town Life,* which had just been published. So impressed was Churchill that he wrote a lengthy article summarizing Rowntree's arguments and urging government action.[40] His social concerns over the next decade were not merely an attempt to establish his credentials with the Liberals but equally the effect on a sympathetic imagination of the discovery of the squalor and greyness in which most British lives were passed. Walking through the streets of Manchester in January 1906, he remarked to a companion: "Fancy living in one of these streets—never seeing anything beautiful—never eating anything savoury—*never saying anything clever.*"[41] But the compassion, powerful and sincere, stopped well short of any fundamental changes in British society. Churchill wanted to see that society improved and made more humane but reacted with hostility to any action he took to be a threat to its basic structure. In holding these views he was no different from most other Liberals and virtually all Tories. The vigor of his actions and the language with which he accompanied them were different, however. His reaction to the railway strike of 1911 showed that he would move forcefully against what he saw as challenges to the government and the order it represented.

The suspicion of Churchill, born then in Labour, was never thereafter entirely eradicated. After going to the Admiralty, Churchill had little time and less inclination to deal with social problems. When he went to the Ministry of Munitions, the pattern of wartime labor relations had been set, both by circumstances and by Lloyd George. Only when he became war secretary in 1919, in an atmosphere of postwar unrest whose effect on him was heightened by his concerns about the spread of communism, did he come again into direct conflict with a now much strengthened Labour party and trade union movement. The British sympathizers with the Russian Revolution and opponents of intervention were to be found mostly on the Left. In a January 1920 speech devoted to denunciation of bolshevism, Churchill lashed out as well at "would-be imitators in this country" and pronounced the Labour party "quite unfitted for the responsibility of government." He qualified this condemnation by adding "at this period in their development," but that did little if anything to mitigate the sting of the remark.[42] Eight months later during another defense of his Russian policies, he referred to that party as a "subversive cause."[43] Even in the "Red Scare" atmosphere prevailing in western Europe and the United States in 1919–20, his attacks were intemperate. The emergence of Labour was the cardinal fact in British domestic politics after 1918 and one for which Churchill was ill prepared. Already suspect on the Left, he turned suspicion into open hostility. Even after the German danger had driven Churchill and Labour together again in the 1930s, misgivings remained.

In some ways these doubts were well grounded because Churchill was never happy with the replacement of the political world of his youth by mass politics. As late as the 1930s he was advocating the restoration of plural voting. His sympathetic concern for the distressed, his romantic regard for the "British nation," and his deep devotion to parliamentary traditions alone prevented him from becoming a complete reactionary in domestic politics. But, as one editorial at the time of his death commented, he failed "to comprehend the basic aspirations of British socialism. . . ."[44] To that extent he was, from 1918 on, a man out of joint with the mood of his country.

Churchill's hostility toward bolshevism abroad and socialism at home had its parallel in his reaction to nationalism in the empire. He had grown up with the late Victorian surge of empire building. He was eight when Britain occupied Egypt, eleven when Gordon fell at Khartoum, and present when Gordon was avenged at Omdurman in 1898. The empire he had known as a young man always would seem to him part of the natural order of things, beneficent and an indispensable prop of British power and greatness. Yet his entire political career would be played out in an era of challenge and dissolution for imperial rule. Churchill's reaction to colonial nationalism was similar to his response to the self-assertion of the British working class. Necessary concessions should be made from a position of strength and always within the framework of the existing order of things, in this case an enduring link with Britain. The proof that this was possible lay, for imperialists of Churchill's generation, in the reconciliation of the defeated Boer republics, a process in which Churchill was an active participant as colonial undersecretary (1906–08). Jan Smuts, the shrewd Afrikaner lawyer, guerrilla chief, and politician, became one of Churchill's most trusted confidants, symbolizing what creative imperial statesmanship had achieved. (That most Boers were less reconciled to the British connection than Smuts, and that the Union of South Africa had been created at the price of surrendering Britain's ability to protect South Africa's blacks, was not fully grasped at the time, or for long after.)

If self-government within the empire was the appropriate path for Canada, white South Africa, Australia, and New Zealand, Churchill's reaction to the unrest that swept the nonwhite empire after 1918 was quite different. It may seem curious to discuss the case of Ireland here, but to many Englishmen the other island had always presented problems more related to those of the empire's backward possessions than to those of Canada, for example. Faced with an Irish guerrilla campaign in 1919–20, Churchill, as war secretary, sponsored the primitive and self-defeating counterinsurgency campaign conducted by the controversial "Black and Tans." When in early 1921 he moved to the Colonial Office, his perspective on Irish matters changed, particularly since repression was not working and was unpopular at home and abroad. He eventually played a constructive part in the negotiations that led to the Anglo-Irish treaty of December 1921 and to the emergence of the Irish Free State. In the process he was genuinely impressed by the Irish guerrilla leader Michael Collins, seeing in him an Irish Smuts. When Collins was killed in the Irish civil war that followed Britain's withdrawal, Churchill's distress was sincere, for he thought that the Irish had proved, like the Boers, that self-government alone would preserve the imperial connection. But if Churchill conceded that the South African analogy applied to Ireland, there was no question of extending it to the nonwhite empire. Here the doctrine of "unfitness to rule" prevailed absolutely.

The storm centers of nationalism after 1918, Ireland apart, were India and Egypt. Churchill believed Britain derived important strategic advantages from both, and that good government under British auspices was preferable to self-government for the empire's nonwhites who were not ready to manage their own affairs. Churchill's racial attitudes were those of enlightened late Victorian imperialism. He believed Britain had a duty and a right to act as trustee for less developed peoples. Concessions to Egyptian nationalism he denounced as a recipe for throwing a country away. But it was India that really aroused him. When the crucial decision was taken by Lloyd George's government in 1917 to announce dominion status as Britain's goal in India—that is, self-government on the Canadian or South African model—Churchill was minister of munitions and on his best behavior.

After the war, however, as the 1917 pledge was embodied in legislation, he made clear his opposition. "An idea was prevalent," he told a meeting of ministers in February 1922, ". . . that we were fighting a rearguard action in India, that the British *raj* was doomed, and that India would gradually be handed over to the Indians. He was strongly opposed to that view of the situation. On the contrary we must strengthen our position in India. . . . He believed that opinion would change soon as to the expediency of granting democratic institutions to backward races which had no capacity for self-government."[45] His most revealing comment on the Indian question was reserved for a "very private" letter. Writing in September 1922 to the wife of the governor of Bengal, Lady Lytton, with whom, as Miss Pamela Plowden, Lieutenant W. L. S. Churchill, 4th Hussars, had been deeply in love twenty-five years before, Churchill told her:

> Ireland . . . is I think going to save itself. They are a proud and gifted race. . . . *Responsibility* is a wonderful agent when thrust upon competent hands. I do not needless to say apply the reasoning to the East. I am sure dear Pamela you will do your best to keep the Flag flying and the prestige and authority of the white man undiminished. Our true duty in India lies to those 300 millions whose lives and means of existence would be squandered if entrusted to the chatterboxes who are supposed to speak for India today.[46]

From this attitude he did not budge for twenty years and in many ways never abandoned it.

Churchill's view of British rule in India as an unbreakable trust ignored not merely Indian nationalism but also growing uncertainty in Britain itself about the empire. E. M. Forster's *A Passage to India* was being written even as Churchill opened his mind to Pamela Lytton. Published in 1924, "of all the novels written about the Empire, except possibly *Kim,* this was the most influential . . . anyone who read it found that the scenes of imperial life never seemed quite the same again."[47] What always presented itself to Churchill as a glorious duty began to seem to many in Britain irrelevant, even rather embarrassing. Perhaps it was fortunate that talk in 1920 of making Churchill viceroy of India came to nothing, although it is possible that in contact with Indian reality his views would have changed. He did, however, have one personal proconsular moment, and one that made it even harder for him to believe that British power was weakening. In early 1921, Lloyd George asked Churchill to take over the Colonial Office. The rationalization of Britain's postwar tangle in the Middle East thus fell to him, and he presided over the last major extension of British imperial power.

With T. E. Lawrence as an adviser, he created a Middle East department within the Colonial Office and then proceeded to Cairo where he presided over a mammoth conference (March–April 1921) that gave to this vast new sphere of British paramountcy the shape it would retain for twenty-five years. Many of the ideas and most of the detail were contributed by subordinates but the driving force was Churchill's, and it is curious that he virtually ignored the entire episode in his memoirs.[48] The client states of Iraq and Transjordan were created, assuaging the uneasy consciences of the Arabophiles who thought that Britain had failed to redeem its wartime promises to the Arabs. Despite this Churchill was not overly enthusiastic about the Arabs. His imagination was engaged by another of Britain's wartime commitments, for he was—and remained—one of the firmest of Britain's "Gentile Zionists," the supporters of the Jewish National Home in Palestine promised in the 1917 Balfour Declaration. He made it clear to a delegation of Palestinian Arabs in Jerusalem in March 1921 that the British government meant to stand by its pledge to Zionism.[49] Churchill had first come into contact with Theodor Herzl's dream of a Jewish state when he was a Liberal member of Parliament for Northwest Manchester (1906–08) where many Liberal activists were Jewish. The romantic in him responded to the dream of a Jewish return to Palestine, and the imperial strategist believed the Jewish National Home, whatever its final form, would always be a British ally because it would always need British support. Looking over his Middle Eastern fief, Churchill might well have thought that there was no reason to despair of the empire.

Churchill's Colonial Office successes, however, were overshadowed and swallowed by a crisis that destroyed not only his second career but also the Lloyd George government. Since the armistice of 1918 the prime minister had consistently supported the Greek vision of a Greater Greece which would incorporate a large section of Turkish Asia Minor, a policy many, including Churchill, had disliked. The Greek adventure collapsed in August 1922 with the defeat of the Greek armies by the resurgent forces of Turkish nationalism led by Mustafa Kemal. As the Turkish forces surged toward the "neutral zone," covering Constantinople and its approaches, still garrisoned by an allied force, Lloyd George tried to save the wreckage of his policy by ordering the Turks to stop. He was now strongly supported by Churchill, reacting as always to a challenge to British power and fearful that triumphant Turkish nationalism would threaten the structure of British influence in the Middle East. A war-weary country was startled to find itself apparently on the verge of a new conflict with Turkey. The rank-and-file Conservatives, long restive with Lloyd George, seized the occasion to revolt against the prime minister and most of their own leaders, rallied by Bonar Law and an obscure junior minister named Stanley Baldwin.

Without Conservative support, the Lloyd George coalition could not carry on. The government resigned and a general election ensued. In the midst of this chaos, Churchill was stricken with appendicitis. His own reelection campaign in Dundee, which he had represented for fifteen years, had to be carried out largely by proxy. His rapport with his constituency was not good; he was no better at the small arts of politics than he had been before 1915. When the results were declared, Churchill was out; Dundee returned a Prohibitionist (the only one ever elected as such in Britain) and a Labourite, E. D. Morel, a wartime conscientious objector. For the first time in twenty-two years Churchill was out of both Parliament and office. The Liberal party, reduced to a shadow of its former self, was unlikely to provide him with a vehicle for a return to either.

Indeed many wondered if Churchill would or should come back. He himself was magnanimous about his defeat: "If you saw the sort of lives that Dundee folk live you would admit they have many excuses."[50] But the "warmonger" label was now firmly affixed, along with "anti-labour." Churchill had always sensed the ambivalence in himself about war. "Much as war attracts me and fascinates my mind with its tremendous situations—I feel more deeply every year what vile and wicked folly and barbarism it all is," he wrote to his wife while watching the German army on maneuvers in 1909.[51] On the eve of war he told her "everything tends towards catastrophe and collapse. I am interested, geared up and happy. Is it not horrible to be built like that? The preparations have a hideous fascination for me."[52] Lloyd George once remarked that Churchill had been waiting all his life for a war to break out, a half truth that by 1922 had become, however, the conventional wisdom about him. Fisher's verdict that *he was a war man*" seemed to say it all. "The tendency to rush into warlike enterprises has been the bane of his life," the *Observer* wrote three days after his defeat, "and unless he corrects that bias all else will be in vain."[53]

Amid the pressures of war, Churchill's obvious gifts could not be wasted, as Lloyd George clearly saw in 1917. The 1922 election, however, expressed a British longing for a "return to normalcy." Perhaps in such a world the fears Churchill aroused would more than offset his obvious talents. On his forty-eighth birthday, two weeks after his defeat at Dundee, Churchill was observed by a fellow Liberal: "Winston was so down in the dumps, he could scarcely speak the whole evening. He thought his world had come to an end—at least his political world. I thought his career was over."[54]

The rebound from despondency was swifter than in 1915, perhaps because of the easier circumstances of his private life. Although he always lived well, Churchill also always had to earn his own way. His parents spent lavishly, and he inherited little. In the two years before he entered Parliament in 1900, he had put together a capital sum of £10,000 from journalism and lecturing. Thereafter he depended on investments, income from writing, and his ministerial salary. Clementine Hozier, whom he married in 1908, brought him great happiness but no money. But in 1921 he unexpectedly inherited, from a distant relative, an estate in northern Ireland worth about £4,000 per year. The following year he purchased Chartwell in Kent and began to convert it into the home of his heart. His projected war memoirs, which he started to compose in the Riviera sunshine shortly after his defeat, had already brought in a £5,000 publisher's advance by February 1923. Exclusion from Parliament was painful, but the black depression of 1915–16 did not return.

In any case he did not expect to stay away from politics long. In November 1923 at West Leicester he fought a by-election as a Liberal. It was a hectic, rowdy campaign with Churchill continually heckled, especially about the Dardanelles, and on one occasion snapping back: "What do you know about that? The Dardanelles might have saved millions of lives. Don't imagine I am running away from the Dardanelles. I glory in it."[55] He trailed the victorious Labour candidate by over four thousand votes. It was his last appearance as a Liberal. When he stood again at another by-election, this time in the Abbey division of Westminster in March 1924, it was as an independent anti-Socialist with substantial Conservative support. He lost to the Conservative candidate by only forty-three votes. When he tried once again at Epping in the October 1924 general election, he billed himself as a "Constitutionalist" and stood with the full support of the Conservative Central Office and party machine. This time, benefiting by a Conservative landslide, he won with a 10,000-vote majority. Not only was he back in Parliament, but he also was immediately invited by Baldwin to join the government as chancellor of the exchequer, traditionally the second-ranking cabinet post. Behind this astonishing reversal of Churchill's fortunes lay the confused state of British politics after the fall of Lloyd George.

The Conservative government, formed in October 1922 by Bonar Law, lacked many leading Conservatives who had been disqualified by their membership until the last minute in the Lloyd George coalition. This forced Bonar Law to fill his cabinet with relative unknowns. One of them, Baldwin, an important figure in Lloyd George's downfall, became chancellor of the exchequer and was therefore in a key position to succeed Bonar Law when illness forced his retirement in May 1923. Most political leaders have their private demons, and Baldwin's was Lloyd George, who he believed had demeaned public life. Having helped to destroy Lloyd George, Baldwin thereafter feared that he might stage a comeback. This fear led him into an ill-judged general election in the autumn of 1923 in an attempt to preempt ground that the Welshman might otherwise occupy. The result was a near deadlock, in which Asquith's Liberals held the balance and put the first Labour government in British history into office (January–November 1924). It is against this background that Churchill's return to office must be viewed. Like Lloyd George before him, Baldwin saw the wisdom of harnessing Churchill's talents to the government lest they be employed against it. He saw as well that a Churchill within the Conservative fold deprived Lloyd George of a potential ally (for the same reason Baldwin also placated the "Conservative coalitionists" left out in 1922). Finally, with the defeat of Labour the key issue, Churchill's credentials were good; he could not be faulted there by even the most rabid Tory.

As for Churchill, he was certainly surprised to be offered the exchequer but soon recovered. His father, Lord Randolph Churchill, had held the same office and his mother had kept the chancellor's official robes after his resignation for Winston's eventual use. The issue that had originally severed Churchill from the Conservatives—free trade versus protection—was in abeyance. (Baldwin had dropped protection after it had helped lose the 1923 election for the Tories.) The violently contentious Irish issue was settled—forever, the British hoped. On new issues—the danger from the Labour party, communism, and Indian nationalism—

Churchill was in harmony with most of the Conservative party. There seemed to be no reason why he should not take root and flourish. In 1925 he rejoined the Tory Carlton Club, from which he had resigned twenty years before.

Yet Churchill's unexpected restoration to high office did not open another period of dazzling activity. In *The Gathering Storm* he skipped lightly over his years as Baldwin's chancellor, and not merely because he was anxious to get to the 1930s and his crusade against appeasement. His years at the treasury were not his most successful, and he must have come to realize how Baldwin, by a combination of luck and shrewdness, had both used and contained him.

Economics was not Churchill's subject either, and for this reason, allied with his desire to consolidate his place in the Conservative hierarchy (for doubts about him were still widespread), he was uncommonly receptive to received wisdom, in this case the orthodoxy of his officials and the financial community. The most controversial result was the restoration of the gold standard in 1925, which was universally held to be correct then as it is now almost universally condemned. What probably most attracted Churchill about the gold standard was its reaffirmation of Britain's return to prewar verities. In fact, it did nothing to cure the underlying weakness of the British economy—the increasing obsolescence of the basic export industries—which had become manifest since the war. John Maynard Keynes argued that, by overvaluing the pound and therefore overpricing British exports, Churchill's action further weakened those industries. Keynes's argument has not gone unchallenged, but it is unquestionable that the most dramatic episode of Churchill's chancellorship was, at best, an irrelevance.

For the rest, Churchill made brilliant budget speeches and showed that his prewar liberalism and social concern were not merely a passing phase by sponsoring in his first budget an extension of the existing Old-Age Pension Law which sharply increased the income of the aged poor. (The government's most important social legislation was the work of Neville Chamberlain, who laid the basis at the hitherto obscure Ministry of Health for his subsequent rise.) But the most significant event of Churchill's time at the exchequer was one he chose to forget entirely when writing *The Gathering Storm*—the general strike of May 1926.

That episode grew out of the troubles of the British coal industry. Afflicted by shrinking markets, falling profits, archaic and reactionary management, and a bitter history of bad labor relations, it detonated the only general strike in British history. Baldwin, an instinctive centrist and conciliator, gave Churchill the job of editing an official government newspaper, the *British Gazette,* which was printed for the duration of the strike. Baldwin later claimed it was the cleverest move he had ever made. It certainly gave Churchill an outlet for his bellicosity and Labour a focus for its anger. A general strike was for Churchill first and foremost an attempt to coerce the government, a challenge to be met and broken. While Baldwin had tried to avert the strike and worked for compromise during it, Churchill, in the *British Gazette's* leading articles, unsigned but with his characteristic impress on them, denounced the trade unions as the enemy and demanded their "unconditional surren-der." The "law and order" home secretary of 1911, the man who called the Labour party a "subversive cause" in 1920, and now the inflammatory editor of the *British Gazette*—Labour's bill of particu-lars against Churchill was long, and long remembered. After the general strike collapsed, Churchill joined Baldwin, in vain, to urge the mine owners to make a reasonable settlement with their workers. But the damage had been done; he had isolated himself from the unions and Labour. Only Hitler would succeed in pushing them together.

The differences between Churchill and Baldwin, apparent enough in connection with the general strike, became strongly marked as the government neared the end of its term and India moved again into the political spotlight. The 1919 Government of India Act provided for a review of its workings after ten years. Baldwin, in fact, appointed a Royal Commission in November 1927 to prevent its composition and terms of reference from being set by a Labour government should the next general election produce one. Just before the 1929 general election, Churchill told Baldwin he could not support Indian self-government. When that election pro-duced a Labour government, Churchill promptly went off on a long tour of the United States and Canada and then settled down at Chartwell to write. He badly needed the money. Chartwell was expensive, he had lost heavily in the American stock market crash, and without a ministerial salary his income from journalism (he signed £40,000 worth of magazine contracts while in the United States in 1929) was indispensable to him. However, neither Chartwell, nor writing, nor the prospect of renewed office, if the Labour government without a clear majority of its own and again dependent on Liberal support should fall, could keep him from brooding over the future of the British raj and moving toward an open clash with Baldwin.

India was another subject that Churchill wrote little about in

The Gathering Storm. The Indian Empire was history by 1948, and it would have served neither Churchill's artistic design nor his political hopes to resurrect his stand in its defense. Yet nothing perhaps is as important, not only to understanding Churchill's position in the 1930s but also to grasping one of his principal war aims and its ultimate failure from 1940 to 1945, as his passionate commitment to preventing complete Indian self-government. Isolated already from Labour, he would isolate himself from the Conservatives over this issue, and only Hitler would rescue him from the political exile he had fashioned. He saw the dangers but could not draw back. The mainspring of his effort was a deep belief that dominion status for India was the wrong goal; it was dangerous for India and enfeebling for Britain. He was convinced that, as he had told Pamela Lytton in 1922, the "political classes" in India were a tiny and unrepresentative minority—"chatterboxes"—and that the withdrawal of British authority would lead to chaos and bloodshed. He knew that the Indian market was important to Britain and above all that the Indian Army represented a vital strategic reserve undergirding the entire British position east of Suez. Greater self-government at the provincial level he had reluctantly accepted in 1919, and he would have swallowed its extension but only subject to final British authority at the Center. Dominion status, complete self-government, was out of the question.

Churchill's breach with Baldwin, although foreshadowed before the election, actually began with the "Irwin Declaration" issued on 31 October 1929 by the viceroy, Lord Irwin (the future Lord Halifax), stating that dominion status was the "natural issue" of India's constitutional development. Baldwin, who had originally appointed him, was much influenced by Irwin's views and was willing to join Ramsay MacDonald, the Labour leader, in making India's next step toward self-government a bipartisan matter. Churchill was not. "My idea," he wrote, "was that the Conservative Opposition should strongly confront the Labour Government on all great imperial and national issues. . . . So far as I could see Mr. Baldwin felt that the times were too far gone for any robust assertion of British imperial greatness. . . ."[56] In January 1931, MacDonald affirmed that India's "full responsibility for her own government" was British policy. Six days later Irwin released Mahatma Gandhi from detention to improve the atmosphere for negotiation. The following evening, 26 January, Churchill, explicitly disassociating himself from the official Conservative leadership, attacked the MacDonald-Irwin policy and was answered not by a Labour minister but by Baldwin. The next day Churchill resigned from

Baldwin's Conservative shadow cabinet. With that move his third political career ended and his "wilderness" years began.

The 1930s are the most difficult part of Churchill's career to assess. On the surface, Nicolson was uncannily accurate. When England's future became dark indeed, the country turned to Churchill. He himself bequeathed to posterity a much-extended version of the same theme. In *The Gathering Storm,* whose widely accepted depiction of this period has by now impressed itself indelibly upon the popular imagination, he presented himself as the one person so consistently right about the menace of Hitler as to make inevitable his return to office in September 1939 and subsequent ascent to national leadership. Yet the reality of Britain during the 1930s, and Churchill's place in it, cannot really be so easily summarized.

The starkest reality of that decade for many in Britain, and one which Churchill largely ignored in *The Gathering Storm,* had nothing to do with the German menace. It was mass unemployment, which hovered around 2 million. The rigid orthodoxy of the government's response did nothing to alleviate it, and the failure to do so aggravated another problem, the defection of loyalties from England's social and political order. The British governing class, shaken by the losses from 1914 to 1918, was beginning to lose the certainty about its role that had until this time characterized it. "In 1939, the ruling circles in Britain did not give the impression of being full of eupeptic optimism," the verdict of one shrewd observer, is, if anything, an understatement.[57] The doubt and intellectual confusion, out of which came the Soviet "moles" in the British establishment—"Kim" Philby, Anthony Blount, Guy Burgess, and Donald Maclean—reflects an important aspect of 1930s Britain and one to which Churchill's defense of the traditional order of things was an irrelevance. "Nothing can save England if she will not save herself," he told an audience on St. George's Day in 1933. "If we lose faith in ourselves, in our capacity to guide and govern, if we lose our will to live, then indeed our story is told."[58] Six years later he was still warning of a "marked decline of the will to live, and still more of the will to rule."[59]

Throughout a period of increasing doubt and uncertainty, Churchill preserved his faith in Britain and fortified it by dwelling on the history of his country, not the history known to professional historians with its endless, careful qualifications but history as creative myth, sustaining a belief in Britain's special mission and destiny. Churchill identified the "spirit of Britain" with "the cause of Liberty," and in late 1937, hard at work on what became his *History of the English-Speaking Peoples,* he told the viceroy of India: "I have come to think myself in the last lap of life that one should always look back on the history of the past, study it and meditate upon it. Thus one learns the main line of advance. On the other hand it is wrong to be bound by the events and commitments of the last few years, unless these are sound and compatible with the main historic line."[60] Looking back Churchill saw England's heroic defiance of Spain, the battlefield triumphs of his great ancestor the first duke of Marlborough during the reign of Queen Anne, and the creation of Queen Victoria's empire. Most of his countrymen looked back and saw the terrible battlefields of the First World War and the long lines of unemployed ever since.

Churchill's ability to sustain his belief in Britain's destiny by immersing himself in an essentially romantic vision of its history was the first factor that set him apart from the mainstream of British politics in the 1930s. The second was a series of quarrels with the rest of the political establishment, which isolated him from virtually every major group within it and made his warnings about Germany seem less the foreboding of a statesman than the latest hobbyhorse to be ridden by a talented, vain, ambitious politician of repeatedly demonstrated bad judgment.

When Churchill broke with Baldwin early in 1931, he might well have suspected that the party leader, whose abilities he always seriously underrated, would not last long. Many Conservatives besides Churchill disliked Baldwin's Indian policy, while two of the most powerful newspaper proprietors, Lords Beaverbrook and Rothermere, were determined to topple him in the interest of a protectionist scheme that went by the confusing name of "Empire Free Trade." But Baldwin held on to the central mass of the Conservative party, beat off the challenge of the press lords, and in August 1931 became the beneficiary of the accident that shaped British politics for the remainder of the decade. Hammered by the full blast of the depression, hopelessly split over how to deal with it, MacDonald's Labour government resigned, but MacDonald himself remained in office at the head of a national coalition, with Baldwin as his principal colleague. In October a bewildered and fearful electorate gave the national government the largest majority in British history—497 seats over the combined total of its opponents, of which 472 were Conservatives. MacDonald remained prime minister, but actual power was Baldwin's, and the Conservative leader did not need, as in 1924, to placate any dissident Conservatives. Churchill's only way back to office after 1931 was to make his peace with Baldwin. Since this would have meant accepting the government's Indian policy, there was no possibility that Churchill would do so. Instead he used his immense talents to fight the India Bill which was, for him, a clear case of a policy incompatible with "the main historic line." As with intervention in Russia, Churchill was far from alone, but as in that episode, it was his zeal and ability that gave the cause he championed both its success and its most forceful spokesman. Certainly, without Churchill, the Tory right would not have been able to fight a stubborn rearguard action for four years, the account of which later filled 4,000 pages of *Hansard,* the official record of parliamentary debates.

Churchill's opposition to Indian self-government intensified when he reflected on India's contribution to British power in an increasingly dangerous world. Lord Linlithgow, chairman of the parliamentary committee charged with shaping the India Bill, wrote to Churchill in May 1933, expressing widespread sentiment: "If you and those who are with you are able to recreate the India of 1900 and—what is a great deal more difficult—fit it with even reasonable success into the world of 1934, I shall be the first to admit my error, and to rejoice in your strength and wisdom." Churchill's reply shows how far beyond the average Tory "diehard" his mind ranged:

> I think we differ principally in this, that you assume the future is a mere extension of the past, whereas I find history full of unexpected turns and retrogressions. The mild and vague Liberalism of the early years of the twentieth century, the surge of fantastic hopes and illusions that followed the armistice of the Great War have already been superseded by a violent reaction against Parliamentary and electioneering procedure and by the establishment of dictatorships real or veiled in almost every country. . . . In my view England is now beginning a new period of struggle and fighting for its life, and the crux of it will be not only the retention of India but a much stronger assertion of commercial rights. As long as we are sure that we press no claim on India that is not in their real interest we are justified in using our undoubted power for their welfare and for our own.[61]

This view of India as an essential prop of British power would color Churchill's policies throughout his coming years of power. So would his preference for benevolent autocracy as the most appropriate instrument of government there.

"Using our undoubted power" to maintain that style of government was to contemporaries one of the most unsettling aspects of Churchill's position on India. He was already known as a man for whom conflict held no terrors. Would he use force to suppress Indian nationalism? In July 1920, defending a decision to censure British officer General Reginald E. H. Dyer, who the previous year had fired upon an unarmed crowd killing almost four hundred in the Indian city of Amritsar, Churchill had declaimed in his most majestic style:

> Governments who have seized upon power by violence and by usurpation have often resorted to terrorism in their desperate efforts to keep what they have stolen, but the august and venerable structure of the British Empire, where lawful authority descends from hand to hand and generation after generation, does not need such aid. Such ideas are absolutely foreign to the British way of doing things.[62]

Yet it was precisely the fear that, if British rule were to be maintained in India in opposition to Nationalist feeling, such methods might have to become "the British way of doing things" that animated many supporters of the Baldwin-MacDonald policy. Moreover, there was a legitimate query to be placed after "undoubted power." The British raj depended on Indian civil servants, soldiers, and policemen who still exhibited considerable reserves of loyalty. Whether this devotion would have continued had concession been replaced by repression in the early 1930s is problematic, and residual Indian loyalty was to be crucial to Britain between 1939 and 1945.

Furthermore, one important constituent of power is the willingness to use it. Churchill argued that, if Britain were known to be willing to use force, it would never be necessary actually to do so. But what if he were wrong? It is more than questionable how much patience the British public still had for what one Labour spokesman on India denounced as Churchill's ultimate reliance on "the lathi, the stick, and after the lathi, the rifle, and after the rifle, the machine gun, . . . government by force which public opinion in this country could not stand. . . ."[63] In fact, Churchill believed not in repression but in the acceptability of power—humanely wielded—in the service of national interest, traditionally defined. But in a society that was becoming unsure about the morality of power and without a consensus on whether the empire was any longer a national interest, he could persuade few.

In that atmosphere he could and did, however, reaffirm for many the belief that he was a hopeless reactionary, frighteningly willing to shed blood for a cause that few wished any longer to defend to the death. Moreover, this sentiment that the raj would soon end was widespread in Anglo-India itself. "I went to India [in 1928] clearly thinking that we were going there to lead India on the way to self-government," recalled one of the most brilliant of the last generation of British administrators.[64] Churchill's Indian crusade also convinced the bulk of the Conservative party that he was unscrupulously ambitious and willing to use any means to discredit the party leadership, with the hope of replacing it. This analysis of his motivations, put about by the government whips during the ferocious political struggle that he precipitated, had just enough foundation in Churchill's well-known ambitions to be extremely damaging to him. It became part of the received wisdom about him, which was summarized by Baldwin in a conversation with one of his intimates in May 1936:

> One of these days I'll make a few casual remarks about Winston. Not a speech—no oratory—just a few words in passing. I've got it all ready. I am going to say that when Winston was born lots of fairies swooped down on his cradle gifts— imagination, eloquence, industry, ability, and then came a fairy who said, 'No one person has a right to so many gifts,' picked him up and gave him such a shake and twist that with all these gifts he was denied judgment and wisdom. And that is why while we delight to listen to him in this house we do not take his advice.[65]

By deleting from his account of the 1930s all but glancing references to the India controversy and stressing instead his record of warnings about Germany, Churchill made himself appear more reasonable to posterity than he looked at the time. He was, in fact, obscuring clear and strong signals about Germany with simultaneous bursts of static about India.

Churchill began pointing to the danger of a German military resurgence even before Hitler came to power. Traveling to Bavaria in September 1932 to examine the site of Marlborough's great victory at Blenheim, he was immediately aware of the strength of the

Nazi movement. "All these bands of sturdy Teutonic youths, marching through the streets and roads of Germany, with the light of desire in their eyes to suffer for their Fatherland . . . are looking for weapons," he warned the House of Commons on 23 November 1932.[66] When they got them, he predicted, they would certainly shatter the European order created at Versailles in 1919. Thereafter he ceaselessly pointed out that Germany was arming fast, while Britain, he claimed, was not rearming rapidly enough to keep pace. He also continually urged a diplomatic strategy which, if backed by adequate military force, would preserve the European equilibrium and contain Germany without war.

On these positions, which he depicted in *The Gathering Storm* as taken up early and unflaggingly maintained, Churchill rested his case before posterity: the man whose consistent accuracy on the one issue that counted made his return to office inevitable. Few personal memoirs have ever had such remarkable success in impressing their author's version of events on subsequent historical writing, especially on textbooks. The popular view of the Western democracies' response to the German challenge is therefore Churchill's, held today even by those who have never read *The Gathering Storm*. "Munich" is and probably will remain an emotionally charged word, not just because it symbolizes a policy that failed but because of Churchill's strictures on that policy and its authors. The Churchillian view of the origins of the Second World War contains a substantial element of truth, but to retrace Churchill's road back to office and power, it is necessary to restore some of the highlights and shadows he omitted.

The experience of the First World War had left a bitter and lasting impression engraved on the mind of the British public. A combination of public mood, financial problems, and the virtual disappearance of credible enemies led to a drastic reduction in Britain's armed forces during the 1920s. The symbol of this declining military power was the "Ten Year Rule," first laid down in 1919, which stipulated that the services should take it as given that there would be no major conflict for a decade. In 1928, when he was chancellor of the exchequer and guardian alike of fiscal orthodoxy and the public purse, Churchill had the rule changed so that the ten-year period began afresh every day, although it could be reviewed any time a governmental department so requested. Only in March 1932 was it finally canceled by the cabinet at the urgent request of the chiefs of staff. Even without the rule, it seems that the 1920s probably would have been a lean time for the services in Britain. Whom, after all, were they preparing to fight? And even after its cancellation in the much different atmosphere of the early 1930s, defense spending did not rise sharply. Only in 1939 did the treasury's grip on service budgets at last begin to relax. Churchill could argue that the international situation in the 1920s was benign, and that responsibility for ensuring that Britain could defend itself rested with those who were in power when that condition changed. Still, it is not surprising that many of those who endured the lash of his rhetoric over the gaps in Britain's arsenal did so with the feeling that here was another example of captious criticism from someone who bore a heavy responsibility himself.

As in the case of India, Churchill was arguing not just with the government but with a widespread mood. The dead of the First World War were buried but far from forgotten. New war memorials were constantly being dedicated. "War books," usually bitterly critical, kept alive the memory of muddle, slaughter, and ultimate disappointment. The mood of the country was deeply pacific and profoundly isolationist, while the belief that rearmament was an admission that another war was on the way made it a tricky issue politically, a fact that Baldwin, acutely sensitive to the national mood, clearly realized. On 29 July 1935, speaking privately to a deputation of Conservatives, including Churchill, about the pace of rearmament, Baldwin was candid:

> Most of you sit for safe seats. You do not represent industrial constituencies; at least not many of you. There was a very strong, I do not know about pacifist, but pacific feeling in the country after the war. They all wanted to have nothing more to do with it, and the League of Nations Union have done a great deal of their propaganda in making people believe they could rely on collective security, and it was a question in 1934 whether if you tried to do much you might not have imperilled and more than imperilled, you might have lost the General Election when it came.[67]

Rearmament only became possible, he added, when the public "had begun to realize what Hitler meant," an enlightenment he believed only events could bring about: "It is not easy when you get on a platform to tell people what the dangers are. . . . I think the one line whereby you can get people to sit up in this country, if they think dictators are likely to attack them . . . but I have never quite seen the clear line by which you can approach people to scare them but not scare them into fits."[68] Baldwin repeated much of this speech in Parliament in November 1936 and thus laid himself open to Churchill's crushing rejoinder twelve years later: "That a Prime Minister should avow that he had not done his duty in regard to national safety because he was afraid of losing the election was an incident without parallel in our parliamentary history."[69]

At bottom, the difference between Churchill and Baldwin was essentially the degree to which public opinion could be led. Baldwin's attitude, Churchill complained at the time and later, did "less than justice to the spirit of the British people."[70] "Tell the truth to the British people," he urged Baldwin in his first speech on the German danger in 1932. "They are a tough people, a robust people."[71] But Baldwin, who told the 1935 deputation "I am not going to get this country into a war with anybody for the League of Nations or anybody else or for anything else," was speaking not only from his own deepest convictions but also out of his instinctive sense of what was possible. Baldwin's appreciation of the depth of the nation's aversion to war was intensified by the peculiar form that the argument on rearmament took, one nicely calculated to scare the public.

That discussion focused almost exclusively on air power. After 1918 it was assumed by almost everyone that the British army would never again operate in strength on the European continent, and its role was defined as "imperial policing." No one seriously challenged that until the eve of the Second World War. Only in February 1939 did the British agree to dispatch a token contingent to France. So when rearmament became a political issue after 1932, even Churchill, responsible as he was for much of the public discussion of the subject, did not argue for a "continental commitment." Similarly the navy, its ships aging but still one of the two largest in the world, was not a matter of intense concern as it had been before 1914. The new weapon of air power, its full potential as yet unknown, dominated the arguments over Britain's defenses. That the Germans were creating an air force in defiance of the Versailles treaty was known; what sort of air force, and for what purposes, was not. The Royal Air Force had made a strategic bombing offensive, aimed at an enemy's industry and work force, its central strategic doctrine, and it assumed a similar aim for the new German air force.

Such an offensive had never been attempted, but one assumption that had to be made by its planners was that the bombers could reach their targets. Conversely, enemy bombers would reach British cities. Baldwin summarized professional wisdom on the subject when he told the House of Commons in November 1932: "I think it is well . . . for the man in the street to realize that there is no power on earth that can protect him from being bombed. Whatever people may tell him, the bomber will always get through."[72] The man in the street had no trouble grasping the apocalyptic possibilities. Films like *Things To Come* (1937), which opened with an enemy obliterating central London from the air, seemed to be not in the least fanciful when viewed against the background of the obliteration of Guernica by the German Condor Legion, or the devastating Japanese attacks on Chinese cities. On the eve of war, experts were predicting that the Germans could drop as much as 100,000 tons of bombs on Britain in the first two weeks. Even cautious writers thought that 125,000 casualties were possible in the first week of such an onslaught, and the Ministry of Health was trying to provide 300,000 beds. Such predictions obviously intensified the desire to avoid war at all costs, a desire common alike to the "appeasers" and the public who strongly supported them.

Churchill, on the other hand, had a different approach. In a newspaper article published in May 1938, he admitted that British cities would be bombed but argued that the damage could be kept to manageable proportions by adequate fighter defenses and a vigorous British bombing attack on "the nests from which the hostile vultures come." He argued his case, however, in a way that many of the *News of the World*'s 4,000,000 readers could not have found reassuring:

> I do not believe in reprisals on the enemy civilian population. On the contrary, the more they try to kill our women and children, the more we should devote ourselves to killing their fighting men and smashing up the technical apparatus upon which the life of their armies depends. This is the best way of defending London, and of defending the helpless masses from the bestialities of modern war.[73]

The lengthy argument Churchill carried on with the government between 1934 and 1936 over the rate at which the German air force was growing (a rate of growth which he overestimated) thus not only further alienated Baldwin's mass of supporters, but it also probably enhanced the fears that lay behind the fervent loyalties Baldwin commanded. "The rank and file . . . will not see the old man bullied as they are intensely and pathetically loyal to him," Churchill's cousin, Frederick Guest, warned him in June 1936.[74]

If the Conservative party would not listen, it might be thought that the Left would have responded to what Churchill had to say about Germany. But apart from his own past and their opposition to the rearmament he demanded, there was another important reason why Churchill initially found no answering echoes from the Liberal or Labour parties. He expressed his views on foreign affairs in a way that ran counter to the perception of the world held by the Left. The sense of moral outrage aroused by Nazi Germany was certainly shared by Churchill to the fullest, but his thoughts were bent on containing the threat of German power and his remedies for that lay along traditional lines. He distinguished sharply between Germany and Italy and was considerably less critical of the latter. He was not particularly forward in condemning Japanese assaults on China, and the intense emotions aroused by the Spanish civil war did not stir him deeply. Instead, fortified by his historical studies, he thought in terms of utilizing the European balance of power to contain Germany. In May 1936 he wrote to his cousin, Lord Londonderry, who was one of the many British visitors to Hitler who came back deeply impressed by Germany:

> You are mistaken in supposing I have an anti-German obsession. British policy for four hundred years has been to oppose the strongest power in Europe by weaving together a combination of other countries strong enough to face the bully. Sometimes it is Spain, sometimes the French monarchy, sometimes the French Empire, sometimes Germany. I have no doubt who it is now. But if France set up claim to the overlordship of Europe, I should equally endeavor to oppose them. It is thus through the centuries we have kept our liberties and maintained our life and power.[75]

This, like the views he held and voiced on India, expressed Churchill's deep and unchanging inner convictions. But in an era when belief in the League of Nations, collective security, and the equal awfulness of all Fascist and militarist regimes were the prevalent orthodoxies of the Left, it commanded as little support there as did his stand in defense of the empire. As Baldwin once remarked, Churchill did not really understand "the postwar mind."[76]

How little he grasped the extent of his own isolation can be seen by Churchill's expectation in 1936 that, since the India Bill controversy had passed, he would be taken back into the cabinet, perhaps even made minister of defense in order to coordinate and accelerate rearmament. Although Churchill's arguments were beginning to have impact, there was no actual chance that Baldwin would take him back, particularly as his heir apparent, Chamberlain, wanted Churchill kept out. The year 1936, which to Churchill had seemed so promising, ended with his political influence at its all-time low, and his reputation for poor judgment reaffirmed. Rashly allowing his romantic inclinations—and perhaps his contempt for Baldwin—full sway, he made himself the principal champion of Edward VIII at the time of the brief, intense crisis that led to the king's abdication. Once again Baldwin proved the shrewder judge of the national mood. On the evening of 7 December 1936, Churchill's pleas on behalf of the king were taken as simply another attempt to attack Baldwin, and he was howled down in the House and ruled out of order by the speaker. Nothing like it had ever happened to Churchill before. He stalked out of the chamber, followed only by Bracken, and told one of the prime minister's entourage, whom he encountered in a corridor, that his political career was over. "Winston . . . suffered an utter defeat. He almost lost his head, and he certainly lost his command of the House," the usually sympathetic Nicolson noted that night in a letter to his wife.[77] Churchill never regretted what he had done, telling Bernard Baruch in a candid New Year's greeting that he always preferred to follow his heart rather than cold calculation. Baldwin's handling of the "King's Matter" made him, as Churchill predicted in that letter, impregnable. When he finally retired in May 1937 after the coronation of the new king, George VI, he handed over his position, as expected, to Chamberlain.

Baldwin, whom Churchill privately dismissed as a "very mediocre intellect" in 1936 and later described as "without detailed executive capacity," was ironically quite perceptive about Churchill's future.[78] Shortly after his retirement, Baldwin remarked that Churchill was a "forceful character and if war should come, the country will want him to lead them."[79] It was this situation that Chamberlain planned to avoid. Utterly lacking Baldwin's shrewdness, empathy for national mood beyond party frontiers, and desire for consensus, he was certainly much more vigorous. He knew his mind and meant to have his way. Like Baldwin, he saw rearmament largely as a deterrent, creating the conditions in which it would be possible to handle Germany's grievances by negotiation. Where Baldwin, however, was vague and intuitive, Chamberlain was brisk, incisive, and to the point:

> You don't need offensive forces sufficient to win a smashing victory. What you want are defensive forces sufficiently strong to make it impossible for the other side to win except at such a cost to make it not worthwhile. That is what we are doing and though at present the German feeling is it is not worthwhile *yet* they will presently come to realize that it never *will* be worthwhile, then we can talk.[80]

That Chamberlain could write this letter in late July 1939 reveals how wedded he was to his own views. His belief that he could achieve his foreign policy goals without war was perhaps his principal reason for not wanting Churchill in the government: "Winston is Public Enemy No. 1 in Berlin," he told the owner of the *Daily Telegraph*, who was urging Churchill's merits upon him. There were other reasons as well. Chamberlain was convinced by past experience that Churchill would be a disruptive influence in the cabinet. As he told Lord Camrose in the same interview,

> . . . he appreciated Churchill's ability but his own experience in Cabinet work with him had not been such as to make him feel that his [Churchill's] inclusion in the Cabinet would make his own task any easier. He admitted that Baldwin had not attempted to control his Cabinet and that therefore Winston had had a much freer rein than he should have done. In any case, however, the result was that Winston's ideas and memoranda tended to monopolise the time of the whole Ministry. If you did not agree with him he was liable to lose his temper in argument and a number of his colleagues found that the easier way was not to oppose.[81]

Since Chamberlain meant to run his cabinet his own way, the temperamental differences between himself and Churchill would probably have made for Churchill's exclusion in any case, but in the circumstances between 1937 and 1939, the root of the problem lay in their different assessments of Hitler's character and aims. Churchill had always feared the aggressive dynamic he sensed in nazism. By 1937 he was gloomily certain that the maintenance of the European balance without war had become rather unlikely. Chamberlain believed, because he wanted to, that Germany could be dealt with by a combination of deterrence and negotiated change in the Versailles order, leading ultimately to a definitive "appeasement" of Europe. The bulk of the Conservative party was as fearful of war, and as solidly behind the quest for lasting peace, as they had been in Baldwin's time, and Chamberlain was much more willing to use ruthlessly his powers as party leader to quell dissent. It was an unpromising situation for Churchill, and yet it was during these years that events began finally to move his way.

Since 1928 Churchill had supported his lavish way of living by lucrative journalism. By 1937 his articles and books had earned him over £100,000, before tax. By the spring of 1938 his expenses and further American stock market losses of £18,000 had placed him in such a precarious financial situation that he had decided to sell his beloved Chartwell. Only the intervention of Sir Henry Stakosch, one of the South African financial magnates who played a large part in his private life, bailed him out and saved Chartwell. Nonetheless, he had to write vigorously, even for him, in order to regain financial stability. His journalism—£20,000 worth of books and articles scheduled for 1939—made his views on the dominant foreign policy issue of the day widely known in Britain as well as to readers throughout Europe and the United States, not to mention those of the *East African Standard, Madras Mail,* and *Times of Malta.* Churchill always cherished a grievance against the BBC for keeping him from broadcasting as often as he wished during the 1930s. His journalism, enforced by his life-style, more than compensated for the BBC's attitude. Together with his amply reported speeches in Parliament, it provided him with a great source of visibility as the most vigorous spokesman for a hard line with Germany.

Not only was it impossible not to know Churchill's views on Germany, but he also was finally beginning to find the political base he had always lacked. In his struggle with Baldwin over India and rearmament, he had aimed his assaults at the Conservative party. He failed to make any dent in its traditional loyalty to its chosen leadership, except on the Right where he rallied a substantial minority. But when Germany and not India became the major issue, he found himself deserted by the Conservative right who feared war against Germany might endanger both the empire and Britain's social order. Therefore, from 1936 on Churchill, by force of circumstances, found himself associated with nonpartisan, anti-Fascist groups like the British Non-Sectarian Anti-Nazi Council to Champion Human Rights and its offshoot Freedom and Peace. These organizations, in fact, depended heavily on the Center and the Left, and they brought Churchill into contact with Liberal and Labour as well as trade union figures and intellectuals of the Left.[82] This was the beginning of the end of his isolation and the first tentative step toward his emergence as a national candidate for war leadership.

Churchill's pragmatism where questions of the balance of power were involved aided this opening to the Center and the Left. He quickly realized that in any anti-Hitler coalition the Soviet Union would be an essential partner. By the spring of 1936 he was entertaining the Soviet ambassador, Ivan Maisky, at Chartwell and beginning to argue that he "would marshal all the countries including Soviet Russia from the Baltic southward right around to the Belgian coast, all agreeing to stand by any victim of unprovoked aggression." He had not changed his mind about communism but, as he stated in his memoirs, " . . . anger must be subordinated to defeating the main immediate enemy."[83] That there were serious practical problems in Churchill's "grand alliance" scheme did not make it any less attractive to many of Churchill's new associates, although it did not endear him to orthodox Conservatives who already feared contamination by association as a result of the Franco-Russian Alliance of 1935. In the same vein, Churchill learned to invoke the name of the league repeatedly in support of what were, in fact, quite traditional views. The cumulative impact was significant. By March 1938 a dedicated Labour party member wrote: "Churchill may be a reactionary in most ways, but he is sound about foreign affairs, and his speeches are a joy to read."[84]

Churchill also began to reach in another direction, one that in the long run was to be of profound importance. He realized that German power in Europe, buttressed perhaps by Italy, could only be balanced by calling in the New World as well as the Soviet Union, or perhaps the Russians could only be involved safely if the Americans were too. At any rate Churchill, half American by birth, as well acquainted with the United States by travel and study as any major British political leader, began to argue in his speeches and articles for greater American participation in European affairs. As in the case of the Soviet Union, however, he did so with his eyes open. In October 1937 he wrote privately: "Although the ideals of the two countries are similar, their interests are in many ways divergent."[85]

None of these political arguments would have mattered in the slightest if Chamberlain had been right about Hitler. The question of whether Hitler was an opportunist drawn on by his perception of Anglo-French weakness, or whether his personality, ultimate goals, and the nature of his regime equally required war, will continue to be debated. Churchill's position, however, was affected by two palpable facts: he had consistently warned about Germany's aggressive intentions, and in 1938 the lull that had followed Germany's remilitarization of the Rhineland came to an end. The annexation of Austria, followed by the buildup of tension over the Sudeten question, culminating in the dismemberment of Czechoslovakia at Munich in September, made the fears of Churchill and the other "anti-appeasers" seem terribly cogent.

Churchill was not the only critic of Chamberlain's policy, but he was certainly the most widely known and the most formidable. When Chamberlain told the House of Commons on the afternoon of 28 September 1938 of Hitler's invitation to a four-power conference at Munich the next day, the Conservative benches erupted in jubilation. Only Churchill, Anthony Eden, Leo S. Amery, and Nicolson remained seated, despite shouts of "Get up! Get up!" from fellow Conservatives. In the subsequent parliamentary debate on the Munich settlement, Churchill delivered a forty-five minute blast, denouncing the agreement as "a total and unmitigated defeat." When the House voted, he abstained (he had originally intended to vote against but finally was brought to abstention by the realization that it was the only parliamentary tactic on which Chamberlain's Conservative opponents could be persuaded to agree). Churchill insisted, however, in remaining ostentatiously seated in the House when the members rose to troop into the division lobby. Less than half of the Conservative abstainers remained with him. Chamberlain was not a man to take opposition lightly, particularly as he was convinced that his policy was both sound and popular, referring in a letter to his sister to "the countless letters and telegrams which continued to pour in expressing in most moving accents the writers' heartfelt relief and gratitude." The prime minister believed that such public reaction could only be a prelude to renewed effort "to make the world a better place."[86] Writing to Churchill, the press magnate Lord Rothermere warned him that "the public is so terrified of being bombed they will support anyone who keeps them out of the war" and advised him to "soft pedal" his opposition to Chamberlain, advice that was ignored.[87] As a friend with whom Churchill broke over Munich later recalled, "if you voted against what he regarded as the national interest that was that—he was prosecution counsel and judge combined."[88]

Fortified by the belief he was right, Churchill faced the intense pressure Chamberlain placed on all the Conservative dissenters through the party machine in their constituencies. "I do not withdraw a single word. . . . I know it has gained for me a greater measure of goodwill from my fellow-countrymen than I have ever previously enjoyed," Churchill told his critics on 10 March 1939, adding four days later, "what is the use of Parliament if it is not the place where true statements can be brought before the people?"[89] The following day German troops marched into Prague, shattering both the Munich settlement and a great many illusions in Britain. The scattered sparks of doubt about British policy, which Churchill had done so much to foster and keep alive, now fused into a blaze that Chamberlain could not ignore. He still hoped to avoid war by negotiation but now had to make unmistakably clear that war would come if Hitler moved again unilaterally.

By the end of the month the British government had guaranteed the territorial integrity of Poland.

Six months remained before war finally came, six months during which the Chamberlain government both prepared reluctantly for it and simultaneously tried desperately to avert it. Public opinion was in many ways more single-minded. Accepting now that war was likely and believing that the responsibility was Hitler's, the public became increasingly receptive to the idea of Churchill's return to office. A public opinion poll published in May showed 56 percent of the respondents wanted Churchill in the cabinet. If war came, Churchill's return to government, as Chamberlain well realized, would be unavoidable.

Churchill's preeminent suitability for war was, in fact, one of the few points of agreement about him among both politicians and the public. Early on the morning of 1 September 1939 the Polish ambassador called Chartwell to inform Churchill that Germany had attacked. That afternoon when Churchill arrived in London, Chamberlain asked him to join his war cabinet. The next thirty-six hours were consumed by Chamberlain's frantic last efforts to preserve peace, at least for Britain and France, but by the late evening of 2 September, war, and with it Churchill, had become inevitable. The former came at eleven o'clock the next morning. That evening the Admiralty signaled to the Royal Navy's ships around the world: "Winston is Back."

Churchill returned to office because Chamberlain's strategy for averting war had failed. The consensus that he belonged in any war government then made it impossible to exclude him. The same two factors—failure of Chamberlain's strategy and public opinion—forced Churchill into supreme power nine months later. But the road from the Admiralty to Number Ten was far from straight and smooth.

Churchill's return did not mean the end of his political isolation, at least in the Conservative party. Chamberlain had not broadened his government by bringing in either the Liberal or Labour parties, nor had he tried very hard to do so. His government still rested on the party basis established by the 1935 general election. With a majority of approximately two hundred seats in the House of Commons and as absolute master of the party machine, Chamberlain seemed to have little to fear. His war cabinet, Churchill apart, was built around a core of his most trusted prewar "inner cabinet" colleagues—Halifax, his heir apparent, Sir John Simon, and Sir Samuel Hoare. To them were added Admiral Lord Chatfield, minister for Coordination of Defense, and Hankey, now a baron and minister without portfolio, and the three service ministers, Sir Kingsley Wood, a staunch Chamberlainite, Leslie Hore-Belisha, and Churchill. None of these men were likely to take Churchill's side in any quarrel with the prime minister. Not only the Conservative party but also the civil service eyed Churchill warily. Such dissent as there was in the Conservative ranks looked rather to Eden than to Churchill for a lead and, with Eden back in the office as dominions secretary, was not likely to cause Chamberlain much trouble. Apart from faithful disciples like Bracken and Robert Boothby, Churchill seemed to have little significant support anywhere in Whitehall or Westminster. This, while true, was misleading. His strength lay in public opinion and his growing acceptability to the Opposition, and that sort of strength would only threaten Chamberlain if the war went badly, a contingency Chamberlain's strategy was designed to avert.

Chamberlain was certainly as determined to beat Hitler as was Churchill. The difference lay in their definition of victory. Chamberlain's strategy after September 1939 was based on assumptions about Germany which were clear but unfortunately wrong, the same weakness that had vitiated his prewar diplomacy. His starting point was his belief that the German economy was already under stress and that the German people were under a corresponding strain. It followed that neither the German war economy nor the regime's popular support could stand much more pressure; therefore, time was working for Britain and France. A strategy of attrition, carried out largely by an economic blockade, would cripple Germany and might prompt internal convulsions that would end the Nazi regime. It was more likely, however, that Germany would become willing to negotiate on terms acceptable to the Allies before this stage was reached. A war conducted and ended in this fashion would avoid the total commitment that many in Britain feared might mean, even if victory resulted, economic ruin, the end of the empire, and further irreversible social change. All this fitted together with the French desire to avoid any direct clash with Germany, if possible, and both governments' fear of the consequences of air bombardment of their cities and industries. Allied strategy, therefore, did not include a plan for victory through decisive battle. The French army stood on the defensive; Britain's Bomber Command was not "unleashed" against Germany for fear of German retaliation. Economic and diplomatic pressure alone remained.

This situation made Churchill's position even more lonely. Bursting with energy and ideas, he was temperamentally in favor of attacking the enemy and, alone in the cabinet, gripped by the sense that time was not an ally. But his attempts to infuse vigor into the war effort were handicapped by the mental gulf that separated him from his colleagues, the suspicion with which he was still viewed, and the clumsy decision-making machinery in which he was enmeshed. The success of Lloyd George's war cabinet in 1917–18 made the revival of a similar mechanism inevitable. In Chamberlain's cabinet, however, the dynamic force Lloyd George had supplied was missing, or rather was to be found only in Churchill, once again as in 1914–15 trying from a subordinate position to impose a coherent pattern on events. Furthermore, the war cabinet was only one of several loosely coordinated bodies with a hand in policymaking. Early in October it organized a Military Coordination Committee (MCC), chaired by Lord Chatfield, on which the three service ministers plus the chiefs of staff served. Finally there was the Chiefs of Staff Committee, which also reported directly to the war cabinet. It was not an efficient system and, in fact, institutionalized delay as the same issue was thrashed out at three different levels. This machinery survived until the Norwegian campaign mercilessly exposed its weaknesses and thus forced the first steps in the construction of a realistic instrument of war direction, a process that Churchill carried to completion when he became prime minister. Meanwhile, a politically isolated and frustrated first lord argued relentlessly, but without much success, for a more vigorous approach to waging war.

Far more than any specific action he took, it was Churchill's energy and the vigor of his imagination that set him apart from his colleagues during the "Twilight War," reinforced the growing consensus that he was the obvious national war leader, and in the end made him Chamberlain's successor. The energy radiated from him. As in 1914 he found the challenge of war exhilarating. His astonishing physical resilience belied his age. Old newsreels preserve the evidence: the sixty-four-year old first lord charging up a ship's gangplank, face set and yet managing to convey that he is enjoying it all, while his entourage pants behind him. His energy and imagination were not always fully informed or well directed, but there was no doubt about his stimulating influence. Long away from the center of affairs, Churchill, despite his efforts to keep informed, had not yet taken the full measure of the changes that twenty years had brought in military technology and consequently in operational possibilities, but neither had Britain's service chiefs. He readily accepted the Admiralty belief that "asdic" (sonar) was the answer to the submarine menace and, like his advisers, underestimated the constraints that air power would place on the navy. Although one of the pioneers of tank development, he had lost touch with advanced thinking on armored warfare and assumed, as did most military men, that defensive firepower retained its ascendancy. Many of his early memoranda refer back to his World War I experience, as if the new conflict might prove a linear extension of the old.

What is interesting, in fact remarkable, is how quickly Churchill began to catch up, while on certain issues he was on target from the beginning. He saw that a coherent production strategy related to a general view of the war's probable development was necessary, that the application of science to the war effort would be vital, and that a passive strategy of encirclement and attrition which surrendered the initiative to Germany could well be fatal. In discussing the relationship of production to strategy, Churchill from the first took seriously his position as a member of the war cabinet, with a responsibility for taking a broad view. He thus had, in his own mind at least, full license for his old urge to cross departmental frontiers. He also armed himself with a formidable weapon for these forays, installing his long-time scientific adviser, the Oxford physicist Frederick A. Lindemann, as head of the "First Lord's Statistical Branch," which dealt not only with naval matters but also examined material submitted to the war cabinet by other departments and provided Churchill with the means to direct searching critiques at them. His chief target was the Air Ministry, where he believed the disparity between resources committed and results, in terms of first-line squadrons available, was indefensible. In fact, he dissented fundamentally from the belief that the Royal Navy and the Royal Air Force could be Britain's principal contribution to the war effort, a point he made to Chamberlain when the war was barely two weeks old:

> The reason why I am anxious that the Army should be planned on a fifty or fifty-five division scale is that I doubt whether the French would acquiesce in a division of effort which gave us the sea and air and left them to pay almost the whole blood tax on land. Such an arrangement would certainly be agreeable to us; but I do not like the idea of our having to continue the war single-handed.[90]

It was not only the related questions of production and strategy that exercised the first lord, but also every aspect of the war effort drew his attention and produced a minute. The chancellor of the exchequer was told on 24 September: "I am thinking a great deal about you and your problem, as one who has been through the Exchequer mill. I look forward to a severe budget based on the broad masses of the well-to-do."[91] Early in October the home secretary was informed that, "in spite of having a full day's work usually here, I cannot help feeling anxious about the Home Front. . . . I hear continual complaints from every quarter of the lack of organisation on the Home Front. Can't we get at it?" There followed thoughts and suggestions on blackout regulations (too severe), meat rations (not generous enough), and the failure to utilize properly the spirit and enthusiasm of the middle-aged ("Why do we not form a Home Guard? . . .").[92] Even the prime minister, with whom Churchill tried to cultivate relations of trust and friendship, was not spared: "As I shall be away till Monday, I give you my present thought on the main situation. . . . I hope you will consider carefully what I write to you. I do so only in my desire to aid you in your responsibilities and discharge my own."[93] None of these proposals endeared Churchill to his colleagues and, indeed, Chamberlain, who had feared precisely this reaction, was irked enough to have a conversation with Churchill which slowed down the flow of Churchillian exhortation, at least in the prime minister's direction. For someone surrounded by dubious friends, someone long suspected of lacking balance and judgment while being all too ambitious, Churchill's conduct was not politically wise, but wise or foolish it was the way he was made. War was a challenge to which he had to respond.

There is another element to be considered in Churchill's relations with his cabinet colleagues, impossible to document but suggesting itself irresistibly. In addition to his long political career, experience of high command in war, and intuitive knowledge of the dynamics of conflict, another factor set him apart. Chamberlain and his cabinet sprang from the Victorian upper-middle class, while Churchill came from one of the great landed families whose history for centuries had been entwined with that of the nation. There was always an aristocratic self-assurance about him, a conviction of having been born to lead. The cautious businessmen who had taken over the Conservative leadership a generation before confronted in Churchill an older, more robust leadership tradition, with more than a dash of Elizabethan buccaneering spirit. In some important ways Churchill and his colleagues were inhabiting different mental worlds. It must have added to the sense of uneasiness he generated, an uneasiness then ascribed to his "faulty judgment," a term vague enough to encompass both specific errors and the opinion that he did not look at issues from the correct angle of vision.

Apart from these issues, others continually arose on which Churchill behaved in a way that continued to reinforce doubts. His instinct for the application of technology to war spilled over departmental boundaries. He forced a reluctant Air Ministry to put photoreconnaissance on a proper footing by threatening to take it over himself; his commitment to the "UP," an antiaircraft rocket that was a favorite project of Lindemann's, was costly in time and effort, and useless. Then there was "Cultivator Number Six," an immense, armored excavating machine that was to approach enemy lines at one-half mile per hour under cover of darkness (but clearly not muffled in silence), digging a five-by-seven-foot trench along which infantry would follow to the attack. The pattern of 1914–15 seemed to be repeating itself. Churchill's energy, enthusiasm, and imagination were creating resentment and confirming adverse views of his judgment, while politically he seemed dependent solely upon the goodwill of the prime minister.

It is at this point that the analogy with 1914–15 begins to break down. At that time Churchill had virtually no political base, was detested by the Conservatives, and was not well liked in Liberal circles. Now support for him, at least as a war minister, cut across party lines. The dissident Conservatives admired him, as did many in the Liberal and Labour parties. Chamberlain needed to foster a national war effort—at a minimum, he needed trade union cooperation—even if he fought the sort of limited war he desired. Churchill was the only minister in his government with "national" appeal. If he resigned on an issue related to the war, there would be trouble. In 1915 Asquith would have had difficulty keeping him. In 1939 Chamberlain would certainly have trouble if he left. Thus, the prime minister could not really dispense with his ebullient first lord but only try to contain him within the framework of his own strategy of limited commitment, unless Churchill ruined himself. On his past record, this was always a possibility.

Symptomatic of Chamberlain's desire to contain Churchill was the first lord's absence from meetings of the Anglo-French Supreme War Council, the body that formulated alliance strategy. The council first met on 12 September 1939 but only on 5 February 1940 did Churchill make an appearance. Chamberlain knew that Churchill had long-standing and carefully fostered contacts both in the French army and, perhaps more importantly, among activist

French politicians like Paul Reynaud and Georges Mandel who also were dissatisfied with the torpor of Allied proceedings. Both Chamberlain and the French premier, Edouard Daladier, preferred that their more aggressive ministers be kept away from the periodic Allied summits. This did not prevent Churchill from constantly pressing for a more vigorous strategy. "Operation Royal Marine" was one of his more imaginative schemes, a typical Churchill package of technological ingenuity and aggressive design. He suggested in September the sowing of specially designed "fluvial mines" in the canals and rivers of western Germany to disrupt the Reich's vital inland water transport. Nothing eventually came of the idea because the French, fearful of German retaliation, stalled until Royal Marine was swallowed by greater events in May. But Royal Marine showed in miniature the determined aggressiveness that Churchill was sure would be necessary to defeat Germany. It showed as well his temperament. The fact that many of the barges on Germany's rivers and canals belonged to neutrals weighed heavily with the British and French governments; it troubled Churchill much less. The ruthless touch in Churchill the war leader was seen more dramatically, however, in his favorite offensive project.

Even before the war Churchill's eyes had been on the Baltic. There, he believed, Germany could be struck a serious, perhaps mortal, blow. His imagination had fastened upon the German industry's need for Swedish iron ore. If those ore shipments could be interrupted, a crisis would arise in German war production. Therefore, almost as soon as he returned to the Admiralty he began to press "Operation Catherine" on the naval staff. To control the Baltic he proposed to take the Royal Navy's five oldest battleships, rebuild them extensively to make them "proof" against mines, torpedoes, and aircraft and then send them into the Baltic accompanied by cruisers and destroyers as well as armored supply ships. The plan shriveled under scrutiny, doubtless fortunately, but only after considerable staff study finally convinced the first lord that it was simply not feasible. His insistence, foreshadowed in 1914–15, in forcing the investigation of project after project and of refusing to accept that the experts knew best until he had probed the limits of their confidence in their own judgment and forced them to meet his rigorous standards of proof was why he alarmed and infuriated so many of them. It also accounts for the irritation threaded through the memoirs of staff officers and civil servants. But if Churchill could not have Catherine, there was another possibility and one he also began canvassing vigorously the moment he returned to office.

When the Swedish port of Lulea was frozen during the winter, the iron ore was transported by rail to the ice-free Norwegian port of Narvik and then, never leaving Norwegian territorial waters, to Germany. Churchill wanted to stop this traffic. The first lord urged the war cabinet to mine Norwegian territorial waters on 19 September, using the precedent of a minefield laid there by the Allies in 1918 to stop U-boats from slipping out into the Atlantic. With ingenious variations, he thereafter relentlessly pressed his case on his colleagues. If he could not have a mine barrier, what about merchant ships, their bows specially strengthened, roaming Norwegian coastal waters, seeking out and ramming, accidentally, German ore carriers? In all these considerations there was more disregard for the fine points of international law, a fact of which Churchill was fully aware. In a long, thoughtful memorandum written for the war cabinet on 16 December 1939, he addressed the central issue: How does liberal democracy confront totalitarian amorality?

> The final tribunal is our own conscience. We are fighting to re-establish the reign of law and to protect the liberties of small countries. Our defeat would mean an age of barbaric violence, and would be fatal, not only to ourselves but to the independent life of every small country in Europe . . . we have a right, and indeed are bound in duty, to abrogate for a space some of the conventions of the very laws we seek to consolidate and reaffirm. Small nations must not tie our hands when we are fighting for their rights and freedom. The letter of the law must not in supreme emergency obstruct those who are charged with its protection and enforcement. It would not be right or rational that the aggressor Power should gain one set of advantages by tearing up all laws, and another set by sheltering behind the innate respect for law of its opponents. Humanity rather than legality must be our guide.[94]

Linked with Churchill's willingness to set aside conventions was his obvious willingness to see the war spread to Scandinavia. At a minimum it would end the iron ore traffic, he argued. Churchill's ideas on interference with the ore traffic were not only based on an attitude toward taking the offensive not widely shared in the government but also on a specific tactical assumption. Britain, controlling the seas, could intervene decisively in Norway while Germany could not. This assumption was generally shared, but the likely impact on world opinion of Churchill's proposed hard line with neutrals was too much for Chamberlain and Halifax. They hoped to win without major fighting, and the information coming out of Germany that winter about plots against Hitler could only have reinforced that hope. The deadlock was complete. Churchill could not institute an offensive project without cabinet support. To his colleagues, however, the risks involved were simply too great. If the war had gone as expected, Churchill might well have found his situation so irksome that he would have once again acted rashly and finished himself politically, but one more time he was lucky. If Britain and France hesitated to strike, Stalin and Hitler did not.

On Churchill's sixty-fifth birthday the Russians attacked Finland, setting off an irrational enthusiasm for aid to the Finns. The Right in Britain and France certainly feared and hated the Soviet Union as much as, if not more than, Hitler. The surprising Finnish victories in the first stages of the war roused great popular enthusiasm. Aid to Finland could give an appearance of martial dynamism to British and French cabinets under criticism for lacking it. But it is hard to envision how anyone could have believed that an Anglo-French war with the Soviet Union would damage Germany. In fact, the sudden spasm of enthusiasm for action in Scandinavia cannot be fully explained except as a perceived safe release from the tensions of the "phoney war." Churchill contributed his share of pro-Finnish, anti-Bolshevik rhetoric but from the beginning looked upon aid to the Finland movement as a way of accomplishing his long-held designs on the Swedish ore fields. Narvik was the obvious base port for an Allied force heading for Finland; the railroad to the ore fields their best, in fact only, line of advance; and the Swedish ports on the Gulf of Bothnia, from which the ore was shipped in the summer, their jumping off point for Finland. Whether an Allied expedition succeeded in helping "gallant Finland" or not, it would certainly place the Swedish ore fields out of Germany's reach, a solution acceptable to Churchill.

With aid to Finland at the top of the agenda, Churchill attended his first Supreme War Council meeting. Action, or at least the appearance of it, was becoming politically necessary and no symbol of action was more potent than Churchill. But if Churchill knew why he wanted to use "aid to Finland," it is difficult to see that anyone else did, except perhaps the French who saw it as a way to keep the fighting safely distant. The entire project quickly drifted into fantasy, with detailed military planning going on side by side with a diplomatic strategy that left a veto on the plan in the hands of the Norwegian and Swedish governments. They had no doubt about whom it was most dangerous to offend and promptly declined to cooperate. Then the discussion was aborted by the Russo-Finnish armistice on 12 March, which caused the fall of the French government, an appropriate final touch. Out of all this confusion came only one positive decision for action. Churchill finally extracted permission to lay a minefield in Norwegian coastal waters. This operation was then delayed yet again in order to try to synchronize it with the launching of Royal Marine, but with the French still adamant about military activity any closer than Karelia, the minelaying was finally set for 8 April 1940. At that point Churchill's offensive urges collided with Hitler's.

The German decision to invade Norway was born in part of the German navy's First World War frustration at being bottled up in the North Sea. As early as 1925 a German naval writer had urged taking Norway in any future war with Britain to ensure access to the Atlantic. Then Hitler began to worry that the Western allies would do precisely what Churchill was urging and interfere with the iron ore supplies. Out of this emerged *Weservebung*, a bold and astonishingly successful gamble. Using air-transported troops and virtually the entire German navy with a recklessness the British never anticipated, on 9 April the Germans overran Denmark, whose airfields they needed as staging points for their transports, and all the principal Norwegian ports. The British misread the meaning of early intelligence indications, and when they began tardily to react, found that the basic premise on which so much discussion had proceeded was false. German air power virtually negated British sea power in Norwegian coastal waters. The British lost the initiative in Norway in the first hours of the campaign. Their improvised responses never produced quite the right combination of forces and leadership to wrest it back, and as the reality of German success sank in, rumblings of discontent became steadily louder in London.

The Admiralty was the ministry most concerned with Norway, and Churchill later wrote that "it was a marvel that I survived and maintained my position in public esteem and parliamentary confidence."[95] The initial signs were indeed ominous. Memories of the Dardanelles were revived, and the government whips began to spread the word that Churchill was responsible for most of the mistakes. Yet it was the Norwegian campaign that made him prime minister. This takes some explaining.

While Churchill certainly had made his share of errors, the actual problem went much deeper. The Germans had the initiative; Allied policy had seen to that. No one in London ever dreamed the Germans would strike as boldly as they in fact did. Interservice cooperation was poor. The command machinery in London was incredibly clumsy. Only time and painfully learned wisdom would change these conditions. Indeed the Norwegian experience led to an important reconstruction of the British machinery for war direction. Chamberlain asked Churchill to take the chair of the MCC just before the Norwegian campaign opened. Of this arrangement Churchill later wrote: "I had, therefore, an exceptional measure of responsibility but no power of effective direction."[96] Moreover, the prime minister did nothing to clarify the confused relationship between the war cabinet, the MCC, and the chiefs of staff. From a subordinate position there was little Churchill could do, and political danger if he tried, as the whispers in the corridors of Whitehall and Westminster clearly showed.

Whether he perceived the political danger, or merely saw the administrative futility of his position, Churchill quickly handed the MCC chairmanship back to the prime minister on 15 April. By late April, however, with failure in Norway looming, he was compelled to force a major reorganization of the central direction of the war. After a meeting of the Supreme War Council in Paris on 22–23 April, Churchill returned to London, brooding on the way the war was developing, and wrote a virtual ultimatum to the prime minister. Pointing out that there was no effective grip on the war effort and that only the prime minister was in a position to provide it, Churchill then added:

> If you feel able to bear this burden, you may count upon my unswerving loyalty. . . . If you do not feel you can bear it . . . you will have to delegate your powers to a deputy who can concert and direct the general movement of our war action, and who will enjoy your support and that of the War Cabinet unless very good reason is shown to the contrary.[97]

The letter never had to be sent. Chamberlain rang and asked Churchill to dine at Number 10. The prime minister doubtless knew what was brewing, since Churchill was not good at keeping his feelings secret. "He cannot really tell lies. This is what makes him so bad a conspirator," Baldwin had mused in retirement.[98] A long after-dinner conversation followed. "I have no record of what passed, which was of a most friendly character. I am sure I put the points in my unsent letter, and that the Prime Minister agreed with their force and justice," Churchill wrote demurely eight years later.[99]

The result of that evening's friendly chat was a directive issued by Chamberlain on 1 May, conferring on Churchill, as chairman of the MCC, responsibility "for giving guidance and directions to the Chiefs of Staff Committee." He also was given the right to summon the chiefs of staff "for personal consultation at any time when he considers it necessary" and, to give his new powers reality, a "suitable central staff," headed by Major General Hastings Ismay, was placed at his disposal.[100] This left Churchill, while now virtually minister of defense, still subject to Chamberlain and the war cabinet. If it was no longer quite responsibility without power, it was certainly responsibility with carefully trammeled power. It was nevertheless, in embryo, the organizational structure that Churchill used ten days later when he became prime minister to grasp immediate and effective control of the entire British war effort. But perhaps what is most startling is that Churchill had confronted Chamberlain with a veiled but palpable threat of resignation and as a result increased his powers at a time when gossip, at least in Conservative circles, was blaming him for misjudgment in Norway and many thought his position weakened in consequence. Was Chamberlain being Machiavellian, giving Churchill enough rope to hang himself? Perhaps, but a more likely explanation is that Churchill's position was, in fact, a much stronger one than it appeared to be, and that the prime minister was well aware of it.

Churchill alone among Chamberlain's ministers had a following that cut across normal party lines, dating back to his consistent opposition to Germany which had begun to tie him into both the Center and Left opinion in the late 1930s. War and his return to office had strengthened his standing as a possible consensus war leader. His vigor and imagination set him apart from other members of the government, an image reinforced by his broadcasts and speeches and by the care he spent on Admiralty public relations. In the autumn of 1939 one left-wing paper, *The Star*, ran a picture of Churchill on its front page, his face set in its best look of glowering determination, accompanied by the caption "this is the man he [Hitler] fears." Churchill's lack of a "progressive" attitude on social and imperial questions was not so much forgotten as set aside as temporarily irrelevant. (Perhaps it was as well for his fortunes that it was not generally known that the minute he entered the war cabinet he again took up his rearguard action on India, an indication of his inflexible resolve that Britain's world power must survive.)

As the bleak uneasy winter of 1939–40 passed into spring and Germany's ability to plan boldly and strike vigorously was contrasted with Anglo-French hesitancy and confusion, many became gripped by the fear that had long nagged Churchill: the Allies were losing the war. Military failure in Norway acted as a catalyst, bringing together those who wanted a more vigorous war administration and encouraging them toward the effort required to force a change. This all surfaced in the "Norway Debate" in the House of Commons on 7–8 May 1940, the most dramatic parliamentary episode of the century. Once the spirit in which the war was being fought became the major political issue, and with it the need for a national government, Churchill inevitably became the obvious man. He alone was acceptable and believable as leader in that context. Lloyd George at seventy-seven, his only possible rival, had become an appeaser some years before and was now quite defeatist.

Chamberlain's 1 May directive was an attempt to head off the rising storm of criticism. What doomed Chamberlain was simply that he and his government, Churchill apart, had completely lost the credibility necessary to sustain a national war effort. Chamberlain did not face this fact until the bitter end, perhaps not surprisingly since most informed opinion expected him to weather the storm. When the venom of the attack on him in the House and the defection of nearly half his normal majority in the ensuing vote of confidence convinced Chamberlain he had to go, he made an effort, before finally giving up, to pass his crown to Halifax, who was acceptable to some Labour leaders but lacked the spirit for the inevitable fight with Churchill. Churchill became prime minister, then, because of a surge of national resolve to beat Hitler, and specifically because the Labour party, without whose wholehearted support that resolve would have been fatally impaired, refused to accept Chamberlain as a war leader any longer.

There were accidental elements in the final stages. Chamberlain, for instance, handled the House of Commons very maladroitly, but looking back forty years later, it is difficult not to see a certain element of inevitability in what happened. Churchill stood for victory. To a nation, most of whose citizens believed victory was essential to the maintenance and even the improvement of their way of life, that was the crucial issue. When Sir Edward Spears, a devoted admirer of Churchill's, noted that the new prime minister's first appearance in the House of Commons was that of "the High Priest of a great religion dedicating a nation to measureless sacrifice . . . ," he caught an essential element in what had happened but missed the central ambiguity.[101]

Churchill stood for the preservation of as much of Britain's traditional social order as possible, and all its world power. Most of the support that had allowed him to displace Chamberlain came from those who hoped and expected sweeping reforms as the reward for their efforts in achieving victory. But before British society could be remade, victory over Germany had to be won.

Notes

1. Herbert H. Asquith to Venetia Stanley, 25 March 1915, *CV3*, pt. 1:742.

2. *OB*, 3:469. Compare Arthur J. Marder, *From the Dreadnought to Scapa Flow: The Royal Navy in the Fisher Era* (London, 1961–70), 2:292. ". . . It was his work during the critical prewar period that will give him a secure place in naval history."

3. Arthur J. Marder, "The Dardanelles Revisited," in *From the Dardanelles to Oran: Studies of the Royal Navy in War and Peace 1915–1940* (London, 1974), 1, 32.

4. Churchill to Asquith, 29 December 1914, *CV3*, pt. 1:344. The colorful remark about chewing barbed wire comes from this memorandum.

5. Churchill to Sir Charles Sargent, September 1919, *CV4*, pt. 2:886. This entire memorandum (886–93), written for the postwar Royal Commission on War Inventions, is worth reading. Churchill is referring to Wells's "The Land Ironclads," a short story published in 1903.

6. Ibid., 886–87.

7. Ibid., 891.

8. Churchill to Arthur Conan Doyle, 1 October 1916, *CV3*, pt. 2:1572. The Royal Commission on War Inventions said much the same thing in its final report of 17 November 1919, citing Churchill's "receptivity, courage and driving force" as chiefly responsible for giving the idea of the tank "practical shape." *OB*, 3:537 n.2.

9. War Council minutes, 13 January 1915, *CV3*, pt. 1:411.

10. Alan Morehead, *Gallipoli* (New York, 1956), 46.

11. Marder, "The Dardanelles Revisited," 1–32.

12. Quoted in Sir Roger Keyes, *The Naval Memoirs of Admiral of the Fleet Sir Roger Keyes* (London, 1934–35), 1:455–56.

13. Lord Beaverbrook, *Politicians and the War 1914–1916*, 1 vol. ed. (London, 1960), 125–26.

14. *FH*, 15.

15. Admiral Lord Fisher to Lord Cromer, 11 October 1916, in *Fear God and Dread Nought: The Correspondence of Admiral of the Fleet Lord Fisher of Kilverstone*, ed. Arthur J. Marder (London, 1952–59), 3:375 (italics in original).

16. Anthony Storrs, "The Man," in A. J. P. Taylor et al., *Churchill Revised* (New York, 1969), 229–74. Storrs, an eminent psychiatrist, has produced the only persuasive "psychohistory" interpretation of Churchill to date.

17. Quoted in *OB,* 3:473.

18. Churchill's own account, "Painting as a Pastime," originally published in *Strand Magazine* (December 1921), has been reprinted in his *Thoughts and Adventures* (London, 1932) and as a booklet, *Painting as a Pastime* (London, 1948). Storrs has pointed out how unconsciously revealing of Churchill's inner self this little essay is.

19. Churchill memorandum, 15 October 1915, *CV3,* pt. 2:1221.

20. Beaverbrook, *Politicians and the War,* 127.

21. Churchill memorandum, 3 December 1915, *CV3,* pt. 2:1306. The entire paper (1303–08) is worth reading.

22. Churchill to Clementine Churchill, 2 February 1915, *CV3,* pt. 2:1410.

23. Quoted in *OB,* 3:793.

24. Quoted in Charles, Lord Moran, *Churchill: The Struggle for Survival, 1940–1965* (Boston, 1966), 794. See also the entry in the diary of David Lloyd George's mistress, Frances Stevenson, 13 February 1934. "Orpen described a scene to me in his studio while he was painting Winston just after he had lost office. W. came to Orpen for a sitting, but all he did was to sit in a chair before the fire with his head bowed in his hands, uttering no word. Orpen went out to lunch without disturbing him and found Winston in the same position when he returned. At four o'clock W. got up and asked Orpen to call him a taxi, and departed without further speech. D. [avid Lloyd George] said it must have been gall and wormwood to him to be useless and inactive. . . ." A. J. P. Taylor, ed., *Lloyd George: A Diary by Frances Stevenson* (London, 1971), 253.

25. Churchill to Jack Churchill, 15 July 1916, *CV3,* pt. 2:1531.

26. Churchill memorandum, 1 August 1916, ibid., 1534–39.

27. Churchill memorandum, 9 November 1916, *CV4,* pt. 1:27–33.

28. Sir Abe Bailey to David Lloyd George, 2 December 1916, *CV3,* pt. 2:1589.

29. Sir George Younger to Lloyd George, 8 June 1917, *CV4,* pt. 1:70.

30. Lord Derby to Lloyd George, 8 June 1917, ibid.

31. Winston S. Churchill, "Naval War Policy 1917," 7 July 1917, ibid., 77–99, deserves to be read in full.

32. *Times* (London), 18 July 1917, quoted in ibid., 99n.

33. Churchill to Sir Archibald Sinclair, 29 December 1917, ibid., 222.

34. Churchill to Lloyd George, 9 September 1918, ibid., 391.

35. Churchill memorandum, 21 October 1917, in Winston S. Churchill, *The World Crisis,* 5 vols. (New York, 1923–29), 4:310.

36. Churchill memorandum, 19 November 1918, *CV4,* pt. 1:419.

37. Churchill speech, 11 November 1922, quoted in *OB,* 4:915.

38. Churchill to Sir William Robertson Nicoll, 31 January 1920: Churchill to Leicester and District Trades Council, 1 September 1920, *CV4,* pt. 2:1024, 1203. The letter to Nicoll, a prominent Liberal editor, was not in the event sent.

39. Churchill to Leicester and District Trades Council, 1 September 1920, *CV4*, pt. 2:1203.

40. Churchill's article is in *CV2*, pt. 1:105–11.

41. Edward Marsh, a civil servant and lifelong friend of Churchill's, quoted in *OB*, 2:111. Marsh remarked that "the italics were his."

42. Churchill speech, 3 January 1920, *CCS*, 2920–21.

43. Churchill to Leicester and District Trades Council, 1 September 1920, *CV4*, pt. 2:1204.

44. *The New Statesman*, 29 January 1965.

45. Conference of ministers, minutes, 9 February 1922, *CV4*, pt. 3:1763.

46. Churchill to the Countess of Lytton, 19 September 1922, ibid., 1986.

47. James Morris, *Farewell the Trumpets: An Imperial Retreat* (New York, 1978), 364.

48. Churchill, *The World Crisis* (New York: 1923–29), 5:491–96. "A Memorandum Upon the Pacification of the Middle East" is all Churchill ever had to say on the subject.

49. Churchill, "Remarks to a Palestinian Arab delegation," 30 March 1921, *CV4*, pt. 2:1419–21.

50. Churchill to H. A. L. Fisher, president of Board of Education, 18 November 1922, *CV4*, pt. 3:2126.

51. Churchill to Clementine Churchill, 15 September 1909, *CV2*, pt. 2:912.

52. Churchill to Clementine Churchill, 28 July 1914, ibid., pt. 3:1989.

53. Quoted in *OB*, 4:892 (italics in original).

54. Sir Geoffrey Shakespeare, quoted in *OB*, 4:892.

55. Quoted in *OB*, 5:19.

56. *GS*, 33.

57. J. H. Plumb, "The Historian," in Taylor, *Churchill Revised*, 168.

58. Speech to the Royal Society of St. George, 24 April 1933, quoted in *OB*, 5:486.

59. *Evening Standard*, "Londoner's Diary" column, 1 September 1938, quoted in ibid., 969.

60. Churchill to Lord Linlithgow, 3 November 1937, quoted in ibid., 480.

61. Linlithgow to Churchill, 4 May 1933; Churchill to Linlithgow, quoted in ibid., 480.

62. Quoted in *OB*, 4:408.

63. Quoted in Robert Rhodes James, *Churchill: A Study in Failure, 1900–1939* (New York, 1970), 220–21.

64. Philip Mason, in *Plain Tales from the Raj: Images of British India in the Twentieth Century*, ed. Charles Allen (London, 1975), 203.

65. Thomas Jones, *A Diary with Letters 1931–1950* (London, 1954), 204.

66. Quoted in *OB*, 5:451.

67. From the official transcript of Baldwin's remarks, quoted in ibid., 776.

68. Ibid.

69. *GS*, 216.

70. Ibid., 217.

71. Quoted in *OB*, 5:451–52.

72. Quoted in ibid., 450.

73. Quoted in ibid., 938.

74. Frederick Guest to Churchill, 19 June 1936, ibid., 759.

75. Churchill to Lord Londonderry, 6 May 1936, ibid., 733.

76. In an interview with F. W. Wilson, political editor of *The People*, 16 May 1924, quoted in H. Montgomery Hyde, *Baldwin: The Unexpected Prime Minister* (London, 1937), 213.

77. Nigel Nicolson, ed., *The Diaries and Letters of Harold Nicolson, 1930–1939* (New York, 1966), 282.

78. Churchill to Londonderry, 6 May 1936, *OB*, 5:733; *GS*, 221.

79. Baldwin to J. P. L. Thomas (n.d. but spring 1938), quoted from Baldwin's papers in Hyde, *Baldwin*, 537.

80. Neville Chamberlain to Hilda Chamberlain, 23 July 1939, quoted in *OB*, 5:1096.

81. Lord Camrose memorandum of conversation with Churchill, 3 July 1939, ibid., 1081.

82. See, for example, Churchill to Lady Violet Bonham Carter, 25 May 1936, ibid., 740. Asquith's daughter was a leading Liberal.

83. *GS*, 448.

84. Helen Wedgwood to her husband Josiah, 17 March 1938, *OB*, 5:918, n.3.

85. Churchill to his literary assistant A. M. Diston, 3 October 1937, ibid., 871.

86. Chamberlain to Hilda Chamberlain, 9 October 1938, ibid., 1009.

87. Lord Rothermere to Churchill, 15 October 1938, ibid., 1009.

88. Sir Patrick Donner, interview with Martin Gilbert, ibid., 1002.

89. Churchill speeches, 10, 14 March 1939, ibid., 1044.

90. Churchill to Chamberlain, 18 September 1939, *GS*, 458.

91. Churchill to Sir John Simon, 24 September 1939, ibid., 459.

92. Churchill to Sir John Anderson, 7 October 1939, ibid., 488.

93. Churchill to Chamberlain, 15 September 1939, ibid., 456–57.

94. "Norway—Iron Ore Traffic: Note by the First Lord of the Admiralty," 16 December 1939, ibid., 547. The entire note (544–47) is worth reading as an example of Churchill at his best as an advocate.

95. Ibid., 650.

96. Ibid., 587.

97. Ibid., 642.

98. Diary entry, 8 December 1937, *Nicolson Diaries*, 314.

99. *GS*, 642.

100. The directive is reproduced in ibid., 643–44.

101. Edward L. Spears, *Assignment to Catastrophe*, vol. 1, *Prelude to Dunkirk* (London, 1954), 138.

> . . . we shall defend our island, whatever the
> cost may be, we shall fight on the beaches,
> we shall fight on the landing grounds, we
> shall fight in the fields and in the streets, we
> shall fight in the hills; we shall never
> surrender.
>
> —WINSTON CHURCHILL
> 4 June 1940

Chapter Two

We Shall Never Surrender

"I thought I knew a great deal about it all," Churchill wrote later of the moment when he took over from Chamberlain, "and I was sure I should not fail."[1] By the time he had written those words, he was already guaranteed against the imputation of failure everywhere except perhaps in the innermost recesses of his own spirit. He also was dictating, at white heat, his narrative of the war years. A great classical scholar has said of Thucydides's *Peloponnesian War* that "no other historical subject is so much the product of its reporter."[2] While Churchill's memoirs cannot hope for the unique authority that Thucydides enjoys, *The Second World War* dominated the history of its period for a generation and remains an interpretation to which subsequent generations will have constant recourse, if only to dispute Churchill's version.

The opening pages of *Their Finest Hour* record Churchill's account of the formation of his government and his methods of business. At first sight, this brief essay on politics and administration is a curious digression, for which the author himself seems to apologize: ". . . the awful battle was now going on across the Channel and the reader is no doubt impatient to get there."[3] Yet it was a digression that Churchill, whose historical sense always leaned more toward narrative than toward analysis, clearly thought to be important. In it he first described the extent of Britain's contribution to Germany's defeat. Even as he wrote, British power and the empire that was its most spectacular manifestation were fading swiftly away. Whether or not he fully grasped the degree to which the war had eroded British power, he could have had little doubt about the increasingly one-sided nature of the "special relationship" with the United States. By pointing out Britain's massive contribution to Hitler's destruction, he was reminding his countrymen of what they had endured and accomplished and encouraging them to remain worthy of their great heritage. He also was reminding his American readers, conscious of Stalin's shadow across Europe, how important partnership with Britain had been in the defeat of a previous tyranny, reminding them as well that Britain's claims to be heard rested on more than its present strength.

Churchill's account of the formation of his coalition and his own methods of work was also important in setting the scene against which his narrative would unfold. His emphasis on national unity, which transcended party ("the attitude of all those I sent for was like that of soldiers in action, who go to places assigned to them at once without question"[4]), struck a note that he maintained throughout subsequent volumes, although only by virtue of excluding nearly all discussion of domestic politics during the war. It has even been suggested that the way the British perceive themselves today has been strongly affected by Churchill's version of their collective behavior during the war years.[5] Unquestionably, he smoothed the edges of political behavior when recording it for posterity, just as he overstated the harmony and camaraderie between Britain and America, or between himself and the service chiefs in matters of strategy and operations.

This polishing process tended to obscure the foundations of his power which rested upon his personality, his vision, and his ability to communicate both so effectively. Churchill had always believed in his destiny. Repeatedly as a young soldier and war correspondent he had asserted to total strangers that he would one day be prime minister. Attaining his dream released incredible energies. "I know how sincere natures gather force and conviction from motion and activity,"[6] he had written in 1911, ironically in a letter opposing women's suffrage. His personal "force and conviction" in his power to lead Britain to victory carried Churchill through five years of ninety-hour weeks, a heart attack, and a near fatal bout of pneumonia. The same personal commitment to victory at all costs, projected in speeches that were a kind of dialogue between himself and his nation's history, was the basis of his astounding hold on public opinion. Within weeks of becoming prime minister his approval rating, measured by opinion polls, passed 90 percent. For the next five years it hovered between 80 and 90 percent, only once slipping to 78 percent. Most of the British believed in their country's superiority; they believed as well that they invariably had won the last battle. Churchill, fresh from writing *History of the English-Speaking Peoples*, shared those beliefs. His speeches gave them memorable expression. His power rested on a consensus, emerging on the eve of war, that saw him as the one figure in public life who adequately incarnated the national determination to survive and conquer.

His power rested also on the revolutionary effect of Chamberlain's fall on the fortunes of the two major political parties. Labour moved from the wings to the center of the political stage, opening the breach through which Churchill stormed Ten Downing Street. Churchill's entente with the Labour party and the trade union movement was strictly for the duration, but it was essential to his position. He could not have become a "national" leader unless Labour accepted him. His relationship with the Conservative party, on the other hand, was highly ambiguous. "Halifax would be the man if Chamberlain is ever got rid of," a British colonel assured Clare Boothe Luce just before Chamberlain's fall.[7] After that event the party still remained in the hands of Chamberlain and Halifax. Only the fortuitous conjunction of the dying Chamberlain's resignation as party leader just after the end of the Battle of Britain and Halifax's lack of desire to fight with Churchill enabled the prime minister to become Conservative party leader. Thus, he neutralized the party as a possible source of opposition and consolidated his power base in a way that Lloyd George had never been able to do. But his conservatism was always a matter of instinct, romantic instinct perhaps, rather than loyalty to party dogma. Ambitious, visionary, a political free-lance with touches of late Victorian liberalism, all describe Churchill better than the party label he wore most of his life. His closest associates—men like Lord Beaverbrook, Brendan Bracken, or Professor Frederick Lindemann—were certainly not party regulars.

This unorthodox element in Churchill's makeup alarmed the powerful Whitehall civil servants who might have presented major problems had Churchill's grip on public opinion and the House of Commons been less sure. The civil service was capable, proud, deeply entrenched, and had a long memory. Churchill was firmly labeled as a difficult minister, indifferent to departmental frontiers, established procedures, and official wisdom. On the eve of Chamberlain's fall, one civil service mandarin confided to his diary that Churchill was "useless," while another was so distressed when Churchill succeeded Chamberlain that he could not bring himself to congratulate the new prime minister. Such reactions seem to have had little effect on Churchill. He had been in politics long enough to know that "the loyalties that center upon number one are enormous."[8] Thus, the urgency of the situation and the impact of Churchill's personality soon swung most of the civil service into line. The same mandarin who would not congratulate Churchill was heard a few weeks later exhorting other officials in Churchillian terms that Britain must not contemplate any result short of victory.[9]

Churchill, however, did not control every facet of government activity, an impression his memoirs, with their broadsides of memoranda cajoling, exhorting, or hectoring every conceivable addressee, tend to give. Powerful departments headed by ministers of some political weight could and did obstruct and even defeat the prime minister. The Foreign Office under Anthony Eden did so over relations with France, while the Colonial Office, in alliance with the Foreign Office, fought stubbornly against Churchill's Zionist sympathies in defense of the official policy on Palestine laid down in the 1939 White Paper. There were also entire areas of domestic policy where the prime minister seldom intervened because his interest was at best intermittent. The central issue was the war.

In that area Churchill indisputably exercised an authority that was almost unquestioned and certainly unshaken throughout the war. Grand strategy was his particular domain. He had sought in vain in 1914–15 to shape British strategy from a subordinate position. Now that he was "number one," he intended to impose his strategic vision on British policy. He was fortunate in finding more suitable machinery through which to work than had existed at any time during the First World War. The obvious failures in strategic planning and interservice cooperation then had led to the creation of the Chiefs of Staff Committee (1924) which offered unified military advice to the government. The chiefs of staff in turn were served by the Joint Planning and Joint Intelligence committees, established in 1927 and 1936, respectively. In Chamberlain's final rearrangement of responsibility for war direction, Churchill had been given the task of presiding over the deliberations of the chiefs of staff and providing them with guidance on behalf of the war cabinet.

Churchill thus became a de facto minister of defense. Once prime minister, he turned the arrangement into the central feature of his own machinery of war direction, becoming formally minister of defense. Under Chamberlain's scheme, Churchill was to be assisted by a small staff directed by Major General Hastings Ismay who was already deputy secretary to the war cabinet. To facilitate matters, Ismay would become an additional member of the Chiefs of Staff Committee, a move Churchill also adapted to his own purposes. Ismay, while remaining part of the war cabinet staff, became Churchill's chief staff officer as well. With his seat on the committee, he was Churchill's link with the service chiefs. Ismay's staff formed the Office of the Minister of Defense and a crucial element in Churchill's success.

Ismay, as the prime minister's personal chief of staff, became a well-known figure, although his role has been rather consistently misinterpreted. He did not advise on policy and would quickly have forfeited the general trust he enjoyed if he had acted in that capacity. He was an indispensable liaison man, a facilitator, and not infrequently a conciliator. Likewise, his two chief subordinates, Leslie Hollis and Ian Jacob (colonels in 1940, generals in 1945), functioned not as advisers but as a "handling machine" to link the prime minister in an orderly fashion to the rest of the government. Enabling an often erratic genius to work within a complex bureaucracy, Ismay, Hollis, Jacob, and the small staff they directed made a contribution that Churchill acknowledged in a single sentence: "The war machine over which I presided as Minister of Defence was capable of enforcing all decisions with precision."[10]

Churchill functioned more efficiently than many had thought possible, in large part because of the administrative arrangements that allowed him to utilize a system within which his previous ministerial experience had always found him to be something of a foreign body. His famous red "Action this Day" label affixed to minutes would not have been so effective a spur, nor his injunction that delays in a favorite plan or project be reported to him so useful a warning, if he had not had his own capable and conscientious staff officers pursuing his papers through the bureaucratic maze.* "In my experience of Service Departments, which is a long one," he told Eden during his struggle to convince the War Office to accept the commando idea, "there is always a danger that anything contrary to Service prejudices will be obstructed and delayed by officers of second grade in the machine."[11] Churchill's staff could not prevent this from happening, but they made it possible for one man to grip the government machine as thoroughly as is possible

---

*An action-this-day minute of 2 August 1940 directs Ismay to collect information on pilot training, report on "plans for lectures on tactical subjects" to troops, ask about scrap metal collection, demand a report on the activities of the Admiralty's salvage department since April, request information plans for use of civil defense workers during an invasion, and require a report "on one sheet of paper" on the development of armored divisions. *FH*, 651. This would start Ismay's staff to making requests and inquiries to a half-dozen departments, all of which would feel the prime minister's gaze on them. Good descriptions of how Churchill's staff, civil and military, functioned can be found in *OB*, 6:322–26, 454–55, 592–93, 891–94.

in a free society. His characterization of his debt to his staff as "immeasurable" is completely accurate.

When he designated himself as minister of defense, Churchill signaled an intention to dominate strategic policy, an intent that could have surprised few. The war cabinet never showed any disposition to challenge his control of this area, and the cabinet's Defense Committee, its direct link with the chiefs of staff, was dominated by the prime minister and minister of defense. British strategy, therefore, would be what Churchill, the service chiefs, and circumstances could make of it.

Churchill's first team of service chiefs was not a strong one. General Sir Edmund Ironside, chief of the Imperial General Staff and a brave, colorful, but not very intellectual soldier, was rapidly replaced on 27 May by General Sir John Dill, intelligent but stiff, reserved, and rather pessimistic, perhaps because he was worn down by private tragedies.* Air Chief Marshal Sir Cyril Newall, chief of the Air Staff and chairman of the committee, was the reverse of Ironside—colorless but capable. Admiral Sir Dudley Pound, chief of the Naval Staff, was, and remains, an enigma. Accidentally succeeding to his position upon the unexpected death of his predecessor on the eve of war, his own health was so uncertain that a medical officer who knew him well doubted his ability to endure the stress of high command in wartime. Pound nevertheless worked successfully with Churchill from September 1939 until his death in October 1943, but he did so at the price, the Royal Navy's official historian has charged, of deferring excessively to Churchill's views.**

From the moment he took responsibility for British strategy, then, Churchill was working with a group of service chiefs who lacked the fire, toughness, and clear strategic vision of their own to challenge him the way the "westerners" of the previous war had challenged Lloyd George. Nor would such a military figure emerge until General Sir Alan Brooke became chief of the Imperial General Staff in late 1941. Churchill was in a position to put his own impress

---

*Dill's wife, paralyzed by disease, was slowly dying. Returning from the pressures of the war and from the prime minister to domestic anguish became so intolerable that Dill would often sit for hours alone in a stupor of exhaustion in his London club. As early as July 1940, Churchill complained that Dill was not as helpful as he should be.

**The question of Pound's relationship with Churchill provoked a bitter argument between the British naval historian Captain S. W. Roskill and the late Professor Arthur J. Marder. Roskill's case can be found in *Churchill and the Admirals* (London, 1977); Marder's in "Winston Is Back: Churchill at the Admiralty, 1939–40," in Marder, *From the Dardanelles to Oran: Studies of the Royal Navy in War and Peace, 1915–1940* (London, 1974), 105–78.

on British strategy, constrained only by circumstances, of which the most pressing was that the initiative in the war belonged to Germany.

"I also rested under the impression of the superior power of the defensive, . . ." Churchill wrote of his prewar views, influenced as they were by his high regard for the French army. "I did not comprehend the violence of the revolution effected since the last war by the incursion of a mass of fast moving heavy armour. I knew about it but it had not altered my inner convictions as it should have done. There was nothing I could have done if it had."[12] That is a concise statement not only of Churchill's position but also of Britain as the German campaign in France unfolded. The BEF operated under French control, and as the German armored thrust paralyzed the French high command, it became increasingly difficult for the British even to discover what was happening, much less to have any impact on it. The extrication of the BEF from Belgium was the work of its commander, General Lord Gort, V.C., his subordinates, and fighting troops (almost all of whom were prewar regulars), aided by the British army's complete motorization and German errors.

The most famous of those errors was the "halt order" from Hitler which stopped General Heinz Guderian's armor on 24 May just short of the Dunkirk beaches and left open the BEF's way home. It was at this point that Churchill made his only important personal intervention in the BEF's struggle for survival, taking a decision for which he subsequently claimed great significance as a factor "which affected the movements of the German armor at the decisive point."[13] This was his order to the brigade of British troops, hastily flung into Calais on 22–23 May, to fight to the end in order to delay the German thrust along the coast toward the Dunkirk beaches. On the evening of 25 May the war cabinet's Defense Committee agreed that Gort should march to the sea as rapidly as possible (a decision Gort himself had already taken), and that the Calais garrison should fight to cover the southern flank of the withdrawal. The signal conveying this decision was sent to Brigadier Claude Nicolson at Calais about nine o'clock in the evening. Churchill sent it in the presence of Ironside and Secretary of State for War Eden, telling Ismay afterward that he felt ill (for years he became emotional when discussing the episode). About midnight a British minesweeper fought its way into Calais's fire-swept harbor to deliver Churchill's message. Nicolson's troops fought on until 27 May. "Calais was the crux," Churchill wrote nine years later. "Many other causes might have prevented the deliverance of Dunkirk, but it is certain that the three days gained by the defence of Calais enabled the Gravelines waterline to be held and that, without this, . . . all would have been cut off and lost."[14] The escape of the BEF was too complex to be ascribed to a single event. Calais was a factor whose importance, although considerable, is difficult to quantify. Certainly it held up one of Guderian's panzer divisions for a day after the halt order had been rescinded on 26 May, and in a situation where hours were precious that was important, although exactly how important will probably always be disputed.*

The whole episode has another significance. Churchill grew up in a world where the heroic defense of beleaguered imperial outposts—Lucknow, Rorke's Drift, Khartoum, Mafeking—excited the British imagination. To the prime minister such episodes showed the martial virtues of the British at their best, and the belief that the defense of Calais had been crucial to the salvation of the BEF reinforced the grip stubbornly held fortresses exerted on his powerful imagination. His attitude toward Tobruk and Singapore later would be strongly influenced by his inclination to view do-or-die defense as a virtue in itself.

In contrast to the struggle of the BEF, which Churchill could only watch "in flickering glimpses," *Their Finest Hour* records in detail the prime minister's involvement in the collapse of the Anglo-French alliance. Despite his affection for France and his range of contacts there, Churchill obviously had not fully grasped the ambivalence with which many Frenchmen viewed the war. His first visit to Paris on 16–17 May was therefore a shattering experience. Discovering that the French high command had lost its hold on the battle and sensing as well the atmosphere of defeat already beginning to permeate the French government, Churchill, as soon as he returned to London on the 17th, asked Chamberlain to chair a committee "to examine tonight the consequences of the withdrawal of the French government from Paris or the fall of that city, as well as the problems that would arise if it were necessary to withdraw the BEF from France. . . ."[15] At 6:30 that evening the

---

*One of the British defenders of Calais, Airey Neave, later made a careful study of the entire episode and found himself concluding only that "it formed part of the series of events, some foolish, some glorious, which saved the BEF," *The Flames of Calais: A Soldier's Battle 1940* (London, 1972), 215.

prime minister met with the chiefs of staff and asked them to examine "British Strategy in a Certain Eventuality." He also took steps to keep himself closely informed about both facts and moods in Paris, appointing Major General Sir Edward Spears, a longtime friend and supporter, whom he had met in France in 1916 and who was currently a Conservative member of Parliament for Carlisle, as his personal liaison with Paul Reynaud. The first week of the German offensive had brought Churchill up against the likelihood that France would leave the war, and with his characteristic resilience in adversity, he took prompt measures to work out an alternative strategy. He did not yet completely despair of keeping France in the war, if only as a government in exile in its North African territories. The events of 10–17 May also plunged him into a controversy over the degree to which it was prudent to commit British resources to France in the hope of encouraging the French to continue fighting. Echoes of that controversy still reverberate.

Britain entered the war with an air force smaller than Germany's but growing at a more rapid rate, and British monthly aircraft production overtook that of Germany in the course of 1939. Of Britain's 1,873 first-line aircraft, only 416 Royal Air Force planes were in France on 10 May. These, plus 1,200 French aircraft, faced 2,750 German planes. The devastating impact of German tactical air power, not only on the course of battle but also on the imagination of the French high command, led to mounting French demands for more British aircraft, counterpointed by claims that British selfishness in holding back aircraft that could have turned the tide of battle fully justified a French decision to consider French interests first, a decision many Frenchmen interpreted as requiring a speedy end to the fighting.

The reality, however, was very different. The French were not beaten by the *Luftwaffe* but by the German army's bold, almost rash, employment of new tactical concepts. When the French fastened on to German air power as the crucial element, Churchill found himself the focus of competing pressures. The French wanted to see more British fighters in their skies, but there was an irreducible minimum of squadrons necessary to ensure the defense of Britain. One version of this clash between French desires and British needs has Churchill, swayed by his feelings for France, prepared to be overly lavish with Fighter Command's precious *Hurricanes* and *Spitfires* and only dissuaded by a resignation threat from Air Chief Marshal Sir Hugh Dowding of Fighter Command. This story, although full of the drama of a clash of strong personalities, has no support in the records and was explicitly denied by Dowding after the war.* In fact, Churchill was certain from the beginning that failure on the ground was the key to what was happening in France. When General Maurice Gamelin, the French commander in chief, told him on 16 May that more British fighters were needed to stop the German tanks, Churchill replied: "No. It is the business of the artillery to stop the tanks."[16]

There was a consensus in the war cabinet, and in the political and service worlds generally, that even the defeat of France would not necessarily be fatal to Britain, whereas to be left defenseless against the *Luftwaffe* would be. Churchill fully shared this viewpoint. And although the French demand for fighter support was reiterated at every Anglo-French conference until France fell, Churchill steadily returned the same answer, finally telling the French cabinet on 12 June: "This is not the decisive point and this is not the decisive moment. That will come when Hitler hurls his *Luftwaffe* against Great Britain."[17] In spite of the fact that the British continually fed replacements to their frequently decimated squadrons in France and all but three squadrons of their metropolitan air force operated at some point over France, the Royal Air Force commitment had the appearance, as the campaign wore on, of a gesture in alliance politics undertaken with no serious hope of changing the course of events. The British approach to the Battle of France was increasingly in the spirit of a letter King George VI wrote to his mother, Queen Mary, after France surrendered: "Personally, I feel happier now that we have no allies to be polite to and to pamper."[18]

This view of events in Europe, a product of centuries of insular experience, would be an enormous source of strength but could not be expected to commend itself to the French. However, it is difficult to read the accounts of the five meetings of the Anglo-French Supreme War Council during the campaign in France without feeling that the French demand for more British fighters changed rapidly from a desperate grasping at tactical straws to a device for establishing a degree of British disloyalty to the alliance that would

---

*The story originated with Beaverbrook, whose considerable skills as a narrative historian were marred by a fondness for drama. A. J. P. Taylor, Beaverbrook's biographer, in his *English History 1914–1945* (New York, 1965), 485, gave it widespread circulation. It has been carefully analyzed and demolished by Patrick Cosgrave, *Churchill at War: Alone 1939–1940* (London, 1974), 191–210. See also John R. Colville's discussion in *The Churchillians* (London, 1981), 146–49, which includes a postwar letter from Dowding to Colville denying the resignation story.

justify a separate peace. Moreover, even the wholesale commitment of Fighter Command to France (not, in any case, administratively possible) would not have turned the tide. As it was, the Royal Air Force lost 959 aircraft, including 477 fighters, during the French campaign, a number close to the frontline strength of the French air force on 10 May.

In retrospect, there was nothing Churchill or the British government could have done to prevent the military collapse in France, or to prevail upon the French government, once Marshal Pétain was in the ascendant, to transfer itself overseas. More important was the development of a strategy for survival without France and one which, in the long term, offered some prospect of victory, for without that even Churchill would have found it hard to sustain morale. This process began when Churchill on 16 May listened "dumbfounded" to Gamelin's despairing exposition of the military situation in Paris. The prime minister's actions upon his return to London set in motion the business of thinking out Britain's new strategy. By the time the last of the BEF reached England, the outline was complete, and Britain's course for the next several years, in some cases for the balance of the war, had been charted.

Churchill's personal contribution to this new strategy had to do less with details than with the spirit that suffused it. Aggressiveness had always been one of his most pronounced characteristics and one that in the past had made many feel uneasy about him. That instinct now perfectly matched the situation. The prime minister announced repeatedly, in public and private, that Britain would do and suffer anything rather than surrender. This position, and the passion and rhetoric that accompanied it, were distasteful, perhaps even embarrassing, to those like Halifax who feared the consequences of total war and hoped that somehow it could be avoided.* This hope surfaced in Halifax's remarks during the war cabinet meetings on 26–28 May. Three weeks later, still hoping, he sent the Swedish ambassador a message through his deputy, R. A. Butler: "Common sense and not bravado would dictate the British Government's policy."[19] Hitler and not Churchill was the nemesis of the foreign secretary's reasonableness. Churchill knew

---

*It was not only senior Conservatives who found Churchill's rhetoric embarrassing at times. A younger member of the House, interviewed by the prime minister for a junior ministerial appointment, was also treated to a graphic description of the government going down fighting in Whitehall. "That is what I have to offer you if you join my government. Can you face it?" "I don't know," was the cool reply. "They are not circumstances to which I am accustomed." Laurence Thompson, *1940* (New York, 1966), 150.

the futility and the danger of further discussion with Hitler, and steadily tightening his grip, he made the desire to explore the possibility of a compromise peace an emotion no longer respectable.* When Hitler made his "peace offer" on 19 July—in effect an invitation to the British to buy peace on German terms—Churchill gave Halifax the job of broadcasting Britain's refusal. The spirit that energized the British by then was that in which Churchill ordered the ruthless, preemptive strike against the French fleet on 3 July, an action characteristically opposed by Halifax.

Churchill's determination never to accept German hegemony in Europe, allied with the upsurge of insular pride and nationalism that he fanned, fused into the essential spirit of the post-Dunkirk British strategy. His specific contributions to that strategy, conditioned as it was both by circumstances and the weapons Britain had available, were not, however, similarly all-pervasive. In part, this was because the formulation of strategy had become the work of highly trained staff officers, and Churchill's credentials in this area were virtually nonexistent. Educated as a professional soldier in an era when professionalism was somewhat suspect in the British army, especially in smart cavalry regiments like his own 4th Hussars, he had left the army as a lieutenant. He read a few standard authorities on strategy while at Sandhurst, but he had never had any formal staff training. The limitations of his military education would leave him unduly prone to discount the administrative problems of modern armies. What he did bring forward from this stage of his career was more an emotion than an idea: the cavalryman's sense of mobility and urge to attack, pressing forward to harry the enemy remorselessly. His considerable gifts as a strategist were the product not just of professional training but more of personal experience filtered through a powerful imagination steeped in history. He had been among the earliest to recognize the stalemate of 1914 for what it was and to seek a strategic alternative. That search had led him to the most painful moment of his career. Writing afterward a memoir-history of the First World War, which also was to be the

---

*The publication of *Guilty Men*, a brilliantly savage attack on the Chamberlainites, written in four days during the Dunkirk evacuation by a team of Beaverbrook's journalists (Michael Foot, Frank Owen, and Peter Howard, using the pseudonym "Cato"), was as much a body blow to the advocates of a compromise peace as any of Churchill's speeches. In a few weeks it sold over 200,000 copies, and its view of the appeasers colored writing on the 1930s for several decades. The compromise peace movement represented the full spectrum of British politics, a fact everyone preferred to forget after the war and to which Churchill never alludes in his memoirs. The best discussion of it is Paul Addison, "Lloyd George and Compromise Peace in the Second World War," in *Lloyd George: Twelve Essays*, ed. A. J. P. Taylor (London, 1971).

public vindication that Asquith would not allow him in 1916, he reaffirmed his belief that an enormous opportunity had been lost by lack of imagination and flexibility.

The aggressiveness of the horse soldier and the determination to be ready to seize fleeting opportunities would be hallmarks of Churchill's strategical style, but all this was leavened by his historical sense. His vast study of Marlborough, followed by the personal survey of the English-speaking peoples, constituted a refresher course, of sorts, on grand strategy. He had reviewed the military history of his country as well as the uses to which British military power had been put in the service of British policy. Throughout the war the idea that arms are ultimately the servant of policy, and that British policy required the restoration in some form of the European balance Hitler had destroyed, were seldom completely absent from his calculations, although occasionally nearly overwhelmed by gusts of pugnacity and emotion. If Churchill's defiant aggressiveness toward enemies came finally into its own in 1940, his strategic instincts could find only limited scope. He moved most surefootedly in the realm of grand strategy, where the movements of armies and fleets achieve not only victory but national objectives as well. In that realm, however, freedom of maneuver was Hitler's alone.

This was true not simply because the German army had routed the Anglo-French forces and made Hitler master of western Europe. It also was true because Britain lacked the resources to challenge Hitler's newly acquired hegemony. Britain's enormous nineteenth-century power, whose aura still enveloped the nation in 1940, was based on a fortunate historical accident—Britain's pioneer industrialization, an asset that had been eroding for almost sixty years. While impressive overall, and in some areas still a pioneer of new technologies, Britain's economy certainly did not enjoy a commanding lead over Germany's, although under Churchill it was to be far better organized and managed. Furthermore, Britain's pre-1914 financial mastery had never been restored after 1918. From the beginnings of rearmament in the mid-1930s, Britain had had to make extensive purchases abroad, especially in the United States, a trend that the outbreak of war intensified. By December 1939 Britain and France had 2,500 aircraft on order from American manufacturers, all of which had to be paid for.

In American eyes Britain had defaulted on World War I debts. (The British, on the other hand, believed they had met onerous repayment terms as long as they possibly could.) By American law, therefore, the British were required to pay cash for whatever they bought. A report to Chamberlain's war cabinet in February 1940 by one of the government's financial advisers warned that, even if all salable British assets overseas were taken over by the government and liquidated at market value and one-third of Britain's £450-million gold reserve sold as well, the balance of payments deficit at the end of one year of fighting—that is, by September 1940—would be £250 million, or 83 percent of the remaining gold reserve. At the same time, the treasury estimated that with the most frugal management Britain's gold and dollar resources would last just until February 1942. The British could only fight by buying from America, but shopping in that market meant speedy national bankruptcy.

Finally, British manpower, although it would be managed with great efficiency, was simply not equal to fielding an army that could contest Germany's dominance of Europe, let alone cope simultaneously with other enemies. From a population of 48 million, Britain had to maintain the world's largest navy and merchant marine, a powerful air force, and its industrial life, all equally vital to survival. The army, therefore, had to be severely limited in size. In September 1939 its target strength was set at fifty-five divisions, and only thirty-two of those would actually be raised from British manpower. The balance would come from Australia, Canada, New Zealand, South Africa, and India, with each country to be equipped by Britain. At its wartime peak, the British army would number slightly under 3 million men. By contrast the German army, which attacked in the west with 126 divisions in May 1940 and would have 296 in January 1944, at its maximum size deployed 4.6 million men. The British had to import to keep their war machine running, somehow pay for overseas supplies, and find a way for an empire that could only put fifty-five divisions in the field to defeat one that disposed of five times that many. And all this presupposed Britain's ability to survive a direct German attack.

The studies Churchill ordered after returning from Paris on 17 May addressed both the issue of survival, and in a necessarily more vague fashion, that of ultimate victory. Chamberlain's committee reported the next day that without France it would be necessary to fight on single-handed until the United States entered the war. To do this a siege economy, with "totalitarian" control by the government of every facet of national life, would be necessary.* The

---

*Chamberlain's committee consisted of Halifax, Maurice Hankey, Sir John Anderson (home secretary), and Clement Attlee. The shakiness of the assumption about American entry into the war, and the prediction of a degree of government control that would be

chiefs of staff, faced with the job of determining just how Britain would survive and win, took a day longer, but the first draft of "British Strategy in a Certain Eventuality" was ready on 19 May. The staff officers who hastily put it together began with worst-possible-case assumptions: Italian entry into the war, eventual Axis domination of all Europe, a direct attack on the United Kingdom, and an assault on Britain's position in Egypt and the Middle East. The only positive notes struck were the expectation that American economic and financial aid would be forthcoming and that the Soviet Union and Germany might quarrel. In such a situation they believed Britain could still survive if the Royal Navy could keep the sea lanes open and if the Royal Air Force could maintain enough control over British air space to limit the damage that the *Luftwaffe* could do to vital factories, ports, and ships. But if the air force failed and the German army came ashore, they warned, the British army would not be able to drive it out again. Essentially the document was an affirmation of faith, as much in Britain's special providence as in its air force.

The chiefs of staff made this fact much clearer in their answer to Churchill's subsequent request for a concise statement of their views on Britain's chances of survival, which was made just before the crucial series of war cabinet meetings on 26–28 May. "The crux of the matter is air superiority" they wrote, adding in conclusion, "the real test is whether the morale of our fighting personnel and civil population will counterbalance the numerical and material advantages Germany enjoys. We believe it will."[20] The sense of Britain's destined survival was even stronger in Churchill. Moreover, the chiefs' of staff paper expressed his own thinking on the defense of the island. As long as the Royal Air Force held the skies over Britain and the navy kept open the sea lanes, a successful direct assault by the Germans was not possible.*

Churchill could do little directly about the air force's ability to carry out its task. Fighter Command had been brought to a high

revolutionary, may be one reason why both Chamberlain and Halifax were willing, perhaps even eager, to explore the possibilities of a negotiated peace.

*Churchill as first lord had been an active participant in Admiralty-War Office arguments over the likelihood of invasion before 1914. The navy's position then was that, providing British naval supremacy was intact, all that was required from the army was a home defense force large enough to compel an attacker to strike in a strength of at least 70,000. An invasion of this size would inevitably be intercepted and destroyed. Brought up against the invasion problem again in 1940, Churchill merely added air power to the calculations: if the air force maintained control of the daylight air, the navy could still contest the passage of any force larger than a raid. This thinking lay behind his determination to limit the commitment of the Royal Air Force in France.

degree of efficiency by Dowding and his subordinates and would be handled by them with great professional skill during the Battle of Britain. The prime minister, however, could and did see to it that it did not lack either the necessary tools or morale-boosting recognition. A long-standing critic of Air Ministry efficiency, Churchill immediately stripped from it aircraft procurement and handed that function over to the newly formed Ministry of Aircraft Production headed by the erratic, mischievous, but undeniably dynamic Beaverbrook, whose eldest son was a fighter pilot. The new minister, backed by Churchill's full power, produced a sharp acceleration in the output of *Hurricanes* and *Spitfires*, bringing the same intensity to the production of aircraft that Admiral Lord Fisher had brought to naval construction in 1914.* In his speeches Churchill also kept the spotlight of public attention focused on the Royal Air Force. Speaking in the House of Commons on 4 June and conscious of the widespread criticism among the returning BEF of the lack of air support, he made a special point to emphasize the air force's contribution to the Dunkirk evacuation, stressing that it was a good omen for the impending clash in the skies over Britain. Throughout the ensuing summer he constantly praised the role of the air force, culminating in his memorable tribute on 20 August: "Never in the field of human conflict was so much owed by so many to so few." The Battle of Britain was won by Dowding and his pilots, but the air of heroic romance that surrounds it owes much to Churchill.

"Sea power, when properly understood, is a wonderful thing," Churchill wrote later.[21] There is no doubt that he numbered himself among those with a proper grasp of its essentials. He had twice been first lord, thought himself well versed in naval matters, and throughout the war took a close interest not only in naval strategy but also in tactics, shipbuilding programs, and the appointment of key personnel. All of this was colored by his passionate commitment to the offensive, which often led him to apply quite inappropriate cavalry analogies to naval warfare. But in the summer of 1940 the prime minister could do little to affect the navy's day-by-day ability to keep open the sea lanes by which Britain lived. As in the case of the Royal Air Force, his contribution lay in other areas. The painful decision taken in early July to eliminate the French fleet as

---

*Beaverbrook's success in increasing the output of fighters was accompanied by a disregard for established procedures that generated much controversy, especially over the effect that his methods had on long-term projects such as the development of heavy four-engine bombers. A good discussion of the issue is in A. J. P. Taylor, *Beaverbrook* (London, 1972), 414–49.

a factor in the balance of sea power was driven through a doubting war cabinet by Churchill and enforced on the reluctant admirals who bore the operational responsibility by the prime minister and Pound.

Although a variety of considerations were present in Churchill's mind, including the impact such action would have on American opinion, there is no doubt that the threat French warships in Axis hands would pose to British survival was the essential element in his decision; it was simply too great a chance to take. But it was a decision that required enormous courage and determination, as well as ruthlessness. Careful study of the episode shows that without Churchill the decision would not have been made.* Yet taking it was deeply painful for someone who had always been a friend and admirer of France. When he explained the government's decision to a silent House of Commons, he scored a great personal victory as members rose to cheer him, marking the first occasion when the entire Conservative party did so. Nevertheless, as he left one of his private secretaries heard him say to a member: "This is heartbreaking for me."[22]

The Royal Navy and Fighter Command might enable Britain to survive, but the spirit of Churchill's administration was not simply survival until a peace settlement could be patched together but victory, total victory. The way to attain that objective was not clear either to the chiefs of staff or the prime minister as they faced up to the consequences of the French collapse. In December 1937 the chiefs of staff had warned the Chamberlain government that Britain could not fight alone against a coalition of hostile powers:

> Without overlooking the assistance which we would hope to obtain from France and possibly other allies, we cannot foresee the time when our defense forces will be strong enough to safeguard our trade, territory and vital interests against Germany, Italy and Japan at the same time. . . .[23]

They strongly suggested that British diplomacy had to find additional allies, or reduce the number of potential enemies. Now

---

*There are two good studies of "Operation Catapult": Warren Tute's popular account, *The Deadly Stroke* (New York, 1973), and a scholarly study by Arthur J. Marder, "Oran, 3 July 1940: Mistaken Judgment, Tragic Misunderstanding, or Cruel Necessity?" in Marder, *From the Dardanelles to Oran: Studies of the Royal Navy in War and Peace 1915–1940* (London, 1974), 179–288. Marder's conclusion is worth quoting: "In the context of the situation on 3 July 1940, with the information available to the Government, that action is both intelligible and defensible," 288.

"British Strategy in a Certain Eventuality" had to confront a situation in which France had been eliminated and no major power was likely to enter the war on Britain's side, while Japan seemed a possible addition to the ranks of its active foes. The chiefs of staff had to explain how to do what their predecessors had declared impossible. It is not surprising that the sections on long-term prospects in their paper were vague and made up largely of a patchwork of prewar ideas with one interesting new twist. They wrote that "the defeat of Germany might be achieved by a combination of economic pressure, air attack on economic objectives in Germany and on German morale and the creation of widespread revolt in her conquered territories."[24]

Prewar strategic thought had emphasized a war of attrition, and this view still prevailed. It was based on the incorrect assumption that Germany's economy was already at full stretch as well as on the hope that American cooperation would allow the British to supplement their traditional naval blockade with "control at source" of those commodities Germany would seek to import. Perhaps, at bottom, it rested on the belief that blockade, so potent a British weapon in past wars, retained its efficacy, a factor quite doubtful now that Germany was able to draw not only upon European but also Soviet resources.

The impact, whatever it might be, of the economic blockade would be greatly intensified by the bombing offensive of the Royal Air Force. This belief also grew out of earlier plans, or in this case, illusions. "Strategic bombing" to break an opponent's morale and industrial backbone had been the *idée fixe* of the air force for two decades. Bomber Command was, in fact, incapable of doing what was expected of it in 1940. This was not fully appreciated at the time, and the pressure to use the bombers was irresistible. A large part of Britain's rearmament effort had gone into creating the bomber force, and although Chamberlain's government, fearing retaliation and hoping for a limited war, had not allowed it to drop anything more deadly than propaganda leaflets on Germany, the advent of Churchill, combined with the German attack in the west, finally unleashed the bombers.

The war cabinet decided on 15 May to authorize bombing operations over Germany. That night ninety-nine aircraft set out for targets east of the Rhine. (The raid demonstrates the measure of Bomber Command's immaturity in that of the seventy-eight ordered to bomb oil installations only twenty-four even claimed to have found their target and no significant damage was done.) Thus began perhaps the most controversial British campaign of the war.

In an October 1917 memorandum to Lloyd George's war cabinet, Churchill had denounced the idea that "terrorisation of the civilian population" by bombing could win a war. Both he and the chiefs of staff were sure British morale would stand up to any pressure by the Germans, yet readily assumed that the Germans would be made of weaker stuff.* This glaring contradiction is perhaps best explained by the fact that in the circumstances of 1940 Bomber Command was the only weapon available with which the British could strike Germany directly. The prime minister certainly saw it this way. In early July Churchill wrote to Beaverbrook:

> We have no Continental army which can defeat the German military power. The blockade is broken and Hitler has Asia and probably Africa to draw from. Should he be repulsed here or not try invasion, he will recoil eastward, and we have nothing to stop him. But there is one thing that will bring him back and bring him down, and that is an absolutely devastating, exterminating attack by very heavy bombers from this country upon the Nazi homeland.[25]

Thus, erroneous estimates of the state of the German economy, the Royal Air Force's belief in strategic bombing, and Churchill's desire to strike back came together to launch the great bombing offensive. Churchill returned persistently during the rest of 1940 to the theme of his letter to Beaverbrook. Early in September, in a general directive on munitions production intended to set guidelines for the next fifteen months, he wrote: "The Navy can lose us the war, but only the Air Force can win it. . . . the Bombers alone provide the means of victory. We must therefore develop the power to carry an ever-increasing volume of explosives to Germany, so as to pulverize the entire industry and scientific structure on which the war effort and economic life of the enemy depend. . . ."[26] In October Newall retired as chief of the Air Staff and was replaced

---

*It is also true that the prime minister saw the bombing of German cities as a reinforcement to British morale once the blitz had begun. He recounts a visit to a bombed area of south London where the crowd shouted to him "let *them* have it too," *FH,* 349. In the early autumn Churchill engaged in a controversy with the Air Staff over random retaliatory raids on German cities, which he wanted the Royal Air Force to launch. Minutes of 6, 19 September and 16 October 1940, *FH,* 363–65. Ironically, the Air Staff opposed him, although the inaccuracy of British target-finding was such that their raids were, in fact, simple random retaliatory blows rather than the punishing strikes on key economic targets they imagined. A careful survey of public reaction during the blitz found the demand for reprisals on Germany surprisingly slight. Tom Harrisson, *Living Through the Blitz* (London, 1978), 314–19. Churchill doubtless took the anger he noticed as confirmation that his own pugnacious desire to strike back was widely shared.

by Air Chief Marshal Sir Charles Portal who came from Bomber Command and was an uncompromising supporter of its offensive. Nonetheless, the prime minister fretted continually throughout the autumn at the slow growth of Bomber Command and at its high losses, minuting that it should not be used during bad weather and that its tactics should be varied to minimize losses inflicted by German defenses. An action-this-day minute at year's end harped on the same theme: "I am deeply concerned at the stagnant condition of our bomber force. . . . I consider the rapid expansion of the bomber force one of the greatest military objectives now before us."[27] It was a case, as Lord Kitchener had once remarked, of making war not as one wished but rather as one could.

If blockade and a bombing offensive were inevitable in view of past experience and the structure of Britain's armed services, aggressive sponsorship of subversion was not. The duke of Wellington had once remarked that he had a horror of revolutionizing countries for political reasons. That was the authentic voice of a power defending the status quo, precisely the position in which Britain found itself under Churchill. But at no point during the Napoleonic wars had Britain's situation been quite as precarious as it was in 1940, and the prime minister was not about to rule out any useful weapon, however unorthodox. Britain, in fact, had had considerable experience in subversion and guerrilla warfare. In South Africa, where Churchill had been a war correspondent, a small force of guerrillas had defied the British for two years (1900–02); in Ireland, the British had confronted the prototype of modern urban guerrilla warfare (1919–21), with Churchill as secretary of state for war directing a clumsy and futile counterinsurgency operation. Furthermore, the British had sponsored the Arab revolt during the First World War, with results generally thought to be satisfactory—and Churchill was a friend and admirer of T. E. Lawrence.

On the eve of war small sections in both the Secret Intelligence Service (SIS) and the War Office were exploring the possibilities of guerrilla warfare and sabotage behind enemy lines in the event of future conflict. During the "phoney war," enthusiastic but ineffective sabotage operations, aimed at raw materials destined for Germany, were mounted in Scandinavia and the Balkans. "A special organization will be required," the chiefs of staff noted when they threw their weight behind the idea that subversion in all its forms constituted a new dimension in warfare and one that the British could profitably exploit. The separate organizations were fused together in July to form the Special Operations Executive

(SOE). Its first ministerial head was a Labourite, Hugh Dalton, already minister of Economic Warfare. Clement Attlee had insisted that Labour control the new agency to preserve the party balance in the coalition. Dalton believed that SOE would find most of its resisters on the European left, and that it should be a revolutionary organization. Churchill, with his romantic imagination fired, seemed to agree. At the 22 July meeting of the war cabinet that put the final seal of approval on the arrangements for SOE's birth, the prime minister turned to Dalton and told him: "Now set Europe ablaze." But, as a careful historian of SOE, and the only one yet to write with access to its archives, has noted:

> There was a paradox at the centre of SOE's existence. Winston Churchill, the body's first weighty promoter, was a duke's grandson, best known to that time as a resolute opponent of what he once called 'the foul baboonery of bolshevism.' Though his government was a coalition, its main political base lay in a conservative majority in the commons more than twice as large as any that party has since enjoyed. Yet SOE's subversive purpose was revolutionary: it was dedicated to the forcible overthrow of nazi dominion in Germany, and of the puppet rulers who depended on the nazis for power. . . .[28]

The contradiction between Churchill's conservative purposes and the radicalizing influence of SOE's sponsorship of subversion, including terrorism, and wholesale questioning of constituted authority would only become fully apparent later in the war.* Meanwhile, SOE, like Bomber Command, was a way to strike back, and counterattack was the essence of Churchill's approach to waging war.

The unwearying search for ways to strike at the enemy was, in fact, Churchill's principal contribution to the new British strategy that took shape after the collapse of France. The pieces of the mosaic were not new, with the exception of SOE, but the spirit that infused the design was, and that spirit was Churchill's. While the offensive urge was strong in him, it was not simply a matter of an

---

*The eminent British military analyst, B. H. Liddell Hart, a consistent critic of Churchill, wrote of the hangover from the resistance, especially "the amoral effect on the younger generation as a whole. It taught them to defy authority and break the rules of civil morality in the fight against the occupying forces. This left a disrespect for 'law and order' that inevitably continued after the invaders had gone." *The Defense of the West* (London, 1950), 53–59. Like many of Liddell Hart's *obiter dicta*, this analysis is both stimulating and debatable but does serve to point out the contradiction between means and ends in the strategy that SOE symbolized.

aggressive instinct to lash out, although that was there. He knew that it would be difficult to sustain the nation's morale indefinitely unless there was some evidence that Britain was doing more than merely surviving. It would be equally hard to impress neutral powers, particularly that most important neutral, the United States, without evidence of both the determination and ability to win that only vigorous counterattack could provide. Finally, when Churchill urged relentlessly a search for ways to strike back he did so not blindly but against the background of an intelligence picture that became steadily clearer until, in the later stages of the war, it was a more complete insight than perhaps any belligerent has ever enjoyed into the enemy's plans, force structure, and problems. Wellington once commented that throughout his campaigns he had always been bedeviled by the problem of discovering what was happening "on the other side of the hill." Churchill knew.

"Ultra," one of the most remarkable intelligence coups of modern times, and certainly the best kept secret of the war, gave the prime minister this vision.* The German armed forces, diplomatic service, state railway system, police, and security forces all protected their radio traffic by enciphering it prior to transmission on a machine (the Enigma) that produced random five-letter groups that could only be unscrambled by another machine whose operator possessed the correct initial settings. By the eve of war Germany's Enigma machines were capable of generating 150,000,000,000,000,000,000 five-letter groups. Not unreasonably, therefore, the Germans assumed that their machine-generated ciphers were unbreakable, but at that moment they had already been penetrated by Polish military intelligence. In mid-summer 1939 the Poles made the details of their cryptanalytic success available to their British and French allies.

Building on the Polish breakthrough, the code breakers at Britain's Government Code and Cipher School, usually referred to as Bletchley Park from its wartime location, gradually began to

---

*The Ultra Secret by Group Captain F. W. Winterbotham, published in London and New York in 1974, first made the story public. Written from memory, without access to documents, it contains many errors of fact and emphasis but did succeed in opening up a completely unsuspected area of World War II historiography and launching a minor historical growth industry. It also unfortunately launched the legend that Ultra gave advance warning of the devastating German 14 November 1940 raid on Coventry, but that Churchill ruled against special precautions lest the Germans realize that their ciphers were being read, 60–61. There is no truth to this story. Coventry, through a failure in evaluating available intelligence, was only identified as the German target a few hours before the raid began, and the prime minister was under the impression that London was the Luftwaffe's principal target for the night.[29]

break into the German cipher systems. On 22 May 1940 the cryptographers broke the principal *Luftwaffe* operational cipher known as the "Red" cipher "currently"; that is, signals in that cipher were read the same day they were sent. Bletchley Park continued to read that particular *Luftwaffe* cipher currently throughout the rest of the war and gradually added most of the other German cipher systems as well. Ultra's greatest days still lay ahead in 1940, but even in its infancy Churchill readily grasped its significance. Early in August he ordered that the most important of the signals decrypted at Bletchley Park should be sent directly to him with notes explaining what was significant and why. A minute of 5 August to Ismay takes on new significance in the light of what is now known about Ultra. In it the prime minister insisted on receiving *"authentic documents in their original form."*[30]

Churchill saw only a tiny fraction of the Bletchley Park intercepts "raw" in this fashion. Most of them were sent to the appropriate government departments, civil and military, and reached him through bureaucratic channels. But just as Lindemann's analysts and statisticians served as an outside check on the Whitehall machine, Churchill's insistence on seeing at least the tip of the Ultra iceberg was a safeguard against receiving intelligence estimates filtered through staff or departmental preconceptions. Ultra gave the British, and later Anglo-American, war effort an insight, unique in the history of war, into the mind of the enemy and endowed Churchill personally with the extra authority that accurate information confers. His discussions with the chiefs of staff or theater commanders started from the same point, as far as intelligence was concerned. The knowledge Ultra provided, although to a lesser extent than it would be later, was of particular significance to Churchill in 1940 because he was engaged in complex and delicate negotiations to provide the one indispensable means that the British would need to defeat Germany, a major ally.*

Bomber Command might bring Germany to its knees, and SOE might kindle sparks of resistance into a blaze. But unless Germany was so crippled by economic warfare, bombing, and widespread revolt in occupied Europe that the British army had merely to mop up an already beaten Wehrmacht, there was no possibility that the British army, facing a long period of reequipment after

---

*The care with which Churchill scrutinized the material that he received from Bletchley Park has been highlighted in *OB,* 6. Hence, this factor must be borne in mind when assessing the prime minister's relations with the generals, especially during the 1941–42 desert campaigns.

Dunkirk, and in any case scheduled to grow only to fifty-five divisions, could reenter Europe in the foreseeable future. On the day the Dunkirk evacuation ended, the prime minister minuted that "the completely defensive habit of mind which has ruined the French must not be allowed to ruin all our initiative. . . . How wonderful it would be if the Germans could be made to wonder where they are going to be struck next, instead of forcing us to try to wall in the island and roof it over." A few weeks later he told Jan Smuts that the "*opportunity for large scale offensive amphibious operations may come in 1940 and 1941.*"[31] On 6 June, Churchill dictated a minute on raising "striking companies" and paratroopers, from which came the commandoes and the British army's Parachute Regiment. He urged the construction of tank landing craft and in July created Combined Operations Command to foster amphibious technique and control raiding operations. An unorthodox royal engineer, Major Millis Jefferis, was taken under the prime minister's wing and given research facilities to develop unusual explosive devices, which he did with gusto and mixed success throughout the war. All of this, however valuable in giving the British the sense they were, or soon would be, striking back, in fact promised no more than the ability to mount nuisance raids on German-occupied Europe. To develop the "large scale offensive" for which he yearned, Churchill needed major allies—a grand alliance such as the one formed to contain Louis XIV, whose fortunes he had studied and chronicled in his life of Marlborough. On 25 June, Churchill wrote to Stalin, pointing out that "the problem before all Europe—our two countries included—is how the States and peoples of Europe are going to react towards the prospect of Germany establishing a hegemony over the Continent."[32] Only frosty silence greeted this overture, and Churchill remarked in his memoirs that he expected nothing else. He could only hope that in time the basic incompatibility of the Nazi and Soviet regimes, each with its own rapacious ambitions, would bring Russia into a marriage of convenience with Britain. In any case, hope in 1940 lay in a different direction. From the beginning Churchill looked to the United States to make victory possible.

Churchill had corresponded with Franklin D. Roosevelt since September 1939, at the president's invitation and with the approval of Chamberlain and Halifax. The 15 May war cabinet meeting that approved the beginning of the bombing offensive also agreed that Churchill should continue his exchanges with Roosevelt. That same day the prime minister sent his first "Former Naval Person" message. Churchill thereafter kept relations with the United States very much in his own hands. Even the powerful Foreign Office was reduced to a junior partner. During the war and afterward in his memoirs and the *History of the English-Speaking Peoples,* Churchill was fulsome about the "special relationship." There is no doubt that much of the sentiment he expressed was genuine, but underneath there was a hard core of calculation. The grand alliance necessary to defeat Hitler needed a catalyst. The Dutch republic had fulfilled that function in the wars against Louis XIV; Britain would do so against Germany. Just as the Dutch had needed major partners and found them in Britain and the Hapsburgs, Britain would have to draw in the United States and, if possible, the Soviet Union to contain and roll back the tide of German conquest. Churchill could do nothing with the Soviet Union; therefore, he concentrated on the United States. Seeking alternately to appeal to both national interest and ideals, to alarm and exhort, he was to work with patience and a subtlety hitherto unsuspected to draw a steadily greater commitment to Britain from the Americans. Because American aid would be essential, if not to survival then certainly to victory, and because the quest for victory was the basis of his administration, he had to study closely American moods, views, and prejudices.

Deferring to the Americans became an instrument in Churchill's political repertoire, because in the last analysis he needed them to achieve his war aims. The United States was the essential ingredient in his grand alliance. He certainly had every intention of defending British interests since victory would lose much of its meaning if British power were to emerge from the war substantially diminished. Yet from the beginning there was a contradiction at the heart of Churchill's American policy. In the wars against Louis XIV, Britain had temporarily set aside a long-standing naval and commercial rivalry with the Dutch in the face of a common foe. But the war marked the beginning of the end for the Dutch as a major power. Anglo-American relations had seldom been warm and since 1919 had often been tense. Churchill, along with Hitler, might persuade the Americans that there was an overriding need for cooperation, but the causes of Anglo-American discord—naval, commercial, and financial rivalries and a deeply rooted American suspicion of British imperial power—would remain. The contradiction could only be resolved if Churchill could enlist American support not only for the defeat of Hitler but also for the maintenance of British power. Attempting to do so was his central activity during the war, masking the failure to achieve the second goal part of the purpose in what he wrote afterward.

Churchill's 15 May letter to Roosevelt struck many of the notes that were to become familiar over the ensuing months. Whatever happened, Britain would fight on, but "the voice and force of the United States may count for nothing if they are withheld too long. You may have a completely subjugated, Nazified Europe established with astounding swiftness and the weight may be more than we can bear." Then came the request for American help with "everything short of actually engaging armed forces." Specifically, Britain wanted destroyers from the mothball fleet of World War I vessels as well as aircraft, antiaircraft guns, ammunition, and financial aid for large-scale purchases of raw materials and other supplies. "We shall go on paying dollars for as long as we can, but I should like to feel reasonably sure that when we can pay no more, you will give us the stuff all the same." Finally Britain's foes had to be kept to a minimum, so the president was asked to "keep that Japanese dog quiet in the Pacific" and invited to use the huge, recently finished, and quite empty British base at Singapore.[33]*

Of all these requests, the two with the greatest long-term significance were the bald statement of proud mendicancy and the assumption that America would shield Britain's Asian empire. When Churchill replaced Chamberlain, all pretense of husbanding Britain's financial resources vanished. Between April and July the estimated 1940 expenditure on iron and steel purchases in the United States rose from £12.6 million to £100 million. The severance from European sources of supply meant that raw material imports from North America would rise from 8 to 24 percent of Britain's imports in that category during 1940. In August the treasury would forecast that over the next twelve months Britain would spend $3,200,000,000 in North America, most of it in the United States, but would only be able to cover those obligations from Britain's gold and dollar resources until December. Churchill clearly intended to spend as if Roosevelt would find a way to keep the goods flowing when Britain's cash ran out, calculating perhaps that orders on a massive scale would constitute a powerful argument in themselves.

Roosevelt's replies to Churchill's initial messages were rather

---

*Churchill printed many of his messages to Roosevelt and some of the president's answers. A good selection from both sides, comprising about a third of the exchanges and carefully annotated, is Francis Loewenheim and Harold D. Langley, *Roosevelt and Churchill: Their Secret Wartime Correspondence* (New York, 1975). Comparing Churchill's version of the note (*Their Finest Hour*, 24–25) with that in the Loewenheim edition, 94–95, several interesting changes are observable. Churchill's version, for example, has "the Japanese" for "that Japanese dog," a process of tidying that, in fact, obscures. A complete edition of the Churchill-Roosevelt correspondence is being prepared by Warren F. Kimball.

cool. With France collapsing and most informed opinion expecting Britain to follow, this is not surprising. The American ambassador in London, Joseph Kennedy, was much closer to the Chamberlain-Halifax wing of the Conservative party than he was to any of the Churchillians, and Washington was aware that sentiment for a compromise peace existed in Britain. Churchill's first breakthrough with the Americans came after the French collapse, when the attack on the French fleet at Oran demonstrated that Britain's announced resolve was not merely a rhetorical flourish. On a January evening in 1941 at the prime minister's country retreat, Chequers, Harry Hopkins, Roosevelt's closest adviser in the early years of the war, told one of Churchill's private secretaries that Oran tipped the balance in the president's mind, convincing him that the British would fight and were worth taking risks to support.

Nonetheless, Churchill's courtship of the United States was still far from easy. Roosevelt, complex, shrewd, secretive, and not infrequently devious, saw that American national interests were involved in sustaining Britain and balking Hitler's bid for European hegemony. He saw as well the approaching November election. He could not move too far or too fast without endangering himself politically. Furthermore, Roosevelt's attitude toward Britain was ambivalent from the beginning. His most perceptive biographer has referred to his "heavily forested interior" and, in comparison with Churchill, assessment of his motives is difficult. Yet, while he wished for Germany's defeat and therefore for Britain's continuing belligerency, he had a vision of the postwar world in which British power, especially British imperial power, would be more sharply reduced than was acceptable to Churchill. Thus for reasons both practical and symbolic, the president could only provide aid to Britain on terms that offered him an answer to domestic critics and enhanced America's position vis-à-vis Britain. Anglo-American competition was submerged, not ended, by the war, or rather it was absorbed into alliance politics, much as Anglo-Dutch competition had been during the conflict that provided Churchill with his paradigm for a grand alliance. It is the mixture of motives on both sides that makes the destroyers-for-bases swap not only the most significant event in Anglo-American relations during 1940 but also the most revealing.

On the British side, there were two reasons for requesting destroyers. As a former first lord, Churchill was vividly aware that the emergency program to build convoy escorts, initiated at the outbreak of the war, would not yield results until 1941. Losses of British destroyers in the Norwegian campaign and at Dunkirk had been heavy, and the concentration of light naval craft in home waters for anti-invasion duties further denuded the convoy routes of escorts. Therefore, the elderly American ships, obsolescent as they were, would obviously be useful, but laid up for twenty years they would need extensive reconditioning and refitting. In fact, only nine of the fifty went into service before the end of 1940.

There was, however, a deeper significance to the transaction. The British ambassador in Washington, Lord Lothian, pointed out that transferring war materials to Britain was a belligerent act by the Americans. A Foreign Office memorandum to the war cabinet stressed that the future of the empire depended on Anglo-American collaboration, while the prime minister, in a statement to the House of Commons on 20 August, emphasized that the proposed arrangement "means that these two great organisations of the English-speaking democracies, the British Empire and the United States, will have to be somewhat mixed up together in some of their affairs for mutual and general advantage."[34] The symbolic value of the American commitment, coming as it did as the Battle of Britain built to a climax and presaging an Anglo-Saxon entente against Hitler, undoubtedly far exceeded the practical value of the fifty destroyers.

In addition, there was symbolism of another sort in the destroyers-bases deal. Even before the fall of France, Roosevelt, a disciple of Alfred Thayer Mahan, had become alarmed over the possible fate of the British fleet, and in a conversation on 25 May, pressed Lothian for a commitment that, in the event Britain surrendered or was successfully invaded, the Royal Navy would be treated as imperial property and sailed to Canada. (He demonstrated at the same time his ambiguous attitude toward Britain by suggesting that any British government in exile establish itself in Bermuda because the Canadians might not like Downing Street on their soil, and republican sentiment in the Americas might be distressed by the presence of a monarchy on the Continent.) Churchill responded in his speech on 4 June: "We shall never surrender, and even if, which I do not for a moment believe, this island, or a large part of it, were subjugated and starving, then our Empire beyond the seas, armed and guarded by the British Fleet, would carry on the struggle, until, in God's time, the New World, with all its power and might, steps forth to the rescue and liberation of the Old."[35] But the next day he privately told Mackenzie King, the Canadian prime minister, "we must be careful not to let the Americans view too complacently the prospect of a British collapse, out of which they would get the British Fleet and the guardianship of the British

Empire, minus Great Britain."[36] He repeated the same thing, more bluntly, to Lothian: "If Great Britain broke under invasion, a pro-German Government might obtain far easier terms by surrendering the Fleet, . . . the President should bear this very clearly in mind. You should talk to him in this sense and thus discourage any complacent assumption on the United States' part that they will pick up the debris of the British Empire by their present policy."[37] Throughout the summer Churchill refused to relieve American anxieties over the future of the Royal Navy, arguing that it would have catastrophic effects on home morale because it would imply that the government thought invasion and surrender likely contingencies.

Doubtless he was right. But he was also deeply sensitive about the symbols of power, and nothing, not even the monarchy itself, was more evocative of British pride, power, and tradition than the ships that flew the white ensign. No question of their passing out of British control could ever be allowed to arise. In an agreed exchange of notes, designed for publication, that marked the consummation of the destroyers-bases deal, the president had to be content merely with asking the rather pointless question as to whether Churchill's 4 June statement that the fleet would never be surrendered or scuttled represented the "settled policy" of his government. The prime minister replied that "it certainly does," adding, "I must, however, observe that these hypothetical contingencies seem more likely to concern the German fleet or what is left of it than our own," thus neatly recalling the memory of the surrender of the kaiser's High Seas Fleet to the Royal Navy on 21 November 1918, the symbol of Britain's total victory over Germany in that contest.[38] The honors in the first round of Anglo-American negotiations were about even. In practical terms, what the Americans received was more valuable than what they gave. In the area of symbols of power Churchill came out ahead. Perhaps this was a good indication of the course the Anglo-American entente would take, for as Churchill once observed, "facts are better than dreams."[39]

Throughout the eventful summer of 1940, Churchill's behavior showed the same pattern: an eagerness to draw all possible support, even if only symbolic, from the Americans and a willingness to give concrete value in return, coupled with an underlying wariness about giving too much. Nine days after Churchill became prime minister, Roosevelt began to receive the daily information telegrams sent to all dominion prime ministers. As the intelligence content of these messages came from the Joint Intelligence Committee's daily summary, the president was receiving Ultra information, although its source was disguised and no American knew about Ultra until much later.*

Similarly guarded openness characterized the British response to Roosevelt's probings of British capacity and will to resist. Rightly distrustful of his defeatist ambassador, in July the president sent Colonel William Donovan, the future founding father of the Office of Strategic Services, on a personal reconnaissance. He was followed by an American military mission, disguised thinly as a "Standardisation of Arms" committee. Exchanges of information on production programs and staff plans grew fuller and intelligence collaboration between the two navies became closer, although complete knowledge of Ultra was still withheld. Churchill apparently worried about American security. The British intelligence community also began to worry about the relatively meager return they received in intelligence exchanges with the Americans. Nevertheless, despite the prime minister's desire to extract a quid pro quo for what Britain gave the momentum built steadily, and the flow became more one-sided because British necessities were more pressing.

In August Churchill personally approved the instructions for a mission to the United States, headed by Sir Henry Tizard, one of Britain's key defense scientists. The Tizard mission carried with it the cavity magnetron valve, a crucial British breakthrough in radar technology, as well as a prototype of the proximity fuse and a great deal of information on developments in the antisubmarine and antiaircraft fields. The designs for the Rolls-Royce Merlin, the power plant of the *Spitfire*, went to America, as did information on British nuclear research. In return, the British received only elderly destroyers, a miscellany of World War I rifles and field guns, and a few Coast Guard cutters and long-range (**PBY** or *Catalina*) aircraft. Meanwhile, British orders for American supplies mounted, and national solvency slowly bled away. A note of irritation crept into some of Churchill's references to the United States. On 21 August, at the height of the air battle, he commented: "There is something rather obnoxious in bringing correspondents down to the air squadrons in order that they may assure the American public that the fighter pilots are not bragging and lying about their figures. . . . I must say I am a little impatient about the American skepticism."[40]

*It has been alleged that William Stephenson, the Canadian who headed the SIS liaison office in New York, passed Ultra information to Roosevelt for Churchill. This, like most of Stephenson's *A Man Called Intrepid* (New York, 1976), is best ignored. Sir John Colville, *The Churchillians*, 61–62, has done a sufficient job of demolishing Stephenson's account.

Churchill did not allow any irritation to sneak into his exchanges with Roosevelt. He did, however, continue to stress well into autumn the danger of invasion, although a key Ultra intercept had advised him on 18 September that Hitler's Sea Lion would not take to the water that year. Winterbotham, the link between Churchill and Bletchley Park, was present in the underground war room at this climactic moment:

> There was a very broad smile on Churchill's face now as he lit up his massive cigar and suggested we should all take a little fresh air. As we surfaced, the air raid was at its height. . . . It was a wild scene . . . Winston stood alone in front, his dark blue boiler suit undone at the neck, a tin hat on his head, his hands folded on his stout stick in front of him, his chin thrust out, the long cigar in his mouth, and just across the other side of St. James's Park, Carlton House Terrace was ablaze: the boom of bombs exploding to the south, the crack and rattle of the AA guns and exploding shells, the red white glow of the fires silhouetting the tall black trunks of the great trees in the park. It was a moment in history to remember, and above the noise came the angry voice of Winston Churchill: 'By God we will get the B———'s for this.'[41]

In less emotionally intense moments Churchill knew that by itself Britain would never "get" Hitler, and, despite the careful priming of the Americans with intelligence and production secrets and the diligent fanning of Roosevelt's fears over the balance of sea power, he had progressed no further forward in eliciting American support since August. One month after Roosevelt's reelection, Churchill decided the time was ripe for another major move. In a letter he subsequently described as the most important he ever wrote, he gave the president on 8 December 1940 a wide-ranging survey of Britain's prospects for 1941. The heart of the letter was a request for additional American action to alleviate the burden of the Battle of the Atlantic and above all to stop Britain's financial hemorrhage that had already drained $4.5 billion, leaving only $2 billion in reserve. "The moment approaches when we shall no longer be able to pay cash for shipping and other supplies."[42]

Thus began the train of events that culminated in lend-lease, which Churchill was to call "the most unsordid act" in history. Enlightened self-interest might be more accurate. What it certainly was, was the end of Britain's career as a self-sufficient great power. This was not noticed at the time, perhaps because the afterglow of the Battle of Britain lingered, perhaps because of Churchill's rhetorical legerdemain, or perhaps because, as Churchill wrote the epitaph of British world power, an imperial force was poised to launch Britain's first successful counteroffensive of the war in the Middle East. There a sunset glow of achievement would touch the empire's arms.

The campaigns of the Second World War in the Mediterranean and Middle East have become particularly identified with Churchill. "This was, for him, after India, the very heartland of the British Empire, worth retaining for its own sake irrespective of its significance in the conduct of the war. The generals who failed to defend it earned his malevolence; those who succeeded his extravagant affection."[43] Although capturing the essence of the case that the war in the Middle East was not entirely a matter of rational calculation where the prime minister was concerned, the web of circumstance that made the Middle East an inevitable concern to British strategists has been ignored. It is more instructive to examine the continuity between Churchill's policies and prewar British strategy and the considerable political dimension of his policies, both of which make it clear that "significance in the conduct of the war" is by no means the only test to be applied.

For a century and a half the heart of British power had been India. The security of the Indian Empire had drawn the eyes of British policymakers to the eastern Mediterranean early in the nineteenth century, led them first to oppose and then to buy control of the Suez Canal, and finally in 1882 to begin the "Temporary Occupation" of Egypt which still continued in 1940. Concern for the security of the Indian Empire was by 1914 joined with concern for oil as the Royal Navy switched from coal. The maintenance of imperial interests in the Middle East was one of Britain's principal War World I aims, and the empire reached its territorial apogee in 1921 with the creation of a vast British sphere of influence running from Cairo through Jerusalem to Baghdad.

Unlike the Indian Empire, Britain's power in the Middle East was not primarily a matter of direct administration but of base rights, special treaty relationships, and the provision of advisers to local governments drawn from groups favorable to, and indeed dependent on, the British. In this sense it was similar to the arrangements by which the United States would control so much after 1945. Churchill had grown up with Britain's empire in the Middle East, serving as a young officer in Egypt and as colonial secretary playing a major role in the postwar settlement of the region in 1921–22. The importance of the Middle East in British official thought increased from the mid-1930s on. With Italy hostile and Germany showing an interest in southeastern Europe, the protection of British interests seemed to require both the creation of a Balkan barrier between the Axis and an area vital to Britain and a tightening of the bonds between the British and those Arab groups with whom Britain had long worked. The first strand of policy led the chiefs of staff to focus on the Balkan states and Turkey as possible allies, and it produced the Chamberlain government's guarantees to Greece and Rumania (April 1939) and the tripartite treaty (October 1939) between Britain, France, and Turkey aimed at maintaining the Mediterranean status quo. The second strand led to the appeasement of Arab nationalism, inflamed over the Palestine question, a decision symbolized by the March 1939 White Paper that tilted British policy decisively toward the Arabs.

These policies constituted Churchill's heritage in the Middle East, and it was an inescapable legacy. Middle Eastern oil was vital to the British war effort; British economic strategy deemed it equally vital to keep it from the Germans. The Balkans were not only a buffer for the Middle East but also a source of vital raw materials and foodstuffs, whose denial to Germany would hamper the German war effort. The quest for an anti-Axis Balkan bloc and the persistent wooing of the Turks was not simply a result of Churchill's personal obsessions but rather the natural outgrowth of previous British decisions and a reflection of the essential position occupied by the eastern Mediterranean and the Middle East in British eyes. In fact, the only part of the prewar approach Churchill refused to embrace was the White Paper.

A long-standing supporter of Zionism, he had opposed the White Paper policy in Parliament, argued in favor of softening it after joining the Chamberlain war cabinet, and once prime minister lost no time in serving notice that he intended to undo it as far as possible. He wrote sharply in late June to his "anti-Zionist and pro-Arab" colonial secretary, Lord Lloyd, about "the very large numbers of sorely needed troops" tied up in Palestine and "the price we have to pay for the anti-Jewish policy which has been persisted in for some years." He further added: "I think it little less than a scandal that at a time when we are fighting for our lives these very large forces should be immobilized in support of a policy which commends itself only to a section of the Conservative Party." In the same letter he indicated the basis of his disagreement with official policy on Palestine: "If the Jews were properly armed, our forces would become available, and there would be no danger of the Jews attacking the Arabs, because they are entirely dependent upon us and upon our command of the seas."[44] The romantic in Churchill responded to the Zionist vision of a Jewish commonwealth arising in Palestine; the imperial statesman assumed it would be a dependable ally in a vital area.

This last consideration in turn leads to the wider question of the Middle East as a factor not only in the war but also in the calculus of British world power, whose conservation Churchill, the Conservative party, and most of the official world regarded as a legitimate British war aim. India was the heart of that power, and the Middle East had been linked with the security of India throughout Churchill's lifetime. Even if the tenure of British power in India had come to seem questionable to many, although Churchill no more accepted this than he did the White Paper policy, the Middle East still remained, because of its oil resources, an essential consideration for British policymakers. Therefore, it was far more than a romantic enthusiasm for empire that rejected the idea of loosening Britain's grip on the Middle East, a proposal that confronted Churchill in mid-June. As disaster mounted in France, the chiefs of staff, at Pound's instigation, discussed the possible abandonment of the eastern Mediterranean, with the Mediterranean fleet retiring to Aden, blocking the Suez Canal behind it. The Naval Staff, with their eyes on control of the Atlantic, essential if American supplies were to reach Britain, suggested another possibility: the Mediterranean fleet could move to Gibraltar.

These proposals drew strong negative reactions from Admiral Sir Andrew Cunningham, the pugnacious commander of the Mediterranean fleet, and from the prime minister. Cunningham told the Admiralty on 17 June that, if the fleet left, Egypt and Malta would fall. That same day Churchill wrote that the departure of the fleet would expose Egypt to an Italian invasion "which would . . . destroy prematurely all our positions in the East."[45] The next day Cunningham, worried that his first response was not strong enough, sent another message, dwelling on the "landslide in territory and prestige" that a withdrawal of the fleet would set off.[46] The chiefs of staff, meeting on 18 June with these proposals in front of them, plus a joint planning staff paper which declared that the case for remaining in the eastern Mediterranean outweighed any purely naval advantages that might be gained by pulling Cunningham's ships out, deferred consideration of the Naval Staff's suggestion. It was never heard of again. A telegram to the dominions on 3 July simply stated as policy that the Middle East would be held as long as possible. Years later Cunningham wrote that the removal of his fleet would have been a major disaster. Like the prime minister, with whom he was to disagree often and vigorously over the next five years, he knew the enormous psychological importance attached to the Royal Navy. If it left the Mediterranean, it would signal the end of the British era in the Middle East.

Hope for Balkan and Turkish allies, oil, denial of resources to Germany, and imperial considerations by no means exhausted the catalogue of reasons for hanging on in the Middle East. On the day before the Naval Staff's proposal was shelved, the newly installed Pétain government in France asked for an armistice. Churchill was deeply sensitive to the need to impress upon neutral opinion that Britain would indeed stay in the war, not merely on the defensive hoping to survive but actively striking back. This was the meaning of Oran, the bomber offensive, the commandoes, and SOE. Only by convincing action were the British likely to attract support, especially from the Americans, and without American backing, the British war effort in a matter of months would sputter out for lack of financial fuel, leaving a negotiated peace the best prospect and capitulation the most likely. "In war," Churchill later wrote, "armies must fight," and if action was a necessity, the Middle East had considerable attractions.

Anglo-French staff conversations in March–April 1939 recommended early offensive action against Italy in North Africa in the event of war. When war came Italy initially remained neutral, but much of the reasoning was still valid even after the collapse of France had precipitated the Italians into the conflict. Italy remained the weaker of the Axis partners. Neither its army nor air force possessed up-to-date equipment, while its large fleet suffered from lack of radar, air cover, and reliable fuel supplies. Over the morale of the Italian armed forces there hung a question mark. Italy's North Africa possessions could only be reinforced by sea, a process the British hoped to disrupt. Italian-occupied Ethiopia, on the wrong side of the Suez Canal, was completely cut off. Moreover, the balance of forces, so hopelessly against the British in Europe, was more favorable toward them in the Middle East. The importance of the area had led to the establishment of a new command structure on the eve of war. General Sir Archibald Wavell was named commander in chief (Middle East), although in keeping with the British committee system of theater command, his naval and air colleagues were his equals rather than the subordinates his title seemed to imply. Wavell, a one-eyed veteran of World War I, tough, inarticulate, shyly cherishing a rather unmilitary fondness for poetry, was a commander of great ability and drive. He immediately began to plan a base in Egypt capable of supporting fifteen divisions.

A nucleus about which to group an imperial force on this scale already existed because the concentration of regular British army units in the Middle East ranked second only to that in India. On the eve of war one of Britain's armored warfare pioneers, Major General P. C. Hobart, had welded the mobile forces in Egypt into a striking force which became the most famous British armored formation of the war, the 7th Armored Division—the "Desert Rats." In August 1939 the 4th Indian Division, a superbly professional force, arrived in Egypt, followed over the winter by units from Australia and New Zealand. More troops were being raised in Australia and South Africa, while the expansion of the Indian Army, long the empire's strategic reserve in the east, was sharply accelerated after the fall of France.

All these gathering forces had to be supplied by the long sea route around the Cape of Good Hope since Italian hostility had closed the Mediterranean route to regular convoys. To remove some of the consequent strain on British shipping and industrial production, the Eastern Group Supply Council was created in October 1940. Based in New Delhi, it coordinated production and procurement from Capetown around the arc of the Indian Ocean to Singapore. The British, therefore, had two principal military reasons for fighting in the Middle East: a local base, capable of handling a considerable buildup of imperial forces and able to sustain itself in part at least from imperial resources, and an opportunity to fight on reasonably favorable terms the least formidable of their opponents.

Finally, in Wavell, the vast, quasi-isolated Middle East command had a leader of unflagging determination, great resource, and a refusal, similar to Churchill's, to contemplate defeat. Sensing the coming French collapse, Wavell sat down on 24 May and drafted a four-page, handwritten worst-possible-case scenario in which he outlined how he would carry on if France collapsed. The chiefs of staff in London were simultaneously preparing a similar proposal, at Churchill's instance, but Wavell went considerably further, including in his paper a worse-case-still situation, discussing how he would continue the fight if Britain itself fell. On the day France sued for an armistice, he issued an order of the day that concluded: "We stand firm whatever happens. Dictators fade away—the British Empire never dies."[47]

Wavell, however, could not stop the collapse of France from

sending shock waves through the Arab world. On the day Pétain asked for terms and Wavell issued his defiant order, the British high commissioner and ambassador in Cairo, Sir Miles Lampson, was hectoring King Farouk to appoint a pro-British prime minister to offset the impact of the war news. "There was some bluster at one moment by H. M.," Lampson wired London that night, "but I said we were in deadly earnest and meant to see that there was a friendly P.M. and government in office who would stand by us loyally [and] co-operate in all we wanted. . . ."[48] The British knew that, despite Lampson's ability to dominate Farouk and despite the White Paper, Middle Eastern opinion would veer toward the power that seemed likely to be victorious. This added another to the many compelling reasons for carrying the war to the Italians as soon as possible. With Churchill in London and Wavell in Cairo, both set on the offensive as soon as possible, it is at first glance surprising that so many disagreements arose and that the prime minister's relations with the commander of Britain's only active theater of operations on land were strained, tinged with suspicion and fraught with misunderstanding from the beginning.

Perhaps the root of the problem was simply that the Middle East was the only place where Britain confronted the Axis on land and the only place where it could hope for an offensive success. Bearing the tremendous burden of trying to encourage neutral opinion to believe that Britain could win (because without allies Britain could not win), Churchill needed military success. Only Wavell was in a position to provide it.

An additional cause was Churchill's method of dealing with the military. Generals as a group he distrusted, suspecting them of hidebound orthodoxy and paralyzing caution. Because of this opinion, he ceaselessly pushed and prodded, displaying his deep suspicion of the regular army mind as well as a refusal to accept the judgments of staff officers and commanders until he had probed and weighed them. But he respected a case articulately presented and stubbornly maintained. Pound could have told Wavell a great deal about the fine art of working with Churchill. For his part, Wavell combined his great talents with a touch of intellectual arrogance. If Churchill distrusted orthodox soldiers, Wavell disdained politicians. Furthermore, he was nearly inarticulate in face-to-face encounters, an enormous handicap in dealing with Churchill, and one that prevented any meeting of minds when Wavell came to London early in August. Churchill was later to comment that Wavell reminded him of a golf club chairman.

Yet despite the lack of empathy, Wavell's visit set in motion

Britain's first successful offensive of the war. Wavell had sent ahead a long list of the equipment that his armored formations lacked. Churchill knew from Bletchley Park's success in reading Italian ciphers that an Italian offensive against Egypt was imminent. When Dill suggested reinforcing Wavell with an armored brigade, an act that would strip the army at home of half its armor while the battle in the skies built to a climax and invasion remained a real possibility, Churchill immediately approved.* The prime minister then engaged in a vigorous argument with the Admiralty, trying to persuade the Naval Staff to run the convoy through the Mediterranean rather than send it by the safer but slower route via the Cape. Although he failed to have the *Apology* convoy routed through the Mediterranean, the risks Churchill was prepared to accept are a measure of his pressing need for success in the Middle East.

Tanks, however, were not all he sent Wavell. Still dissatisfied after his conversations with the commander in chief, whom he had minutely cross-examined about the use Middle East command was making of its resources, he sent a long signal following Wavell back to Cairo. This "General Directive for Commander-in-Chief, Middle East," specified the troop movements necessary to concentrate 56,000 troops in Egypt by 1 October and laid down as well the tactics to be followed in using them both to defend the Delta area and to counterattack.[49] It was a remarkable signal, usurping the functions not only of the War Office but also of Wavell and his staff, and is a measure of Churchill's doubts about Wavell.

The breach which opened during Wavell's London visit would never be closed as long as he remained in Cairo. Indeed, it widened as soon as he returned. The Italians overran British Somaliland, a strategically insignificant but embarrassing defeat. Churchill immediately pointed out to Wavell that the light British casualties reported seemed to show a less than stubborn defense. Wavell shot back that "a big butchers' bill is not necessarily evidence of good tactics."[50] Dill later remarked that that phrase aroused greater anger in the prime minister than he had ever seen, as well it might considering Churchill's long struggle against huge "butchers' bills" in 1914–15 and the price he paid personally and politically for that fight.

Disagreements over military matters were not the sum total of Churchill's quarrels with Wavell. The Middle East appointment

---

*Formal war cabinet approval came on 15 August, the day Wavell left on his return trip to Cairo and the day of the *Luftwaffe's* first major attack, "Eagle Day."

was not only military but proconsular as well. Wavell's responsibilities took in the entire British sphere from the Sudan through Cairo and Jerusalem to Baghdad and the Persian Gulf. Conscious of the fragility of Britain's position and sharing the Arabophilia common among British soldiers and officials in the area, Wavell had consistently taken his stand in support of the "official line" on Palestine which ruled out arming the Jewish settlers, a policy Churchill wanted and began arguing for virtually from the moment he became prime minister. Although Wavell was by no means the only opponent of Churchill's pro-Zionist impulse, his position made him one of the most important.

This particular Churchill-Wavell quarrel peaked in late November. The S.S. *Patria,* carrying illegal Jewish immigrants being deported from Palestine, blew up and sank in Haifa harbor with the loss of 267 lives.* The war cabinet promptly decided as an act of clemency to allow the survivors of the disaster to remain in Palestine; that is, they decided to make an exception to the White Paper policy. Wavell immediately tried to have the cabinet decision reversed: "From military point of view it is disastrous . . . certain result will be great increase of anti-British feeling. . . . This is serious." The cabinet stood by its decision, and Churchill told Wavell that, if the Arabs' "attachment to our cause is so slender as to be determined by a mere act of charity of this kind, it is clear that our policy of conciliating them has not borne much fruit so far. What I think would influence them much more," the prime minister concluded, perhaps with a recollection of Wavell's "butchers' bill" telegram, "would be any kind of British military success."[51]

By the time Churchill administered that rebuke, Wavell was on the verge of launching the first successful British ground offensive of the war. On 11 September, two days before the Italian offensive finally lurched reluctantly over the Egyptian frontier, Wavell had directed his chief of staff to begin planning a counteroffensive. The Italian advance ran out of steam four days and sixty miles later. On 21 September the preliminary outline of the British counterstroke was complete. Over the next three months the Italians remained stationary, while Wavell and his subordinates planned "Operation Compass." Although Wavell planned to attack, neither the prime minister nor anyone else in London was informed.

---

*Saboteurs under orders from Haganah, the underground Jewish army in Palestine, had affixed explosive charges to the *Patria's* hull, planning to disable the ship and prevent it from sailing for Mauritius where its passengers were to be interned. Miscalculating the quantity of explosive necessary, they tore out the ship's bottom instead.

Autumn was a time of great strain for Churchill. The Battle of Britain had been won and Sea Lion postponed, but the blitz and the Battle of the Atlantic posed equally serious long-term problems without the alleviating exhilaration of the summer. The British were trying to keep Vichy and Spain from becoming unequivocal partners in Hitler's "New Order." Victories would argue the British case strongly in Madrid and Vichy, but apart from victory in the skies over England, the British had yet to show any real capacity to hit back. An attempt to establish General Charles de Gaulle's Free French movement in West Africa had led to an embarrassing fiasco at Dakar in September, precipitating an outbreak of recriminations between Churchill and Australian prime minister Robert Menzies, who questioned both the strategy and the lack of prior consultation with Britain's commonwealth partners.* Churchill had no major success to show in his campaign for American support since the destroyers-bases deal, and Britain's financial resources were nearing exhaustion. Yet an offensive, whose political significance would be as great as its military, was being planned, unknown to anyone in London. In October Churchill, still unhappy at the lack of vigor in the Middle East and convinced that Wavell was producing too few "teeth" (fighting units) in proportion to the size of his administrative "tail" (support units), decided to send Eden on a mission of investigation.**

Eden arrived in Cairo on 15 October, but only two weeks later did Wavell break the news of Compass to him. Wavell's concern for security is understandable. Egypt was a neutral country with many anti-British Nationalists and a large resident Italian colony. But if he had had his way, Eden would have departed unaware of his plans, so deep had the gulf of suspicion become between

---

*Arthur J. Marder made the Dakar operation the subject of *Operation 'Menace': The Dakar Expedition and the Dudley North Affair* (London, 1976). The Churchill-Menzies exchange is in *FH*, 718–22. The Dakar expedition was plagued by a chapter of accidents reminiscent of those that played havoc with the Dardanelles attempt. Churchill, however, was much more cautious in pushing the commanders involved, obviously remembering the charges he had been living down for twenty-five years.

**The size of Wavell's administrative tail was in part a function of the need to build up a large base area in Egypt. Churchill, however, remained suspicious throughout the war that British, and later Anglo-American, administrative support was on far too lavish a scale. He was fighting a trend that began with the impact of the industrial revolution on warfare, but a glance at the ratio of combat to support troops in British, American, and German armies makes it obvious that his complaints were far from groundless. (Germany had 300 divisions made up from 4.6 million men; the United States, 90 from 8.2 million; and Britain, 35 from 2.9 million.) A good statement of Churchill's case at this time is his minute of 9 December 1940 to Secretary of State for War Eden, which discusses and questions not simply the use of troops in the Middle East but also the entire structure of the British army. *FH*, 695–97.

Churchill and the commander in chief. Wavell's behavior is indicative not only of his attitude toward Churchill but also of the degree of independence he had enjoyed up to this time despite Churchill's doubts, a proconsular latitude the prime minister never again permitted. "I purred like six cats," he wrote of his reaction to the news Eden brought back. While he may have purred, he also noted and remembered. "I was myself so pleased that our generals would take the offensive that I did not worry unduly about the result," he recorded acidly nine years later.[52] The event that forced Wavell to tell Eden, and therefore Churchill, about Compass was the arrival on 28 October of news of the Italian attack on Greece, a turning point in the Mediterranean war.

Britain had guaranteed Greek independence in April 1939. Well before that Britain had a special relationship of its own with Greece, going back over a century to Lord Byron and other British philhellene enthusiasts for Greek independence. Although Wavell's resources were scanty, there was no question of not aiding Greece. Failure to do so would be a political defeat of the first order and would end any prospect of creating an anti-Axis Balkan bloc. Eden, who, although secretary of state for war, was most attuned to the management of foreign affairs, immediately began to press Wavell to send as much aid as possible to Greece. It was in the hope of keeping his losses within limits that Wavell revealed the secret of Compass to Eden. Churchill's mind ran along the same tracks as Eden's, however. On 4 November he told the war cabinet that Britain could not afford to allow Greece to fight alone. Therefore, from the Middle East a few squadrons of Royal Air Force bombers and fighters were provided, together with antiaircraft protection for the fields from which they operated. Suda Bay in Crete, long coveted by the Royal Navy, also was occupied, a situation that benefited the British more than the Greeks. Fortunately the rapid collapse of the ill-planned Italian offensive and the success of the ensuing Greek counterattack relieved the British of the need to provide any further aid beyond their initial, essentially token, contribution.

For the first time since the fall of France, however, British troops were back on the European continent, in the politically sensitive Balkans where their air bases put Germany's Rumanian oil supplies at risk, a factor that would have an important effect on Hitler's strategy. Meanwhile, Wavell would continue to plan his attack, only now to the accompaniment of a stream of cables from London in which the prime minister sought to establish the date for Compass, which Wavell refused to divulge. Churchill did so while stressing the larger issues which were always present in the forefront of his mind:

> It seems difficult to believe that Hitler will not be forced to come to the rescue of his partner. . . . It might be that Compass would in itself determine action of Yugoslavia and Turkey, and anyhow, in event of success, we should be able to give Turkey far greater assurances of early support than it has been in our power to do so far. One may indeed see possibility of centre of gravity in Middle East shifting suddenly from Egypt to the Balkans, and from Cairo to Constantinople.[53]

During the inevitable reaction from Churchill's version of the war that began with the publication of Lord Alanbrooke's diaries in 1957,* there was a great deal of sympathy with those British generals who suffered constant oversight and frequent badgering by that opinionated amateur, the prime minister and minister of defense. Yet now, in the light of the Ultra revelations, it is obvious that Churchill was not as unreasonable as he seemed and occasionally sounded, nor were the commanders always as right as their memoirs and apologists would have it. Churchill needed, with the threads of an enormously complex game in his hands, to know exactly what Wavell was planning as well as the time sequence he envisioned. The commander in chief in Cairo, primed by his own code breakers, had before him a good picture of his Italian adversary, but only in London was the picture of German activities discernible. Germany and not Italy was the dominant consideration, and by the eve of Compass it was growing steadily clearer that Germany was turning east.

In one of his flashes of prophetic insight, Churchill had written to Smuts in late June that he expected Hitler to move east, perhaps without even attempting to mount an invasion of Britain. After it became plain that Sea Lion was off at least until spring, the prime minister became more certain that Hitler's next offensive would be in that direction. But what exactly would its target be? The prime minister suspected it would be the Soviet Union and said so to a group of senior officers at the end of October. But no hard evidence

*Arthur Bryant, ed., *Turn of the Tide, 1939–1943* (New York, 1957) and *Triumph in the West, 1943–1946* (New York, 1959) blended contemporary diary entries by the man who succeeded Dill as chief of the Imperial General Staff in November 1941, his postwar "Notes on My Life," and linking passages by Bryant, a writer of colorful popular history. As the first major critique of the Churchill version, it enjoyed a wide readership but today is generally recognized as unfair not only to Churchill but also to Brooke, who appears in Bryant's selections as a man in the grip of perpetual choler.

as yet supported his intuition. Other evidence, however, began to accumulate that could signal a German move southeast toward the eastern Mediterranean. From the British point of view, the deployment of German military power there would be exceedingly dangerous. A German military mission arrived in Rumania on 7 October and was joined by a *Luftwaffe* mission on the 23d. The German air force was the most careless user of the Enigma machine and a correspondingly fruitful source for British intelligence. By early November Balkan items began to show up in Bletchley Park's daily harvest. There was no certainty yet, and at one moment in December Churchill briefly decided a drive through Spain against Gibraltar was the most likely German move.

There was enough evidence though for the prime minister to decide that the first priority in the Mediterranean had to be the creation of a Balkan front to hold German power as far away as possible from an area vital to Britain. British success in drawing Turkish and Yugoslav help would be conditioned by both Wavell's offensive and by the quantity of aid Britain could give. Thus, the future was mortgaged even before Sir Richard O'Connor's Western Desert Force attacked the unsuspecting Italians at 0730 hours on the morning of 9 December 1940, spearheaded by those twenty-six and one-half-ton British infantry tanks, quaintly known as *Matildas*. Brought out by the *Apology* convoy, these tanks were a fearsome weapon, their armor proof against any guns the Italians had.

O'Connor's success was crushing and so total that Wavell quickly allowed the offensive, which he had originally conceived as a limited spoiling attack, to expand into a major drive to destroy the Italian field army in North Africa. Over the next two months O'Connor did just that. As Roosevelt, cruising in the Caribbean, read Churchill's admission that Britain was broke, the Western Desert Force was racing toward Tobruk, having already taken over 70,000 prisoners and destroyed eight Italian divisions. But at the same time, Enigma intercepts began to show unmistakable evidence of strong concentrations of German armor and air in Rumania and the beginning of a forward movement into Bulgaria. Had a major German thrust directed at the Middle East begun, an attack which Hitler's naval commander, Admiral Erich Raeder, like Churchill, thought could be fatal to Britain?

Threats to the British imperial system at the end of 1940 were not confined to the danger that the Germans might erupt into the Middle East. Lord Curzon, one-time viceroy of India, had told a cabinet committee in April 1920: "India . . . had always been and must always be the pivot and focus of British interests in the East."[54]

The Indian Empire still retained its critical importance in the minds of British officials and certainly in that of the prime minister. Yet it was threatened from within and without by the forces of Indian nationalism and by the expansionism of Japan which imperiled the entire structure of British power in the east. Amid the pressures and distractions of his first six months in office, Churchill had had to turn his mind to political and military strategies to contain these threats as well.

Curzon's identification of the primacy of India in the British imperial system expressed a consensus in the political and official worlds which had taken shape at the end of the eighteenth century and endured until after World War I. Churchill's Indian policies should be viewed in the context of that consensus. He certainly thrilled to the romance of empire and, like De Gaulle, believed that his country needed a dimension of the grandeur that empire brought. Churchill also had his share of color bias, which seems to have been especially pronounced where Hindus were concerned. But his position on India was not shaped by either *Boy's Own Magazine* imperial romanticism or by racial feelings. At most, these heightened his rhetoric. Churchill had held key positions in the shaping of imperial defense policy off and on for forty years, particularly in the crucial years after World War I when the settlement of the Middle East and the acceleration of constitutional change in India raised the question of the Indian Empire's future role in imperial security.

The vast British network of trade, influence, and territorial rule stretching from East Africa to China had been made possible by British control of Indian military resources. Therefore, the key issue for policymakers concerned with imperial defense after 1918 was to prevent constitutional change in India from disrupting the Indian contribution to imperial security by fettering Britain's use of the Indian Army. That army, a professional fighting force larger than the regular British army, paid for from Indian revenues and capable of rapid expansion, had been the empire's strategic reserve in the east for a century. Compromise with the rising forces of colonial nationalism in various parts of the empire seemed necessary after 1918 so that British control of the essentials—foreign affairs and defense—could be maintained by conceding the widest possible measure of autonomy in other areas to local elites who would continue to collaborate with Britain.

This policy also had the advantage of lowering the profile of imperial control and thus avoiding some of the antagonism that direct administration aroused among Nationalists. By keeping empire out of the headlines, it had the merit as well of keeping it out of British domestic politics, where public enthusiasm for it was no longer certain and where the Labour party did not share the consensus on imperial matters of the pre-1914 era. Britain had maintained its imperial desiderata in Egypt by such an arrangement, and Churchill had been the architect of a parallel settlement in Iraq. But in India, the devolution of power to local Nationalists promised to threaten rather than safeguard imperial security, precisely because internal autonomy would threaten free disposition by Britain of Indian resources; that is, the tax revenues that supported the army and London's discretionary power over its use.

Faced with a rising tide of nationalism and the need to attract support for the new constitutional arrangements of 1919, even the government of India had begun to argue with London over the extent of the imperial defense burden borne by India. "In India where taxation is not imposed by representatives of the people, a high level of taxation maintained for purposes which India strongly argues are not in India's best interests, form a ready weapon for the extremist agitator in his campaign for fomenting racial hatred, and can only form a grave political danger," wrote Edwin Montagu, secretary of state for India, in a December 1920 cabinet paper that reflected the fears of the viceroy and his advisers.[55]

Churchill, a participant in the 1919–22 discussions on imperial defense, remained acutely conscious of the dilemma that constitutional change in India presented to the managers of Britain's security. Not to offer concessions to the political classes in India was to court an explosion; to offer control of the Indian Army, however, was to risk a fatal weakening of the empire's security. The solution was the division of responsibility known as "dyarchy." Indian control over most areas of provincial government was balanced by continued British control at the Center.* This division safeguarded ultimate British control of India's military resources, although it could not prevent increasing attention by Indian politicians to the use Britain made of those resources. Churchill remained convinced that Britain's essential security needs required continued British control at the Center in India, whatever concessions were made to the Indian political classes in the provinces.

Beneath his colorful rhetoric during the 1931–35 India Bill controversy lurked his unshakable belief that the British imperial

---

*In the provinces certain powers continued to be "reserved" to the British governor: police, justice, and land revenue, which produced most of the government's income. All these had an obvious bearing on the internal security of India and therefore its capacity to play its accustomed role in imperial defense.

system would be fatally compromised by Indian self-government. Churchill's constant references to the report of the Simon Commission, which in 1930 recommended fuller provincial self-government but made no commitments about the Center, were not merely a debater's cudgel with which to belabor the Baldwin-MacDonald policy but reflected his unwillingness to consider any devolution of power in Delhi. The 1935 act, in fact, retained considerable British powers under the federal arrangements for India's central government. The failure to bring the complex federal portion of the act into operation by 1939 meant that the viceroy and his officials still disposed of the even more ample powers left in their hands by the 1919 act.*

This was the political situation that Churchill found on returning to office in 1939. The viceroy, Lord Linlithgow, had declared India at war the moment the king-emperor went to war with Germany. This legally correct but politically obtuse act had deeply offended most Indian political opinion, and during October the Congress party ministries in the provinces had resigned in protest. Churchill made it clear in cabinet discussions that he was in no hurry to resume a political dialogue with Indian nationalism. The situation as it existed when he took over from Chamberlain suited him well, with the Center as much under British control as it had been in 1914; most of the provinces in the hands of the governors under Section 93 of the 1935 act, which provided for the breakdown of ministerial government; and the remainder controlled by reliable, and mostly Muslim, Indian cabinets.

Throughout the war the prime minister was not to budge on two crucial points: there was to be no further constitution making until the peace, when victory would have enhanced Britain's bargaining power, and there could be no compromise on the issue of ultimate British control over Indian military resources. Churchill's secretary of state for India, Leo Amery, was a disciple of Lord Milner, guru to a generation of British imperialists. But Amery quickly came up against the basic flaw in Churchill's logic. The prime minister was thinking not in mid-Victorian terms but in 1919–22 terms. British opinion, however, had moved on. Whatever

---

*The failure to implement fully the 1935 act has often been ascribed to Churchill's fight against it, which markedly delayed its passage through Parliament. This charge has been effectively demolished by R. J. Moore, "The Making of India's Paper Federation, 1927–1935," in *The Partition of India: Policies and Perspectives, 1935–1947,* ed. C. H. Phillips and E. M. D. Wainwright (Cambridge, MA, 1970). Moore is generally critical of Churchill but believes the act was in fact unworkable.

the war meant to conservative imperialists, it did not mean the defense of the raj to the average Briton.

Indian opinion was changing as well, and the prime minister's intention of extracting the maximum military effort from India would best be attained by cooperation rather than confrontation with that country's political classes. The viceroy, trying to dampen the resentment that his declaration of war had aroused, announced in October 1939 that the 1935 act would be open to renegotiation after the war. Amery restated this position as soon as he took office in May. The collapse of France, Britain's precarious situation throughout the summer, and the need to draw a much larger force from India for the Middle East all pointed to the need for a fresh attempt at drawing Indian nationalism into wholehearted collaboration with the war effort.* Amery and Linlithgow therefore began to discuss a promise of dominion status within a year of the war's end and the addition, meanwhile, of Indian political leaders to the viceroy's executive council, currently comprised exclusively of British officials.

Dominion status, however, meant full responsible government; Indian politicians on the executive council meant a threat to exclusive British control of the Indian military machine. Amery discussed the matter with Churchill in mid-July, with predictable results. "Secretary of State has shown me the telegrams which have been passed on secret and personal file and for the first time I realize what has been going on," ran the opening of a distinctly minatory telegram from the prime minister to the viceroy on 16 July. "You must remember that we here are facing the constant threat of invasion. . . . In these circumstances immense constitutional departures cannot be effectively discussed in parliament and only by the Cabinet to the detriment of matters touching the final life and safety of the state." His pointed conclusion was that "I am sure that I can count on you to help us to the utmost of your power."[56] Nine days later Churchill accused Amery at a cabinet meeting of dealing behind the backs of his colleagues. It is a measure of the

---

*The 4th Indian Division had gone to the Middle East in August 1939; the 5th division was preparing to follow it. The Indian Army, 183,000 strong at the outbreak of the war, had grown by May 1940 to about one-third larger according to prewar mobilization plans which stressed controlled expansion to double the size of the army while preserving quality. Then France fell. The revised 1940 expansion program called for five (later six) infantry divisions and an armored division. Before this was completed, the 1941 program— four more infantry divisions and another armored division—was superimposed on it. By the war's second anniversary, India had 1 million volunteers under arms.

dominance Churchill had already attained that the cabinet immediately asked him to take over the further drafting of the viceroy's proposed statement.

Churchill's formulary, the style of which Amery disclaimed responsibility in a private letter, became the "August offer," a statement made by Linlithgow on the 8th. All the more generous features of the original had been expunged. Dominion status as Britain's final goal was reaffirmed, as was the October 1939 pledge, but no deadline was set. "Representative" Indians would be added to the executive council, which could, and in the event did, mean simply some of Britain's "moderate" Indian collaborators. Impatience with the whole business was perhaps the dominant note in Churchill's draft: "It is clear that a moment when the Commonwealth is engaged in a struggle for existence is not one in which fundamental constitutional issues can be decisively resolved."

In the generally vague and anodyne offer there was one quite striking aspect. India's minorities, the most important of which was the 100-million strong Muslim community, were assured that Britain would never set up in India any political structure "whose authority is directly denied by large and powerful elements in India's national life."[57] Indian Muslims thereafter considered this a pledge that they would not be forced into a "Hindu Raj," a state dominated by the majority. It was a step toward the partition of the subcontinent. Churchill's motives sprang directly from an approach that viewed India primarily in terms of its contribution to British power. A third of the Indian Army was Muslim. If reassurances were needed, they should be targeted where they would most benefit the war effort.

Churchill saw Hindu-Muslim antagonism as a safeguard for British power. His Middle Eastern experiences had taught him that local rivalries could often serve imperial interests when contending groups looked to Britain as a referee and safeguard. In any case, India was making its contribution to the war effort without further concessions. Recruiting for the army was proceeding well, and those Hindu groups that traditionally served were coming forward in large numbers, thus confirming Churchill's belief that the Hindu politicians were unrepresentative of the "real" India. The August offer was intended to be the prime minister's last word for the duration. That it was not was due to two fundamental miscalculations, which were to bedevil Churchill's attempt to maintain the structure of British power in Asia and finally to stultify it.

Amery faced a hostile cabinet on 25 July, ready to concede to the prime minister's views, with one important exception. Clement Attlee supported him, although he acquiesced in the cabinet decision. Attlee's dissent was symptomatic of the erosion of the consensus on India that had once united Conservatives like Curzon to Liberals like Montagu and mavericks like Churchill. A different consensus had emerged within the Labour party, typified by a weekend country house gathering which took place in June 1938 while Churchill was writing his *History of the English-Speaking Peoples*. The house was "Filkins"; its owner, Sir Stafford Cripps, a wealthy barrister and left-wing Labour politician. His guests were two leading Indian Nationalists, Jawaharlal Nehru and B. K. Krishna Menon, whom he brought together with a group of future Labour cabinet ministers—Attlee, Aneurin Bevan, Richard Crossman, and Harold Laski of the Labour party Executive Committee, and Leonard Barnes, colonial expert of the Fabian Society, a Labour think tank. The purpose of the meeting was to discuss the mechanism by which the next Labour government would transfer power to Indian hands. Labour too wanted to protect British interests but thought that could be left to a treaty with a free India; Churchill believed the most vital British interest in India would automatically be lost when an Indian government replaced British authority. Labour's willingness to devolve power expressed the public mood more closely than did Churchill's passion for imperial security.

The second miscalculation involved the basis of British authority in Asia. That always had rested, in large part, on what can be best described by the Hindustani word *Iqbal*, meaning the aura of continuing success. With Britain facing multiple threats in the summer of 1940, Churchill had to set priorities. In August, at the same time as he laid down his political strategy for India, he decided to relegate the danger from Japan to a lower priority than the war in the Middle East, thereby furthering a process that ended eighteen months later at Singapore in the irrevocable shattering of Britain's *Iqbal*.

The rise of Japanese sea power, followed by the growth of Japanese expansionism, had created a problem for British policymakers even before the First World War. Initially the British co-opted the Japanese into their imperial security system by the 1902 Anglo-Japanese alliance. But in the long run Japan's aims and Britain's interests in Asia were irreconcilable. When he was Herbert Asquith's first lord, Churchill, during a 1912 discussion of imperial security in the western Pacific, remarked prophetically that, if British sea power were ever shattered, "the only course open to the five million of white men in the Pacific would be to seek the protection of the United States."[58]

The aftermath of the First World War did, in fact, shatter British sea power in the Pacific, although in a way no one could have foreseen in 1912. Under pressure from the United States, seconded in this instance by Canada, the British terminated their alliance with Japan. Churchill, by then colonial secretary, argued strongly that if the choice lay between Japanese and American friendship he would unhesitatingly choose the latter. At the same time, the British agreed to accept parity at sea with the Americans in order to forestall a naval race with the United States. Even without the Washington naval treaties, domestic political and financial constraints would have kept the British from building a fleet much larger than the one they maintained during the interwar years. That fleet was not capable of simultaneously fighting in both hemispheres while British interests could be challenged in Asia and Europe. The Singapore naval base was an attempt to square this circle. Designed on a scale that would allow it to accommodate a major portion of the Royal Navy, its existence would enable the British to shift the fleet rapidly eastward to meet any Japanese threat. Even as the base was planned, however, the great flaw in the strategy built upon it was obvious. If the Japanese chose their time with care, they might challenge Britain at a moment when war in Europe, or even a serious threat there, prevented any substantial eastward movement of the fleet.

British strategy never escaped from this dilemma. The only answer lay in finding a new Pacific ally who could contain Japan. An Anglo-American alliance would serve this purpose but was not attainable. There was some sentiment in Whitehall in the early 1930s for obtaining freedom of action to confront Germany by seeking a renewed entente with Japan, reverting to the pre-1914 pattern, even at the cost of angering the Americans. But this too was not practical politics. By 1937, when the commitment to send the fleet to Singapore was reaffirmed for the benefit of Australia and New Zealand at that year's Imperial Conference, the likelihood had almost dwindled. On the eve of war Chamberlain, in messages to the Australian government, had begun to qualify the promise heavily, and British planners increased the time Singapore would be expected to hold out on its own from three to six months.

Churchill fell heir to all this when he returned to the Admiralty in 1939. He had already indicated in a letter to Chamberlain that the Baltic and the Mediterranean would be the decisive naval theaters in a contest with Germany and Italy, while a Japanese threat would be a distraction to be ignored until the issue of the war in Europe was clear: "We must bear the losses and punishment, awaiting the final result of the struggle."[59] Churchill was therefore, in this as in other areas, in harmony with official thought well before his return to office. During the life of the Chamberlain war cabinet a strategic consensus emerged in London concerning the threat from Japan, which formed the basis of Churchill's own policies later. Australia and New Zealand could not be left in a state of anxiety over their safety, especially if they were simultaneously to be asked for a contribution to the European war. Therefore, in November 1939 the Pacific dominions were assured that Britain would cut its losses elsewhere and come to their aid if they were threatened with invasion, a rather different position than that embodied in the promise to base a fleet at Singapore to prevent such a threat from ever arising. In fact, British planners expected that a southward thrust by Japanese of such dimensions as to threaten the Pacific dominions would bring the United States into the war. The American fleet would then become Japan's main preoccupation. The deterrent to a Japanese threat that would activate Britain's promise thus became American sea power.

The new prime minister's first message to Roosevelt on 15 May read: "We are looking to you to keep that Japanese dog quiet in the Pacific, using Singapore in any way convenient."[60] The rapid strategic reassessment Churchill inaugurated two days later led the British to toss overboard even the shreds and tatters of their prewar strategy. A message to the dominions on 13 June admitted frankly that there was nothing London could now do to meet a Japanese threat. No fleet would sail for Singapore; keeping Japan in check would have to be left to the Americans. The matter could not be left there, however. No formal alliance bound the United States to Britain and the British dominions. The Pacific dominions had relied on British protection, and Britain wanted to draw on their manpower for the imperial war effort. But unless they were satisfied about their own security, they were unlikely to be enthusiastic over the war in the Middle East. Neither Churchill nor the chiefs of staff were anxious to be diverted from the struggle on hand by Far Eastern alarms, but neither the emerging strategic design for the European war nor the prime minister's determination to maintain Britain's world role would be served by standing fast on the 13 June telegram, with its stark avowal of Britain's inability to defend its eastern interests.

In late July and early August another strategy for the Far East was hammered out, a counterpart to the new approach to the European war that had taken shape in June. This strategy rested on air power. Singapore would be defended by an air striking force that could intercept and cripple any Japanese amphibious expedition. To provide advanced air bases, however, the entire Malay peninsula would now have to be held (formerly attention had focused on Singapore and its immediate hinterland). This in turn would require a much-enlarged garrison, first to defend Malaya until the Royal Air Force was built up and then to guard the widely scattered air bases. Thus, lacking a fleet the chiefs of staff fell back on air power; lacking the aircraft to implement that strategy immediately, they fell back once again, this time on a large army garrison that was not yet available either. There was an element of make-believe in this situation, but in the summer of 1940 there were compelling reasons for make-believe. It reassured Australia and New Zealand. Vital as well was the morale of the British community in Malaya, whose rubber and tin exports were the colonial empire's chief dollar-earners. There was finally the hope that bluff and the lingering aura of power would dissuade Japan from an attempt to take advantage of Britain's situation.

The strategic makeshift that became official British policy in August 1940 represented the best the planners could do under the circumstances, which is probably the most persuasive defense of its shortcomings. However, it was not the only British strategy for dealing with the menace from Japan. Churchill also had a policy that he was in a position to enforce, because for none of the chiefs of staff was the Far East a priority matter. The prime minister was very specific on a vital point: Britain could fight one war with a chance of success, or lose two by trying to provide against contingent dangers from Japan as well. He hoped that Japan could be deterred from war by British bluff and American pressure. If Japan attacked, he was relying on the United States to become involved in the resulting hostilities, an event that would make Japan's entry well worthwhile.

Like many in the West, Churchill misunderstood the nature of Japanese political society and the way it made decisions. He also shared the widespread underestimation of Japanese military efficiency. These factors coalesced into a willingness to gamble on averting a Japanese war, allied to an acceptance that forfeits would have to be paid if the gamble failed. When the chiefs of staff moved to put some teeth into the new strategy, the distinction between their position and Churchill's immediately became obvious. The navy had nothing to send to Singapore, and the air force showed little inclination to produce any of the 336 modern first-line aircraft they had declared sufficient to defend it. The War Office, however, was prepared to bolster Malaya's garrison with newly raised Indian units. Churchill fought this move strongly; he wanted every available man, gun, and aircraft for the Middle East, particularly after Mussolini's attack on Greece and the unveiling of Wavell's Compass plans opened new vistas there. Over the next twelve months Churchill did his best to see that as little as possible was diverted to Malaya. He was willing to make time-buying concessions to Japan, as he did in agreeing to close the Burma Road supply line to China during the summer of 1940. He would make none on the principle of concentration of effort.

The prime minister's view of Japan as at worst a serious nuisance was not shared by Australians, whose security was directly threatened. Churchill's relationships with the self-governing dominions were complicated. Canada, with its Atlantic orientation and American ties, tended to follow the British lead in strategy since British strategy met Canadian needs as well. Remote New Zealand also tended to trust the Mother Country, while South Africa's Premier Smuts was one of Churchill's most highly regarded associates. To the prime minister this pattern fitted the logic of the situation. Britain was the senior partner in imperial defense, carrying the chief burden of the war effort. The dominions were too sparsely populated and, with the exception of Canada, too underdeveloped industrially to provide more than limited manpower and raw materials. In the nature of things they were bound to be someone's junior partner, but they were nonetheless newly sovereign nations, jealous of their status and the use made of their troops.

Australia especially saw matters in this light, expecting a fuller measure of consultation over strategy than Churchill was ever prepared to accord. Angry exchanges between London and Canberra at the time of the Dakar expedition foreshadowed a difficult wartime relationship in which Churchill never managed to find quite the right touch, perhaps because he did not completely accept the implications of dominion sovereignty. If, therefore, his gamble— that Japan would either be "rational" or, at worst, containable with American aid—should fail, not only would serious losses of territory, resources, and prestige result but also a crisis in the Commonwealth's relations.

This scenario, however, lay in the future, and, as the autumn of 1940 turned to winter, Churchill could look back on the months since May with considerable satisfaction. Advancing steadily from the wings to the center of the political stage during the twilight war, his entente with Labour had made him the one national candidate for war leadership at a moment when one was desperately needed. His own shrewdness, administrative skills, and inspirational qualities had enabled him to fasten his grip on government and popular imagination. Two opportune deaths in the autumn allowed him to complete the process by seizing control of the Conservative party machine, giving him a political base of his own. Chamberlain's death left the party leadership open, and Churchill did not hesitate to grasp what would otherwise have gone to Halifax. He had no intention of playing Lloyd George to Halifax's Bonar Law. A few weeks later Lord Lothian died suddenly in Washington, and Churchill could disembarrass himself of Halifax as well. The foreign secretary was shunted to Washington, solaced by a nominal continuing membership in the war cabinet.

Halifax's place was filled by Eden, a calculated move on Churchill's part. The Foreign Office was one of the most powerful of Whitehall's bureaucratic satrapies, and Eden was the darling of many younger Conservatives. But the likelihood that Eden would in any way threaten Churchill's hold on the party was virtually nonexistent. At the end of September, the prime minister had told Eden that he would retire at the end of the war and that he looked upon Eden as his successor.* Although personally fond of him, Churchill also sensed what was to become so tragically apparent when fifteen years later Eden finally did succeed him. For all his considerable gifts, Eden was soft at the center. As far back as 1936 Churchill had described him, in a letter to his wife, as a "lightweight."[61] Eden, once made crown prince, would never use his powerful ministry to challenge Churchill.

Autumn was a time of extensive reconstruction in the war cabinet, a process that tended to strengthen Churchill's position. He had already brought Beaverbrook into the cabinet in August, and while Beaverbrook had no fixed political alignment, he had no independent power base either. His tenure of high office depended on his ties to Churchill. Chamberlain's office was filled by Sir John Anderson, a pompous but enormously capable ex-civil servant,

---

*The intention of retiring at the end of the war was not simply voiced for Eden's benefit. One evening in December 1940 at Chequers, the prime minister told a member of his staff, John R. Colville, that he had no wish "to lead a party or class struggle against the Labour leaders who were now serving him so well. He would retire to Chartwell and write a book on the war . . . he was determined not to prolong his career into the period of reconstruction." Colville diary, 12 December 1940, quoted in OB, 6:943.

technically nonparty but in fact Conservative, who became manager of the home front, a technocrat without political following and operating on Churchill's delegated power. It is true that orthodox Tories were also brought in, but one was Eden and the other, Sir Kingsley Wood, chancellor of the exchequer, was a Chamberlainite who had switched sides at the crucial moment in May. In fact, the only new face in the war cabinet with the power to challenge the prime minister was Ernest Bevin, former head of the giant Transport and General Workers Union and now minister of Labour and National Service. Bevin managed the nation's manpower, a symbol of Churchill's wartime entente with Labour, and in this area he reigned as supreme as Churchill did in his. Subject to that, Bevin staunchly supported the prime minister for the next five years. By the end of 1940, Churchill enjoyed a degree of dominance over his colleagues that Lloyd George had never attained. Only military failure, or a breach with Labour, could unseat him.

If the prime minister's political base had become almost impregnable by the end of 1940, his grand strategy had similarly taken firm shape. Britain's survival in that year had been assured as much by German errors as by British skill. Churchill's basic contribution was to avert the kind of moral collapse that had occurred in France and that the Halifax strategy of negotiation risked. Britain's long-term strategy for victory, however, bore a firm Churchillian imprint. He knew that American help and eventual participation were crucial, and he worked tirelessly to enlist American support, paying whatever he had to while striving to keep vital British interests intact. His reward had been the essentially symbolic destroyers-bases deal, a clear breach of neutrality that signaled an American willingness to underwrite the British war effort. That effort could never by itself produce armies capable of reentering the Continent, but perhaps economic warfare waged by heavy bombers might drain German power. Then would be the moment for SOE's "secret armies" to spring to life, and spearheaded by British forces, administer the coup de grâce.

Meanwhile, Britain would fight the war it could and safeguard a key position in the structure of its world power by gripping the Middle East. Politics in India would be suspended for the duration and, with luck, in the Far East all would remain quiet. In *Their Finest Hour* Churchill summarized 1940 in a throbbing peroration, but an even more succinct rendering of the spirit in which he met his destiny is to be found in the acceptance speech he made to the Conservative party meeting that elected him to the leadership: "I have always served two public causes which I think stand supreme—the maintenance of the enduring greatness of Britain and her Empire and the historical continuity of our Island life."[62]

"Looking back on the unceasing tumult of the war," wrote Churchill in 1950, "I cannot recall any period when its stresses and the onset of so many problems all at once or in rapid succession bore more directly on me and my colleagues than the first half of 1941."[63] Underlying this sense of continuous, mounting stress was the failure of the offensive strategy put together in response to the French collapse. Writing to President Roosevelt, the prime minister succinctly described the policy to which Britain had adhered since June:

> The form which this war has taken, and seems likely to hold, does not enable us to match the immense armies of Germany in any theatre where their main power can be brought to bear. We can, however, by the use of sea-power and air-power, meet the German armies in regions where only comparatively small forces can be brought into action. . . . If . . . we are able to move the necessary tonnage to and fro across salt water indefinitely, it may well be that the application of superior air-power to the German homeland and the rising anger of the German and other Nazi-gripped populations will bring the agony of civilisation to a merciful and glorious end.[64]

In the first six months of 1941 that policy failed everywhere with the crucially important exception of the war at sea, where the Germans lacked both the command structure and resources to carry out Hitler's 6 February 1941 Directive 23 ordering the strangulation of the British Isles by his navy and air force. By June 1941, when the German assault on the Soviet Union brought the British both a major ally and breathing space, they were in the same position they had been in one year before; that is, able to survive but without any clear idea of how to win.

Since victory was the central pillar of the Churchill administration, the sense of being in a tunnel, whose end could not be glimpsed, aroused an uneasiness that led to the first serious questioning in Parliament of the central war direction. The bombing offensive, on which the prime minister had placed many hopes, was proving to be a fiasco. As yet, SOE had virtually nothing to show for its efforts. The Americans, while sympathetic, were as far as ever from entering the war, and the British as far as ever from having any adequate defense against an increasingly hostile Japan. In the Balkans and the Middle East, where prospects had seemed so bright at the close of 1940, an unbroken series of defeats had been counterpointed by an imperial crisis, as Arab Nationalists moved to exploit Britain's plight. The army general staff, convinced that invasion was still possible, fought Churchill's desire to reinforce the Middle East to avert political as well as military catastrophe. By June the British effort to wage offensive war seemed a palpable failure. Only Hitler's obsession with his Soviet venture prevented the Germans from pressing their advantages in a way that possibly would have been fatal to Britain's ability to fight on and almost certainly to the Churchill administration. Little wonder the prime minister unhesitatingly embraced his new Soviet ally.

Churchill initially had reposed his greatest hope for a successful offensive in Bomber Command. Its high loss rate and slow expansion troubled him precisely because of his conviction that here was the weapon with which Britain could inflict such punishment on the German heartland as to alter the shape of the war. He clung to this vision into the late winter of 1940–41. In a directive setting the maximum size of the army at thirty-six divisions, he ruled that it was "impossible for the Army, except in resisting invasion, to play a primary role in the defeat of the enemy. That task can only be done by the staying power of the navy, and above all by the effect of air predominance."[65] But, as the prime minister reiterated his belief in victory through the employment of heavy bombers, within Bomber Command an uneasy realization was spreading that only a minority of its sorties ever found their targets. In October 1940, Portal's successor at Bomber Command, Air Chief Marshal Sir Richard Pierse, estimated that only one-third of all short-range attacks and one-fifth of the long-range ones—that is, those flown over Germany—reached their intended targets. Those figures in fact were optimistic.

At this point priorities changed. A committee studying Germany's oil situation reported that the synthetic oil plants, which produced 83 percent of Germany's supplies, were the weak point in the German war economy. Accordingly, the chiefs of staff recommended in early January that oil should be Bomber Command's primary target. It did not remain so for long. At Churchill's direction in March, supporting the navy's efforts against the U-boat superseded oil, and in July Germany's inland transport system became the principal target. Beneath these changing priorities there was a growing sense that, because Bomber Command could only hit large targets, and because its enormous demands on the British war effort—the new four-engine heavy bombers took 76,000 man hours to build, five times what it took to complete a *Spitfire*—could only be justified if what it hit were crucially important, its priority target should be German morale. In fact, in their January recommendation the chiefs of staff indicated that they were moving in this direction:

> The evidence at our disposal goes to show that the morale of the average German civilian will weaken quicker than that of a population such as our own as a consequence of direct attack. The Germans have been undernourished and subjected to a permanent strain equivalent to that of war conditions during almost the whole period of Hitler's regime, and for this reason also will be likely to crack before a nation of greater stamina.[66]

The assumptions made concerning the degree of strain on the German economy and population since 1933 were completely erroneous. Exactly what "evidence" was found regarding German reaction to air attack is hard to say, although the Foreign Office was circulating reports, derived from anti-Nazi German refugees, of poor German morale. Perhaps the question is unimportant since this assumption, like the one six months earlier that Britain could fight on, was at bottom a matter of belief and not of reasoned conviction. This element of blind faith was much more pronounced in a paper that the elder statesman of British air power, marshal of the Royal Air Force Lord Trenchard, the RAF's founding father, sent Churchill in early May: "*History has proved that we have always been able to stand our casualties better than other Nations. . . .* All the evidence of the last war and of this shows that the German nation is peculiarly susceptible to air bombing . . . there is no joking in the German shelters as in ours. . . . This, then, is the weak point that we should strike and strike again." No bomb that hit Germany was wasted, Trenchard concluded, thus arguing that Bomber Command should be given a priority target it could hardly miss.[67]

Churchill, who in September and October 1940 had been arguing for raids on Germany to weaken its morale, circulated this jejune document to the chiefs of staff. With the predictable exception of Portal, they found the arguments overdrawn and preferred to concentrate on inland transport, although the prime minister began to question the concept of long-term priority targets. Doubts about what the air force was actually hitting had now taken firm hold among Churchill's staff, and Lindemann set a member of his statistical section, D. M. Butt, to examine the photographs taken by the bombers as they released their loads. Butt's study would not be finished until late August, but as the first half of 1941 drew to a close, Bomber Command had failed to live up to the expectations its existence had aroused in the prime minister one year before.

While SOE had almost as little to show for its efforts as did the Royal Air Force's bombers, it managed, largely by accident, to look like it had gotten results. Churchill had breathed life into SOE in July 1940. Thereafter his attention to its activities tended to be intermittent, although he always rallied to its defense when it was assailed by any of its numerous foes in Whitehall, where the services and the Foreign Office saw it as a dangerously undisciplined competitor for influence and resources. Dalton's original hope that European socialists and trade unionists would become the backbone of resistance was rapidly displaced by the concept of "secret armies." Major Colin Gubbins, a regular soldier who had been involved in War Office planning for guerrilla warfare in 1938–39 and who, as a major general, would eventually become executive head of SOE in 1943, was the principal sponsor of the idea. Impressed by the "underground armies" being organized by the Polish and Czech governments in exile, Gubbins argued successfully that the development and arming of such forces should be SOE's chief task. This, however, was a long-term policy, dependent upon SOE's acquiring aircraft and supplies on a scale quite out of reach in 1940–41. Furthermore, the essence of the secret army idea was that such organizations should remain quiescent, avoiding destruction at German hands until the time came to explode them, like so many mines, under the Germans when liberating armies drew near.

This policy of passivity, in conjunction with SOE's failure to make much headway developing underground networks in western Europe, but for a fortunate coincidence might well have cost the organization the confidence of the prime minister, whose idea of resistance was much more activist. From one of its forerunners SOE had inherited a fairly extensive network of agents in the Balkans. As German attention swung east and southeast in late 1940, Churchill told Dalton that the Balkans were the "acid test" for SOE. In fact, it accomplished nothing worthwhile there, nor could it have given the realities of German power and British powerlessness. In Yugoslavia, however, the failure was concealed by a chain of fortuitous events. Agents of SOE had been in touch with those sections of the Yugoslav political world that opposed collaboration with the Germans. When the Yugoslav government, headed by the regent, Prince Paul, bowed to German pressure and adhered to the Tripartite Pact, it was overthrown by a coup in Belgrade on 27 March. Churchill exulted that Yugoslavia had "found its soul" and showered congratulations on Dalton, although SOE's contribution to the coup had been marginal, and all its arrangements to sabotage Balkan resources that the Germans needed had failed. Nevertheless, SOE seemed to have been successful and in an area particularly subject to the prime minister's scrutiny.

The Balkans and Middle East appeared full of possibilities as 1941 arrived. These bright hopes then perished in a succession of defeats so continuous and bitter that they called into question the entire strategy that had involved Britain there. Churchill warned Wavell early in January that the exploitation of Compass would have to come to an end at Tobruk in order to free resources for Greece. The commander in chief protested, drawing from Churchill a direct order: "We expect prompt and active compliance with our decisions. . . ."[68] However, when Wavell went to Athens on 15 January for discussions, the Greeks made it plain that British forces would only be welcome if they came in strength sufficient to hold as well as to provoke a German attack. Wavell thus got a breathing space in which to carry his campaign to a victorious conclusion— almost. After O'Connor's final victory at Beda Fromm on 6 February little stood between Wavell and the remaining Italian base at Tripoli but disorganized and demoralized remnants. Had O'Connor indeed pushed on, Tripoli might have fallen and the next two years of fighting in North Africa would have been avoided. However, O'Connor's forces were exhausted (the 7th Armored Division was down to a dozen tanks when it was withdrawn to rest after Beda Fromm), Tripoli was still nearly four hundred miles ahead, and Italian reinforcements were pouring in. More ominously, the German air force had arrived in the Mediterranean one month before. Despite Ultra indications as early as 9 February of the imminent movement of German army units to Tripoli, intelligence evaluations in London and Cairo did not rate highly the possibility of rapid German intervention in North Africa.

Thus a stable defensive flank in the desert seemed possible at a time when the indications of a German forward move in the Balkans grew stronger. The cautious Greek general, Joannes Metaxas, who had turned the British down in January, had meanwhile died and his successor as prime minister, Alexandros Korizis, was more anxious to embrace British help. To draw together all the strands of British policy in the theater, and because of his continuing reservations about Wavell, Churchill decided to send Eden, accompanied by Dill, on another mission to the Middle East. It was on 12 February that the prime minister drafted a directive for the Eden-Dill mission. On the same day the commander of the

German "blocking force" arrived at Castel Benito airfield in Tripoli. His name was Erwin Rommel.

The Italian failure in Greece, followed by their disastrous defeat at the hands of O'Connor and Wavell, changed the direction of the Mediterranean war. Hitler had flirted briefly with an attack on Britain's position in the Mediterranean basin but rejected it. However, an Italian collapse had to be prevented and the new British foothold in Europe erased before Barbarossa began. The *Luftwaffe* in Sicily and the German troops arriving on Rommel's heels in Tripoli were to prevent the one; "Operation Marita," ordered by Hitler on 13 December 1940, would see to the other. There matters would be left until the Wehrmacht returned victorious from the Soviet Union. From this decision flowed the corollary need to coerce Bulgaria and Yugoslavia into Germany's embrace to enable the German army to enter Greece. Neither Churchill nor anyone else in London knew all of this. Ultra told of the continual movement east and southeast, but the Germans' ultimate goal remained unclear.

What was clear was that Germany would be in a position to attack Greece in the spring and that British aid might animate a general Balkan front against the German thrust. "It was not what we could send ourselves that would decide the Balkan issue. . . . Our limited hope was to stir and organise united action," Churchill later wrote.[69] In March 1941 he signaled to Eden: "Let us visualise clearly what we want in the Balkans and from Turkey, and work towards it as events serve. . . . Together Yugoslavia, Greece, Turkey, and ourselves have seventy divisions mobilised in this theatre. Germans have not yet got more than thirty." Greece was an inescapable political obligation, but it was Turkey that Churchill and the chiefs of staff considered the real prize. With the Turks, the Greeks, and, if possible, the Yugoslavs, the British would have what Churchill described as "a good pad on our right hand to protect our Middle Eastern interests," while forcing Germany to "attack in mountainous regions and with poor communications at heavy odds."[70]

Was this policy realistic? It certainly overrated both the stopping power of the brave but obsolete Balkan armies and the likelihood of Turkish intervention and at the same time underrated the speed and fury with which the Germans could move, certainly a curious lapse after two years of war. Churchill defined success for the policy as holding the Germans for a few months. His attitude was that, since the Greek commitment was politically inescapable, the maximum effort should be made to turn it into a catalyst, bringing about the most embarrassment for the Germans. This posture did not really fit into any coherent picture of how the war would end, only into the consensus on defending the Middle East and into the prime minister's personal belief that Britain had to keep fighting back in order to attract allies. When he told the House of Commons in June that "all the great struggles of history have been won by superior will-power wresting victory in the teeth of odds or upon the narrowest of margins," he was voicing his deep inner conviction that determined aggression was the essence of war.[71]

The decision to go to the aid of Greece with more than a token force was, therefore, certainly congenial to Churchill's temperament but not simply his idea. Indeed, once he had sent out Eden and Dill as delegates of the war cabinet, he relinquished much of the initiative to them, several times sharply questioning whether the plans to which they agreed were sound. On the eve of Eden's departure from Cairo for Athens, the prime minister warned him: "Do not consider yourselves obligated to a Greek enterprise if in your hearts you feel it will only be another Norwegian fiasco. If no good plan can be made, please say so. But of course you know how valuable success would be."[72] Eden, Wavell, and Dill sat down on 22 February at the Greek royal palace of Tatoi with the king of Greece, Korizis, and General Alexander Papagos, the Greek commander. Prior to the meeting, King George II insisted that Eden meet privately with Korizis, who then read a declaration that Greece would fight Germany alone if necessary. Since the previous British offer could not have left the Greeks with any doubt about Britain's willingness to come to their aid, the declaration smacks of a negotiating ploy to increase Greek leverage in the ensuing talks. The "staunchness" of King George at this moment, however, counted heavily in his favor with Churchill, and British attachment to the Greek royal family would shape the politics of liberation between 1943 and 1945.

The Tatoi Conference played a crucial role in the ensuing chain of disasters. The key issue was the British desire to have the Greek troops, thinly spread along the Bulgarian frontier, pulled back to a better defensive position upon which the arriving British force could then concentrate.* The British record of the meeting

---

*The bulk of the Greek army—fifteen divisions—was facing the Italians in Albania. The position agreed to at Tatoi on 22–23 February, the so-called "Aliakmon Line," would have covered the flank and rear of the Greek armies from any German thrust coming from Bulgaria or through a complacent or conquered Yugoslavia.

shows agreement on this point; the Greek record has vanished. But Papagos later claimed that no firm agreement had been reached, and he certainly took no steps to implement the understanding, probably because he never intended to abandon Thrace and Greece's second city, Salonika, in advance of a German attack. Eden and Dill only discovered how mistaken they were about Papagos's intentions when they returned to Athens for a second round of conferences one week later. In the interval they had met in Ankara the Turkish leadership which deployed the encouraging evasiveness that it was to use with such success over the next three years. "Turkey undertakes . . . to enter the war at some stage," Eden reported wearily to Churchill.[73] When the foreign secretary reached Athens, a signal from Churchill was waiting, indicating that doubts were growing in the prime minister's mind:

> I am absolutely ready to go in on a serious hazard if there is reasonable chance of success, at any rate for a few months. But I should like you to so handle matters in Greece that if . . . you feel there is not even a reasonable hope, you should still retain power to liberate Greeks from any bargain and at the same time liberate ourselves.[74]

On the day Churchill composed this signal, Bulgaria formally adhered to the Tripartite Pact and German forces began to stream over the Danube; on the day he read it, Eden discovered that Papagos had ignored the principal item in the Tatoi agreement. A British force made up of the 6th Australian and 2d New Zealand divisions, with a British armored brigade, was poised for dispatch to Greece. The dominion governments had been assured that the Greek expedition was a carefully calculated military risk with good prospects of success. When Eden reported the true situation, there was consternation in London.

While wanting a Balkan front, Churchill had had premonitions for some time of possible disaster in Greece. The new situation, revealed in Eden's message, led the chiefs of staff to produce a pessimistic evaluation which implied but, perhaps in deference to Dill, stopped short of stating, that the expedition should be canceled. Churchill sent this news to Eden, accompanied by his own thoughts in which he reflected that "we must liberate Greeks from feeling bound to reject a German ultimatum. If on their own they resolve to fight, we must to some extent share their ordeal." But the sharing, he hoped, would be a purely token affair: "Rapid German advance will probably prevent any appreciable British

Imperial forces from being engaged." He also was quickly readjusting his diplomatic strategy. "Loss of Greece and Balkans is by no means a major catastrophe for us, providing Turkey remains honest neutral," Churchill told Eden, revealing the fears for the northern flank of Middle East Command that underlaid all British thinking on southeastern Europe since 1939.[75]

If Churchill had been as ruthless in overriding military advice as he is often thought to have been, the British expedition to Greece might well have ended at this point. Eden, however, prodded by his ambassador in Athens and supported by Dill, Wavell, and Sir Henry Maitland Wilson, commander of the force destined for Greece, argued strongly for going ahead for reasons as much diplomatic as military: "To have fought and suffered in Greece would be less damaging to us than to have left Greece to her fate. . . ."[76] This curious reversal of roles, with Churchill arguing for caution and Eden (and rather less understandably Dill and Wavell) arguing that the political ramifications of not helping Greece might be catastrophic, ended with the war cabinet, with the visiting Australian prime minister present, agreeing to allow the expedition to sail. Characteristically, Churchill stressed in his signal to Eden that full responsibility now rested on the cabinet, that is, on himself.

Was that risk well taken? The answer can only come from an examination of what risks the decision makers believed they were running in relation to the goals they sought. Eden thought in Foreign Office terms: to woo Turkey and Yugoslavia and to impress Vichy, Spain, and, not least, the United States, the British had to stand by the Greeks and not merely with flourishes of rhetoric and token air force squadrons. Although he had headed the War Office for five months, Eden was not disposed to question the generals searchingly in Churchill's style. It is typical of his essentially surface knowledge that Eden became an advocate of Wilson's claims to high command, based on nothing more substantial than Wilson's background in Eden's old regiment. The foreign secretary could see the diplomatic advantages—and for him that was crucial—but what about Dill and Wavell? Dill had been considered well before 1940 as a future chief of the Imperial General Staff. A former staff college commandant, he was reputed to have one of the best brains in the army. When Dill left London, he was dubious about a Greek expedition, yet once in Cairo he deferred to Wavell without, it seems, losing his pessimism over the outcome. On several occasions he spoke gloomily of impending "bloody noses" in Greece. Churchill's subsequent complaint that "this . . . was not in harmony with any statement he made to us" seems remarkably mild under the circumstances.*[77]

What then of Wavell? One of the most senior generals in the British army, senior in fact to Dill in the army list, he was also the only one with any victories to his credit, which reinforced his demonstrated capacity to act independently of Churchill. Eden and Dill allowed themselves to be guided by Wavell, and Wavell stubbornly adhered to his belief that the Greek expedition was militarily sound, although after the war he was to defend his decision on political grounds. Even after Papagos's action had offered him a way out, Wavell fatalistically clung to the enterprise, quoting British General James Wolfe's famous dictum: "War is an option of difficulties." Beneath Wavell's stolid exterior lurked a dangerous capacity for gambling that all would somehow come out right.

Finally, there was Churchill, obviously dubious and offering Eden, Dill, and Wavell repeated opportunities to say no. Yet, as in the case of Dakar, he allowed the men on the spot to go ahead. Since one was chief of the Imperial General Staff and the other his heir apparent, it would have been perhaps difficult to overrule them, although he commented later: "I am sure I could have stopped it all if I had been convinced."[78] He too could see political advantages—"you know how valuable a success could be"—and his temperament disposed him to favor the aggressive over the cautious. "It was one of my rules that *errors towards the enemy* must be lightly judged," he wrote retrospectively about Dakar.[79] Thus "Operation Lustre" went ahead, with perhaps none of the decision makers actually convinced it would stop the Germans, even for the few months that the prime minister had defined as success.**

---

*Throughout the late winter and spring, Dill conducted a running battle with Churchill over the likelihood of a German invasion attempt in 1941, a real danger he believed in spite of the mounting evidence of heavy German concentrations in eastern Europe. There will always be a gap in the history of Britain's central war direction because Dill, who died in 1944, left nothing behind him which his thinking could be reconstructed. The best record of the war from Dill's perspective is the account by one of his closest War Office associates, Director of Military Operations Major General Sir John Kennedy, *The Business of War*, ed. Bernard Fergusson (New York, 1958). Kennedy saw Dill as soon as he arrived back in London on 10 April: "He spoke of . . . Greece, and said he feared a bad mistake had been made," 90. Why then, as professional head of the British army, had he not stopped it? Dill's behavior over both Greece and the invasion question makes Churchill's loss of confidence in him understandable.

**Further down the chain of command pessimism was even deeper. The Australian and New Zealand commanders, Major Generals Sir Thomas Blamey and Sir Bernard Freyberg, were sure that Lustre was doomed. Neither protested to Wavell, nor did either exercise his right to communicate his concern to his own government.

Churchill had carefully kept Roosevelt informed as the decision to mount Lustre took shape. If impressing neutral opinion was
one of the expedition's purposes, the outcome was bitterly ironic.
Roosevelt, for the first time, tentatively questioned the entire British
Middle Eastern strategy. Subsequently, Churchill rationalized the
Greek expedition by elevating it to causal status in light of the
German failure to take Moscow. In fact, the need to mount a hasty
attack on Yugoslavia after the 27 March coup caused more
derangement to German plans than did Marita, for which they had
been preparing since December. In any case, the entire complex of
Balkan campaigns mattered far less to the German failure in the
Soviet Union than did the inherent flaws in the Barbarossa plan.
But the Greek campaign did have a wrenching effect on British
strategy, for it opened a three-month run of disasters that represented the lowest point in the war for Britain and its prime minister
and that distorted the pattern of British strategy in a fundamental
and irreversible way.

Creating the expeditionary force for Greece had meant strip-
ping the desert flank of equipment (one British armored unit was
reduced to using captured Italian tanks), experienced troops, and
veteran commanders. Despite the Ultra indications of German arri-
vals in Tripoli, Wavell and his intelligence chief, Brigadier Norman
Shearer, were sure they would have a respite of several months
before a serious Axis counterattack could be mounted. And so they
would have if Rommel had done what his superiors expected and
ordered. Instead, sensing the weakness in the British position, the
most brilliant battlefield opportunist of the war lunged forward on
the last day of March. The British forces collapsed like a house of
cards, drawing Rommel forward in an improvised pursuit like
O'Connor's against the Italians. Wavell's intervention compounded
a confused situation, and it was only by a slender margin that
Tobruk, alone among the winter's conquests, was held.

Watching from afar, Churchill, who had not realized until the
eve of Rommel's offensive that the veteran 7th Armored Division
had been withdrawn to Egypt for rest and refitting, was dis-
mayed. He knew from Ultra how few Rommel's forces were, and
in a message to Eden, sounded for the first time a note he was to
repeat often, a deep uneasiness about the fighting qualities of
British troops: "Far more important than the loss of ground is the
idea that we cannot face the Germans and that their appearance
is enough to drive us back many scores of miles. . . . Sooner or later
we shall have to fight the Huns."[80] He need not have worried.
Equipment, training, and leadership, rather than fighting spirit,

were the problem then and later in the desert, although British commanders and their troops were more sensitive to casualties than in the First World War as, despite his rhetoric, was Churchill.

On 6 April, the day Wavell decided to hold Tobruk, the German Balkan campaign opened. The *Luftwaffe* smashed Belgrade, killing 17,000, while simultaneously German troops swept into Greece. Within a week Papagos told Wilson that the British should evacuate to spare Greece unnecessary devastation. When this suggestion was reported to Churchill, he heartily concurred. Wavell informed the Greek king on 21 April that British forces would leave as rapidly as possible. The navy, in fact, withdrew 50,000 of the 58,000 transported to Greece, although all supplies and equipment were lost.*

Once again the British had displayed technical skill only in withdrawing. Faced by defeat on two fronts, Churchill immediately took steps to hang on to the essentials—Egypt and the eastern basin of the Mediterranean. Cunningham was subjected to intense pressure—exerted largely through Pound—to block Rommel's supplies, if necessary, by sinking the battleship *Barham* at the mouth of Tripoli harbor, a reckless scheme illustrating the prime minister's mounting frustration. On 18 April he drafted a directive on priorities to Wavell, which was endorsed and sent by the chiefs of staff: "Victory in Libya counts first."[82] Within forty-eight hours he decided to back that priority with a boldness that shows him at his best, just as his pressure on Cunningham showed him at his emotionally pugnacious worst.

On Sunday, 20 April the prime minister was spending the weekend in the country, and on that morning he was working in bed. He read, and brooded over, a signal from Wavell revealing how little armor was available after recent losses in Greece and the desert. This was the catalyst of decision. "I resolved not to be governed any longer by the Admiralty reluctance, but to send a convoy through the Mediterranean direct to Alexandria carrying all the tanks which General Wavell needed."[83] Ismay was summoned and sent back to London with an imperious directive for the chiefs of staff: "The fate of the war in the Middle East . . . may turn on a few hundred armoured vehicles. They must if possible be carried there at all costs. . . . The Admiralty and Air Ministry

---

*Churchill had worried that the troops involved in the Greek venture were mostly from the dominions: "I feel very much the fact that we are not using a single British division."[81] In fact, British troops formed the largest contingent and suffered the greatest losses.

will consider and prepare *this day* a plan for carrying this vital convoy through the Mediterranean."[84] The service departments were given until noon Monday to have their plans ready. Dill drove another nail into his professional coffin by protesting that the tanks should stay at home in case of invasion, although the previous summer he had willingly agreed to part with a much higher proportion of Britain's available armor. Churchill overrode all opposition, and on 12 May the *Tiger* convoy reached Alexandria with 240 tanks, only one ship having been lost en route. "I had not realised what a strain it had been on all concerned," wrote Churchill in calm retrospect.[85]

Certainly a great deal more than Wavell's ability to resume the offensive rode with *Tiger*. The fate of the commander in chief now rested on the use he made of the tanks sent to him by the prime minister at great risk, for Churchill had clearly overridden his military advisers as he had so disastrously been suspected of having done in 1914–15. That decision had to be vindicated by success. Furthermore, a British victory was necessary to shore up the entire imperial position in the Middle East which was swaying under the impact of German victories.

The kingdom of Iraq was not only a British creation but also one over whose birth Churchill had presided. The Hashimite royal house in Iraq cherished its British connection but Arab Nationalists there, as elsewhere, saw in the British their principal opponent. The German and Italian ministers in Baghdad found ready listeners; the 28,000-strong Iraqi army, British equipped and trained, resented its mentors; and the leader of the Palestinian Arab resistance to British authority, the Grand Mufti of Jerusalem, had found shelter in Iraq. As it had to the Irish before them, Britain's moment of danger seemed to Iraqi Nationalists the right hour to strike. Nuri as-Sa'id, whose connection with the British went back to the legendary days of Lawrence of Arabia and the Arab revolt, was the only Iraqi figure of note on whom the British could rely, apart from the royal family.

Ironically, Nuri began to lose control the moment Churchill became prime minister. That event ended a plan that Nuri had been promoting to accelerate the creation of an elected legislative council in Palestine. Promised by the 1939 White Paper, this would have produced an Arab majority in the council, which itself was the first step toward an independent Palestine. Churchill would have none of this; his policy was ultimately to undo the White

Paper. Deprived of the political coup of posing as the successful champion of the Palestine Arabs, Nuri's influence waned. Rashid Ali-al-Gailani, whose allies were the Grand Mufti, the Axis diplomats, and the army, became the dominant figure in Baghdad. Rashid Ali's military allies moved on the night of 1–2 April 1941. The regent of Iraq fled, and as Rommel surged forward and the German avalanche poured over Yugoslavia and Greece, Churchill and Wavell faced revolt within the vast Middle Eastern base area.

Churchill's reaction was to order Wavell to put together a scratch force from the British units in Palestine to cross the intervening desert to Baghdad and overawe Rashid Ali's followers. At the same time, he asked the government of India to send troops to Basra at the head of the Persian Gulf. The commander in chief (India), General Sir Claude Auchinleck, promptly diverted the leading brigade of an Indian division bound for Malaya. Wavell however argued that he could not take on any more troops and urged a political solution. Behind this situation lay an argument that neither Churchill in his memoirs nor Wavell's biographers chose to discuss.

Wavell was a strong supporter of the pro-Arab tilt in British policy that had produced the 1939 White Paper. Churchill violently opposed this policy and had already clashed with Wavell. "General Wavell, like most British military officers is strongly pro-Arab," he wrote dismissively early in March.[86] The essence of the difference between the prime minister and the commander in chief lay in the fact that Wavell thought placating Arab nationalism was vital to success in the Middle East, while Churchill simply did not rate the Arabs highly as either a political or military force. Wavell's reluctance to face yet another military commitment was doubtless colored by his belief that, had Churchill been more amenable to official wisdom on the matter of Palestine, the Iraqi revolt might never have happened. Churchill's refusal to accept Wavell's advice to negotiate was not only founded on his disdain for Arab military prowess but also on a desire to forestall any discussion of further concessions to Arab opinion on the Palestine issue.

Wavell was certainly under intense strain. To the desert and Greek campaigns was added the Iraqi problem and pressure to launch a preemptive strike at Vichy-controlled Syria and Lebanon. But Churchill was also under great stress and had to keep in mind not only the continuing problems of the blitz and U-boat campaign but the interlocking complex of Middle Eastern problems and their impact on large issues of alliance politics as well. Wavell's conquest of Italy's East African empire made it possible for Roosevelt to declare the Red Sea no longer a combat zone. American shipping could now carry supplies directly to Suez. Basra was another possible port of entry for American equipment, but not unless Iraq was firmly under control. The Australian government, uneasily conscious of the lengthening shadow of Japan, chose this moment to voice its doubts over the prime minister's priorities by asking on 24 April, as one of its divisions was being withdrawn from Greece, how the British government proposed to cope if Suez and Gibraltar fell to the Germans and Japan seized that moment to strike. These reverses and pressures produced a sudden violent explosion from Churchill.

The prime minister was spending the weekend at Chequers working on a major speech for broadcast on Sunday evening 27 April, aimed at American opinion. Churchill was his own speech writer, and the artist in him brought to the task of crafting a speech an edgy, nervous intensity. Afterward, he relaxed over dinner, accompanied by quantities of champagne. Ismay was present, together with David Margesson, secretary of state for war; Alan Brooke, commander in chief, Home Forces; and Lindemann. Major General Sir John Kennedy, director of Military Operations at the War Office, had come down from London for the evening. He and Dill had been reviewing Wavell's contingency plan for an evacuation of Egypt, first drawn up in May 1940 and since updated. When the prime minister asked him for his views on the Middle East, Kennedy responded that a German attack from the west and north might be too much for Wavell to parry. The last contingents of British and dominion troops waited on Greek beaches; Rommel was on the Egyptian frontier; Wavell, whom the prime minister had long suspected of not making the best use of his resources, was reluctant to take action in Syria and Iraq; Dill, it was becoming obvious, was a broken reed; the Australians had more than hinted that they expected the loss of Egypt; and now this. "Wavell has 400,000 men. If they lose Egypt, blood will flow. I will have firing parties to shoot the generals," the prime minister shouted in his most celebrated outburst of the war against the army high command. Kennedy tried to explain that a prudent commander prepared for setbacks as well as for success. Thus Wavell's plan, "Mongoose," the worst-possible-case scheme for the evacuation of Egypt, was revealed to the prime minister. "This comes as a flash of lightning to me. . . . War is a contest of wills. It is pure defeatism to speak as you have done," Churchill snapped.[87] Several times later in the evening the prime minister returned to his theme that willpower was decisive in war.

The argument had momentous consequences. The next day a minute went to Dill, demanding to see Wavell's contingency plan. Later in the day Churchill issued a directive, whose strident tone is evidence of the sense of almost intolerable pressure under which the prime minister labored. First he made explicit his own Far Eastern strategy, brushing aside in doing so not only Australian fears but also the policy agreed to the previous August:

> It is very unlikely . . . that Japan will enter the war either if the United States have come in or if Japan thinks they would come in consequent upon a Japanese declaration of war . . . it may be taken as almost certain that the entry of Japan into the war would be followed by the immediate entry of the United States on our side. . . . There is no need at present to make any further dispositions for the defence of Malaya and Singapore, beyond the modest arrangements which are in progress. . . .

The heart of the directive, however, dealt with the Middle East:

> The loss of Egypt and the Middle East would be a disaster of the first magnitude to Great Britain, second only to successful invasion and final conquest. . . . It is to be impressed on all ranks, especially the highest, that the life and honour of Great Britain depends upon the successful defence of Egypt. It is not to be expected that the British forces of the land, sea and air in the Mediterranean would wish to survive so vast and shameful a defeat as would be entailed by our expulsion from Egypt. . . . All plans for evacuation are to be called in. . . . No surrenders by officers and men will be considered tolerable unless at least 50 percent casualties are sustained by the unit or force in question. . . . Generals and Staff officers surprised by the enemy are to use their pistols in self-defence. The honour of a wounded man is safe. Anyone who can kill a Hun or even an Italian has rendered good service. The Army of the Nile is to fight with no thought of retreat or withdrawal.[88]*

In one sense Churchill's directive can be explained as the emotional reaction of a tired and aggressive man to the multiple difficulties with which he was beset. While true, that however would

---

*Churchill did not reproduce this directive in his memoirs, but John Kennedy did in his, published in 1958. J. R. M. Butler in his official history, *Grand Strategy*, vol. 2, *September 1939–June 1941* (London, 1957), had by then already printed it, minus however the exhortation to "kill a Hun or even an Italian," 557–58.

not be the whole truth. The 28 April directive was born of a profound concern that Britain's ability to wage successful war, attract powerful allies, and thus survive and win were imperiled by professional caution and a lack of fighting spirit in the army. It also signaled a degree of intense, personal commitment to the war in the Middle East that thereafter would never diminish. The Churchill administration stood for the waging of vigorous war against Germany. If it could not do so successfully in the desert where, as Churchill knew from Ultra, Rommel's small German force was at the end of its administrative tether, it was unlikely to do so anywhere. That would spell defeat for Churchill's policy and for the prime minister personally. Churchill stood as well for the maintenance of Britain's imperial grip, but ironically in underlining his determination to fight and win in the Middle East, he was sealing Singapore's fate.

Finally, the argument over the defense of Egypt completed his disillusionment with Dill as chief of the Imperial General Staff. Prompted by Kennedy, Dill responded to the directive by opening a long argument, conducted on paper, that ran on until late May. Dill and Kennedy still feared invasion and adhered to the official policy that Singapore and not Egypt was second in priority to Britain. Churchill had been convinced for months that Russia was Hitler's target for 1941, and he was sure that Britain's war effort stood or fell by what happened in the Middle East. Ismay later wrote that this argument finally shattered Dill's credibility as the government's principal strategic adviser. But he lingered on in office until the late autumn, a situation that left a partial vacuum at the center of Britain's war direction and endowed Churchill with even greater latitude.

Despite the prime minister's almost frenzied efforts to control the situation, the next six weeks saw British fortunes in the Middle East steadily worsen. Under protest, Wavell pushed a scratch force across the desert toward Baghdad and assembled another for use in Syria, where German and Italian planes were refueling on their way to Iraq. At one point Wavell offered a conditional resignation to Dill, to which the prime minister responded:

> Our view is that if the Germans can pick up Syria and Iraq with petty air forces, tourists and local revolts, we must not shrink from running equal small-scale military risks and facing the possible aggravation of political dangers from failure. For this decision we, of course, take full responsibility, and should you find yourself unwilling to give effect to it arrangements

will be made to meet any wish you may express to be relieved of your command.[89]

The day before Churchill sent this telegram, the German airborne attack on Crete had begun. Despite an Ultra picture of German intentions as complete as any the British would ever have and the presence in command of the British forces of Lieutenant General Sir Bernard Freyberg, V.C., a much-wounded paladin for whom Churchill had a special affection, the Germans won in a week, a result the prime minister blamed not on Freyberg but on Wavell.* In the midst of Cretan debacle, the *Bismarck* broke out into the Atlantic, sinking the battlecruiser *Hood* and nearly escaping to Brest before Ultra allowed it to be cornered and destroyed on 27 May, the day Wavell told Churchill that Crete was lost. After observing Churchill at a cabinet meeting on the previous evening, a Foreign Office official, Sir Alexander Cadogan, noted in his diary: "Poor Winston very gloomy—due of course to 'Hood' and Crete . . . will recover all right if we get a bit of good news. Tonight he was almost throwing his hand in. But there is a bit of histrionic art in *that*."[90]

Churchill's depression was not all assumed. The waspish Cadogan might blame the "sensational ineptitude" of British commanders, but murmurs were beginning to be heard that fastened the responsibility for the unbroken series of military setbacks on the prime minister and in particular on his single-handed management of British strategy. Those murmurs had grown loud enough after the evacuation from Greece that Churchill had insisted on a vote of confidence in the House early in May. By making himself the issue, he forced even his critics to vote for him (477 to 3), since he had established himself beyond challenge as the symbol of the nation's resolve. But his resounding triumph in the House did not actually answer criticisms of his methods. Indeed, those criticisms reflected reality, for, as Dill's credit declined, Churchill was managing British strategy, especially in the Middle East, more completely than ever. If he were to continue to do so, however, that strategy

*Churchill was convinced that Wavell should have provided more tanks to defend the airfields, whose loss to the Germans was the turning point of the battle. Colonel Robert Laycock, whose commando unit had fought on Crete, dined at Chequers with Churchill after his return. One of Churchill's secretaries, John R. Colville, noted that "quite unconscious of the effect his words would have, Laycock remarked that if we had had a dozen tanks Maleme [airfield] and Crete itself could have been saved. I could almost hear a large nail being driven into Wavell's coffin." John Wheeler-Bennett, ed., *Action this Day: Working with Churchill* (New York, 1969), 62. This is based on Colville's wartime diaries. Although the dinner at Chequers took place after Churchill had decided to relieve Wavell, it could only have confirmed the prime minister in the soundness of his judgment.

had to produce victory, not over the Iraqis or the Vichy garrison of Syria but over the Germans.

The *Tiger* convoy had been a great risk, and Churchill fretted continually about the delay in bringing the tanks it carried into action against Rommel. Clementine Churchill recalled her husband's anxiety and anger expressed weekend after weekend at Chequers over Wavell's delay in mounting his attack, code named "Battleaxe." The prime minister's wife was not the only one aware of Churchill's impatience. The pressure on Wavell was ceaseless. On one occasion he was told: "Our first object must be to gain a decisive military success in the Western Desert," and again on another: "There is a storm of criticism about Crete, and I am being pressed for explanations on many points. Do not worry about this at all now. Simply keep your eye on Syria, and above all Battleaxe. These alone can supply the answers to criticisms."[91]

Behind the pressure, however, lay more than temperamental combativeness and political necessity. On 27 April an emissary from the German army's high command, General Friedrich Paulus, had arrived at Rommel's headquarters. By exceeding his orders Rommel had won a great tactical success but left himself badly overextended. This situation was reported by Paulus to Berlin and by Bletchley Park to Churchill. The sense of opportunity, fleetingly within reach for a victory that would resolve so many difficulties, added a compulsive urgency to Churchill's telegraphic battering of Wavell. At length Battleaxe was ready, although Wavell was pessimistic about its chances, telling Dill "the measure of success which will attend this operation is in my opinion doubtful."[92] The delay had allowed Rommel to catch his breath and get most of the newly arrived 15th Panzer Division into action. Battleaxe opened on 15 June. Churchill could not bear to await the news in London. "Knowing that the result must soon come in, I went down to Chartwell, which was all shut up, wishing to be alone," he wrote in 1950. "Here I got the reports of what had happened. I wandered about the valley disconsolately for several hours."[93]

Battleaxe had failed. British tanks were neither as mechanically reliable nor as powerfully gunned as their opponents, and British forces had not been handled with anything like the tactical flair that characterized Rommel and his subordinates.* Many of

---

*British armored tactics were inferior to those of their German opponents, a legacy of developments stretching back to 1918. Problems of tank design and armament as well as of tactics would continue to bedevil the British throughout the desert campaigns. In 1942 British Lieutenant General Sir Bernard L. Montgomery solved them but only by never fighting the sort of tank battle at which the Germans excelled. By then circumstances had

these factors were beyond Wavell's control, but the prime minister had come to the end of his patience. "He gives me the impression of being tired out," Churchill told the chiefs of staff during the argument over Iraq.[94] On 4 June he had already appointed Lieutenant General Sir Robert Haining, who had been vice-chief of Imperial General Staff, to the newly created post of intendant general to oversee the huge base establishments in the Middle East which the prime minister was sure could be more efficiently managed. An even more important move to limit the commander in chief's power then followed. In April Wavell, Cunningham, and the Royal Air Force commander in the theater, Sir Arthur Longmore, had jointly suggested that they needed resident political guidance on the numerous problems that arose. On 7 June the prime minister's son Randolph, serving in the Middle East with the commandoes, sent a telegram through Lampson: "Why not send a member of the War Cabinet here to preside over whole war effort?"[95] This, Churchill later wrote, settled the matter in his mind. Haining's appointment and the decision to install a war cabinet member in Cairo reflected not only Churchill's displeasure with Wavell but also his determination to exercise even closer control over Britain's only land campaign, one to which his fate seemed increasingly bound.

Then came Battleaxe, and Churchill decided that the new arrangements in the Middle East required a new commander as well. Sacking Wavell outright might have presented problems, but fortunately there was another way to disembarrass himself of the commander in chief. The alacrity with which Auchinleck had responded to the need for troops in Iraq had favorably impressed the prime minister, particularly in contrast to Wavell's hesitancy and complaints. Churchill therefore proposed to have them exchange posts. "I found that these views of mine encountered no resistance in our Ministerial and military circles in London," he wrote demurely in his memoirs.[96] In fact, the prime minister's dissatisfaction with Wavell was shared by many in London. Dill, pessimistic as ever, played no part in the change, an eloquent comment on the degree to which he had become peripheral. On 21 June, the day Churchill sent Wavell and Auchinleck news of the change of command, Kennedy returned to the War Office from a week's leave. Dill's opening comment to him was "I suppose you realize we shall lose the Middle East?"[97] Only later that day did Dill receive copies of the prime minister's signals to Cairo and Delhi.

changed considerably. Neither Wavell nor Auchinleck could escape from the necessity of fighting Rommel with a flawed weapon.

One week later Churchill named Oliver Lyttleton as minister of state and war cabinet delegate in the Middle East.

Like Churchill, Lyttleton was a political outsider. After distinguished war service in France from 1914 to 1918, he had gone into business. Churchill brought him into Parliament and then into the government as president of the Board of Trade. With Wavell gone, a Churchillian as war cabinet representative in Cairo, and Haining deputed to shake up the rear area administration, the prime minister hoped for more responsiveness from Middle East command than he had had from the Wavell regime. The dismissed commander in chief received Churchill's message stoically. He had already told Dill he was tired and ready to go. Wavell simply commented that Churchill was right and the theater needed a fresh commander. He did, however, ask to return home on leave, a request Churchill refused, telling Dill he would not have Wavell sitting in his club in London and acting as a focus for complaints against the central direction of the war. The day after Wavell's dismissal Germany attacked Russia, ending British isolation and providing a major ally, yet also profoundly altering Britain's status, and that of its leader, in the war against Germany.

One of the many effects of the continuous setbacks in the Balkans and the desert during the spring of 1941, and one that especially distressed the prime minister, was the impact they had on his campaign to draw a steadily greater commitment from the United States, culminating in active participation. Since the destroyers-bases deal, Churchill had felt reasonably secure about receiving American aid, and the passage of lend-lease justified his expectation that Roosevelt would find a way to keep supplies flowing. But American money and material were only part of what Churchill needed. As it became increasingly apparent during the first half of 1941 that the offensive strategies available to the British could cause the Germans little serious inconvenience, let alone damage, and that in the one theater where they were in contact with the German army they were barely hanging on, active U.S. participation seemed steadily more important. In June a planning paper made explicit Britain's need for American intervention: "The active belligerency of the United States has become essential for a successful prosecution and conclusion of the war."[98]

Well before June Churchill had known that the way to bring the Americans into the war was by encouraging a steadily deepening participation in the Battle of the Atlantic. Ian Jacob, writing just after Pearl Harbor, summarized this aspect of Churchill's strategy: "His policy during 1941 was to draw the Americans slowly but surely further across the Atlantic so that a clash with Germany would be inevitable sooner or later. . . ."[99] Churchill's hopes were bolstered by Roosevelt's interest in sea power. A Mahanian and a former assistant secretary of the navy in the Woodrow Wilson administration, the president maintained a particular and detailed interest in naval questions that he did not exhibit where army or air force matters were concerned. Sensing this, the prime minister shrewdly played to it from the moment he came into office. The fate of the French fleet and the future of the Royal Navy were vital weapons in Churchill's ultimately successful effort to extract an American commitment to Britain's survival.

Once the presidential election was past and lend-lease had averted bankruptcy, at least until after the war, Churchill pressed the next stage of his campaign. Roosevelt sent Hopkins to Britain in January 1941 to assess the situation and Churchill personally. Hopkins brought a verbal commitment from Roosevelt to Britain's victory. As encouraging as this was, the prime minister now looked at the impending Anglo-American staff conversations as the occasion of the next important American step toward belligerency. The British had hoped for staff talks the previous autumn, rather unrealistically in view of the presidential election. Now that negotiations were firmly scheduled, the prime minister took great care over their management. The absolutely crucial issue was American participation in the war against Germany and everything else was to be subordinated to this, even if it meant undercutting his own policy in other areas. The British delegation had been cautioned to show "deference" to American views on the Pacific, and when the Admiralty showed a disposition to argue its own views on Pacific strategy, Churchill quashed it firmly. The Americans should be told, he minuted, that the British "loyally" accepted their views on the Pacific: "The first thing is to get the U.S. into the war. We can settle how to fight it afterwards."[100]

In pursuit of this goal, the prime minister went so far as to welcome a proposal, made at the end of April, to move the American Pacific Fleet to the Atlantic, even though he had repeatedly made plain that he counted heavily on American sea power to deter Japan. In fact, compared to the war against Germany, Japan was a secondary concern to the prime minister, who would have welcomed a Japanese attack that brought America into the war. In October 1940 he told Eden that Britain would declare war on Japan even if Japan attacked only U.S. possessions. The American suggestion represented a deeper commitment to the Atlantic war and therefore a step closer to belligerency. He was enraged that

Rear Admiral H. V. Dankwerts, the Admiralty representative in Washington, had been cool to the proposal. But Dankwerts was merely reflecting an official policy that saw the United States as the shield that Britain could no longer provide for its Far Eastern interests.

Churchill took endless pains over every matter connected with the United States. All statistical material on the British war effort was centralized in Lindemann's office so that no conflicting estimates reached Washington. In the same spirit, the service departments were reminded that everyone in contact with the Americans should reflect "a clear and consistent picture of our requirements." Halifax was warned not to let the multiplication of British missions in the United States interfere with the prime minister's direct communication with Roosevelt: "Do not discourage the President from posing his questions direct to me or allow any of the Naval Staff to do so." Anyone who in any way discouraged American forward movement immediately drew the prime minister's wrath. "Who has been responsible for starting this idea among the Americans that we should like their destroyer forces to operate on their own side of the Atlantic rather than upon ours," an action-this-day minute demanded of the Foreign Office and the Admiralty. "Whoever has put this about has done great disservice, and should be immediately removed from all American contacts."[101]

Because Roosevelt's policy was to keep Britain in the war, the pressure of events added its persuasion to Churchill's and brought a deepening of American involvement. March saw the passage of lend-lease and the completion of "ABC-1," the basic Anglo-American strategic document of the war, which made the defeat of Germany the first priority. Staff contacts thereafter became intense and continuous, although the British were not yet ready to reveal Ultra to the Americans. Roosevelt extended the eastern sea frontier of the United States halfway across the Atlantic on 18 April and declared a state of "unlimited national emergency" on 27 May. These American moves, comforting as they were, were far from the active belligerency that Britain needed. The extension of the U.S. security zone and unlimited national emergency did nothing, in fact, to relieve the strain of the deadly struggle with the U-boats. In April, when 654,000 tons of shipping were lost to German submarines and aircraft, Churchill stopped further publication of figures on losses. By the eve of Barbarossa, Churchill's American strategy had been successful only in getting material aid, accompanied by friendly but essentially toothless gestures. The United States was still committed only to helping Britain fight Hitler.

The price of American assistance, however, mounted steadily. Lend-lease masked bankruptcy and the certainty of enormous postwar problems. Britain was tied to American policy in the Pacific without the compensation of any U.S. commitment to shield British interests. In fact, the Americans were ostentatiously disinterested in Singapore. In the war against Germany, Churchill's desire to involve the Americans led him to seek Roosevelt's approval of every major British initiative. Each step in the Balkans was accompanied by a message to the president. When Vichy seemed about to move the damaged *Dunkerque* from Oran to Toulon, Churchill appealed to Roosevelt to stop the transfer by pressuring the French, at the same time warning the Admiralty that "no attack should be made upon the *Dunkerque* unless or until an answer is received from President Roosevelt which expresses no objection."[102] Such flattery and solicitation of the president's views eventually produced a response that, although described by Churchill as "a moving exchange," was both unexpected and unwelcome. "Even if you have to withdraw farther in the Eastern Mediterranean, you will not allow any great *debacle* or surrender," Roosevelt wrote on 1 May, adding that "in the last analysis the naval control of the Indian Ocean and the Atlantic Ocean will in time win the war."[103]

Churchill vigorously rebutted this assumption while simultaneously, hammered by disaster and facing criticism in the press and the House, making an open request for full American belligerency, as hopeless a request as Reynaud's frantic appeal the year before. The exchange highlighted a fundamental problem in Churchill's approach to the United States. It was based on the unspoken assumption that British strategy was fundamentally correct and would become alliance strategy. The pride engendered by Britain's year "alone," fostered by Churchill as a prop to British endurance, when added to the insular sense of superiority with which the British viewed the outside world, gave rise to the belief that the British were, and would in some sense always remain, the senior partner. In fact, the reality was very different. Many Americans, like the president, had mixed feelings about the British. Their appeals for aid gave the impression, misleading but long-lived, that somehow the United States had "saved" Britain in 1940, hardly the basis for the relationship the British anticipated. Finally, deep suspicions of British imperial power and purpose led many Americans to view the war in the Middle East not as an inescapable necessity but rather as a strategic aberration caused by concern for the future of British power.

Thus British strategy seemed questionable, while British

military performance seemed as poor as Cadogan privately labeled it. If and when they entered the war, the Americans meant to fight it rather differently. Churchill's concentration on the Atlantic as the key to American belligerency obscured for him the fact that it would not be the U.S. Navy, which thought largely in terms of a contest with Japan, that would shape American strategy against Germany but instead the U.S. Army. Neither Mahan nor the strategy of scarcity the British had had to adopt in 1940 had any appeal to Army Chief of Staff General George C. Marshall and his planners. Only a major campaign to crush the German army would justify the 200 divisions of which they dreamed. Furthermore, American military thought, shaped by the Civil War, specifically by Generals Ulysses S. Grant and William T. Sherman, emphasized the death grapple with the enemy's army, a situation that could only occur in Europe. Roosevelt's 1 May message was the first indication, faint but unmistakable, that American belligerence would mean a fundamental challenge to the strategy which events had fastened to Churchill. But American belligerency would have been welcome at any price in May 1941.

Relief from almost intolerable strain came, however, not from Roosevelt but from Hitler. As the Ultra indications of German redeployment to the east mounted, a dispute broke out in London over what they meant. Dill and the army general staff stubbornly clung to the belief that Germany's main aim for 1941 remained the defeat of Britain and that invasion therefore remained a real danger. Only on 12 June did the Joint Intelligence Committee, on which the service intelligence directors sat under a Foreign Office chairman, accept the imminence of a German attack on Russia. Knowledge of how precarious Britain's situation was and how welcome a Russo-German war would be doubtless made the London intelligence community reluctant to believe a development so favorable to Britain was actually taking shape. The prime minister, however, had made up his mind months earlier that Russia and not Britain was Hitler's prime target. Although Churchill had occasionally spoken during the summer and autumn of 1940 of a German attack on Russia, certainty only came to him in March 1941.

The prime minister had insisted the previous summer on receiving the more significant intercepts directly from Bletchley Park. Toward the end of March, as German pressure on Yugoslavia and preparations for an attack on Greece peaked, *Luftwaffe* Enigma traffic revealed the transfer from the Balkans to Cracow of three panzer divisions, an SS division, and the headquarters of Panzer Group Kleist which had controlled the German armored thrust to the Channel in May 1940. Following the Belgrade coup this transfer was halted, and Enigma traffic revealed the astonishingly rapid buildup against Yugoslavia. But it was the initial transfer of armor that clarified matters for Churchill. He wrote in his memoirs: "To me it illuminated the whole Eastern scene like a lightning flash. . . . The sudden movement to Cracow of so much armour needed in the Balkan sphere could only mean Hitler's intention to invade Russia in May. . . . The fact that the Belgrade revolution had required their return to Rumania involved perhaps a delay from May to June."[104] Churchill immediately sent a warning to Joseph Stalin. The prime minister was furious when the British ambassador in Moscow delayed handing the message over because he believed the Russians would dismiss it as a "provocation." The delay, however, was meaningless; Stalin ignored dozens of reports streaming in from all quarters, including those of his own agents.

Whatever Stalin might make of Churchill's warning, the prime minister was certain that the Wehrmacht was going east. Furthermore, his sense of history told him that this time it would not be a quick campaign. The Foreign Office, the service intelligence departments, and the Ministry of Economic Warfare all agreed that Russia would be quickly defeated. The prime minister disagreed. He also saw a new alliance, the grand alliance he needed, taking shape. On 15 June, the day after the Joint Intelligence Committee estimated that the German army would be in Moscow in a month and back on the Channel ready for invasion six weeks after that, Churchill advised Roosevelt that "every source . . . some most trustworthy" pointed to a German attack on Russia. "Should this new war break out, we shall, of course, give all encouragement and support to the Russians, following the principle that Hitler is the foe we have to beat."[105] Through the American ambassador, John G. Winant, Roosevelt sent verbal approval.

Churchill went down to Chequers on Friday, 20 June, in a state of high nervous anticipation. A planned broadcast was postponed from Saturday to Sunday "when I thought all would be clear." At dinner on Saturday night Churchill told his guests that a German attack on Russia was certain.* At four o'clock the next morning his private secretary, John R. Colville, was awakened by a telephone call from London. Barbarossa had begun. Mindful of Churchill's orders that once he had retired for the night he was

---

*It was after this dinner, while walking on the croquet lawn, that Churchill, reminded of his anti-Communist past, remarked: "If Hitler invaded Hell I would make at least a favourable reference to the Devil in the House of Commons."[106]

only to be disturbed for an invasion of England, Colville brought the news to the prime minister with his breakfast tray at eight o'clock. Having thought about his reaction for weeks, Churchill's only response was that the BBC should be ready to carry a broadcast at 9:00 P.M. It was one of his most powerful performances: "We have but one aim and one single irrevocable purpose. We are resolved to destroy Hitler and every vestige of the Nazi regime. From this nothing will turn us—nothing. . . . Any man or state who fights on against Nazidom will have our aid."[107] Britain was no longer alone, but the prime minister would never again dominate the war against Hitler.

Churchill later identified Pearl Harbor as the moment when he was certain of victory, but it was Barbarossa that sealed Hitler's fate and altered Britain's position as well. For one year Churchill had stood as the embodiment of Britain's will to survive as an independent nation, and the prime minister's prestige, plus the moral capital accumulated during that period, would be one of Britain's chief assets during the remainder of the conflict. His greatest contributions had been the providing of a voice and focus for the will to fight on, the rationalization and energizing of the war machine, and the vision to see that an offensive strategy alone would attract the support that Britain had to have to win. His determination never flagged in spite of the obvious fact that the British army's leadership, equipment, training, and technique were below what was needed to beat the Germans. But due largely to Churchill's determination, Britain's armies continued to fight until circumstances produced the alliance that Churchill had always known had to come into being before Hitler could be destroyed. That alliance was nearly complete by June 1941. Now a new challenge confronted the prime minister. Maintaining Britain's world position, while sustaining its ties with two states more powerful than itself and hostile to the British empire, was a task that would prove more difficult than defeating Hitler.

Notes

1. *GS*, 667.
2. M. I. Finley in his introduction to the Penguin Books edition of *Thucydides: The Peloponnesian War.*
3. *FH*, 17.
4. Ibid., 8.
5. Maurice Cowling, *Religion and Public Doctrine in Modern England*

(New York, 1980), 285. Cowling's entire essay on Churchill (283–312) is an interesting interpretation.

6. Churchill to Sir Edward Grey, 20 December 1911, *CV2*, pt. 3:1474.

7. Clare Boothe Luce, *European Spring* (London, 1941), 158, quoted in Brian Gardner, *Churchill in Power: As Seen by His Contemporaries* (Boston, 1970), 32.

8. *FH*, 15.

9. The civil servant was Sir Edward (later Lord) Bridges, secretary to the war cabinet. This story is found in Sir John R. Colville, *The Churchillians* (London, 1981), 130–31.

10. *GA*, 150.

11. Churchill to Anthony Eden, 8 September 1940, *FH*, 467.

12. The first quotation is from *GS*, 475; the second from *FH*, 43.

13. *FH*, 78.

14. Ibid., 82.

15. Ibid., 54–55.

16. Ibid., 49.

17. Ibid., 154. A footnote indicates Churchill drew here from Hastings Ismay's memory of the meeting.

18. King George VI to Queen Mary, 27 June 1940, in John Wheeler-Bennett, *King George VI* (London, 1958), 460.

19. E. L. Woodward, *British Foreign Policy in the Second World War*, 5 vols. (London, 1970–76), 1:204fn.

20. Churchill printed the chiefs' of staff summary answer, which includes the terms of reference he set, *FH*, 87–89. "British Strategy in a Certain Eventuality" is partially reproduced and the remainder paraphrased in J. R. M. Butler, *Grand Strategy*, vol. 2, *September 1939–June 1941* (London, 1957), 209–15. The original is in PRO, CAB 66/7, WM (40)/68, 25 May 1940, the date when the final draft was approved by the war cabinet.

21. *FH*, 281.

22. Colville, quoting from contemporary diary notes in his introduction to Warren Tute, *The Deadly Stroke* (New York, 1973), 17.

23. Quoted in Michael Howard, *The Continental Commitment* (London, 1972), 119.

24. Quoted in Butler, *Grand Strategy*, 2: 212–13.

25. Churchill to Beaverbrook, 8 July 1940, *FH*, 643.

26. "The Munitions Situation: Memorandum by the Prime Minister," 3 September 1940, ibid., 458.

27. Prime minister to secretary of state for air, 30 December 1940, ibid., 711.

28. Michael R. D. Foot, *SOE in France: An Account of the Work of the British Special Operations Executive in France 1940–1944* (London, 1966), 129.

29. The intelligence background to the Coventry raid is covered by N. E. Evans, "Air Intelligence and the Coventry Raid," *Journal of the Royal United Service Institute* (September 1976): 64–74; and F. H. Hinsley

et al., *British Intelligence in the Second World War* (London, 1979), 1:528–48. See also Ronald Lewin, *Ultra Goes to War* (New York, 1978), 99–103; and Colville, *The Churchillians*, 62–63.

30. Churchill to Ismay, 5 August 1940, *FH*, 654 (italics in original).

31. Churchill to Ismay, 4 June 1940, and Churchill to Jan Smuts, 27 June 1940, ibid., 243, 228 (italics in original).

32. Churchill to Joseph Stalin, 25 June 1940, ibid., 135.

33. Churchill to Franklin D. Roosevelt, 14 May 1940, in Francis Loewenheim and Harold D. Langley, *Roosevelt and Churchill: Their Secret Wartime Correspondence* (New York, 1975), 94–95.

34. *FH*, 409.

35. Churchill speech, 4 June 1940, ibid., 118.

36. Churchill to Mackenzie King, 5 June 1940, ibid., 145.

37. Churchill to Lord Lothian, 9 June 1940, ibid., 400.

38. The exchange is printed in ibid., 413–14.

39. *GS*, 667.

40. Churchill to secretary of state for air, 21 August 1940, *FH*, 327.

41. F. W. Winterbotham, *The Ultra Secret* (London, 1974), 59–60.

42. Churchill to Roosevelt, 8 December 1940, in Loewenheim and Langley, *Roosevelt and Churchill*, 122–25, contains the text; the words quoted are on 125.

43. Howard, *Continental Commitment*, 141.

44. Churchill to Lord Lloyd, secretary of state for the colonies, 28 June 1940, *FH*, 173.

45. Churchill to first lord of the Admiralty, 17 June 1940, ibid., 639.

46. S. W. Roskill, *Churchill and the Admirals* (London, 1977), 150.

47. John Connell, *Wavell: Soldier and Scholar* (London, 1964), 240. The text of Wavell's worst-possible-case paper is on 229–31.

48. Diary entry, 17 June 1940, in Trefor Evans, ed., *The Killearn Diaries 1934–1946* (London, 1972), 121.

49. The extent of Churchill's interrogation of Wavell can be judged from two of his minutes: prime minister to General Ismay, for General Wavell, 10, 12 August 1940, *FH*, 425–27; the "General Directive" is in ibid., 428–32.

50. Quoted in Connell, *Wavell*, 265.

51. Wavell's protest of 30 November 1940 and Churchill's response of 2 December 1940 are printed in Bernard Wasserstein, *Britain and the Jews of Europe 1939–1945* (London, 1979), 71–72.

52. *FH*, 543, 609.

53. Prime minister to Wavell, 26 November 1940, ibid., 346–47.

54. Quoted in John Darwin, *Britain, Egypt and the Middle East: Imperial Policy in the Aftermath of War 1918–1922* (London, 1981), 169.

55. Quoted in ibid., 255.

56. Churchill to Lord Linlithgow, 16 July 1940, in John Glendevon, *The Viceroy at Bay: Lord Linlithgow in India* (London, 1971), 170–71. Glendevon, Linlithgow's son, drew from his father's papers for this book.

57. The full text of the August offer is in N. Mansergh and E. W. R. Lumby, eds., *India: The Transfer of Power 1942–1947*, vol. 1, *The Cripps Mission* (London, 1970), 887–89.

58. Churchill memorandum, n.d. [February 1912], *CV2*, pt. 3:1512.

59. Churchill to Chamberlain, 25 March 1939, quoted in Patrick Cosgrave, *Churchill at War: Alone 1939–1940* (London, 1974), 62.

60. Churchill to Roosevelt, 15 May 1940, in Loewenheim and Langley, *Roosevelt and Churchill*, 95.

61. Churchill to Clementine Churchill, 8 January 1936, *OB*, 5:696.

62. *CCS*, 6:6295.

63. *GA*, 3.

64. Churchill to Roosevelt, 8 December 1940, *FH*, 559–60.

65. "Army Scales: Directive by the Minister of Defence," 6 March 1941, *GA*, 791.

66. "Report by the Chiefs of Staff on Air Bombardment Policy, January 7, 1941," in Charles Webster and Noble Frankland, *The Strategic Air Offensive Against Germany* (London, 1961), 4:190.

67. Lord Trenchard's paper on "The Present War Situation Mainly in so far as It Relates to Air," 19 May 1941, is reprinted in ibid., 194–97; the quoted sentences are on 194–95 (italics in original).

68. Churchill to Archibald Wavell, 10 January 1941, *GA*, 19.

69. *GA*, 95.

70. Churchill to Eden, 28 March 1941, ibid., 169.

71. Churchill speech, 25 June 1941, *CCS*, 6:6444.

72. Churchill to Eden, 20 February 1941, *GA*, 70.

73. Eden to Churchill, 28 February 1941, ibid., 97.

74. Churchill to Eden, 1 March 1941, ibid., 98.

75. Churchill to Eden, 6 March 1941, ibid., 102.

76. Eden to Churchill, 7 March 1941, ibid., 106.

77. *GA*, 202.

78. Ibid., 101.

79. *FH*, 493 (italics in original).

80. Churchill to Eden, 3 April 1941, *GA*, 205–06.

81. Churchill to Eden, 14 March 1941, ibid., 108.

82. Chiefs of staff to Wavell, 18 April 1941, ibid., 227.

83. *GA*, 246.

84. Churchill to chiefs of staff, 20 April 1941, ibid., 246–47 (italics in original).

85. *GA*, 232.

86. Churchill to secretary of state for the colonies, 1 March 1941, ibid., 742.

87. John Kennedy, *The Business of War*, ed. Bernard Fergusson (New York, 1958), 104–07.

88. Directive by prime minister and minister of defense, 28 April 1941, Kennedy, *Business of War*, 108–10.

89. Churchill to Wavell, 21 May 1941, *GA*, 324.

90. David Dilks, ed., *The Diaries of Sir Alexander Cadogan 1938–1945* (London, 1971), 380.

91. Churchill to Wavell, 28 May and 3 June 1941, *GA,* 326–27.

92. Wavell to Sir John Dill, 28 May 1941, ibid., 339.

93. *GA,* 343.

94. Churchill to chiefs of staff, 6 May 1941, ibid., 258.

95. Randolph Churchill to prime minister, 7 June 1941, ibid., 348.

96. *GA,* 345.

97. Kennedy, *Business of War,* 133.

98. Quoted in Butler, *Grand Strategy,* 548.

99. Colonel E. I. C. Jacob, "Diary of the Arcadia Conference," quoted by courtesy of Lieutenant General Sir Ian Jacob.

100. Churchill minute, 17 February 1941, quoted in Roskill, *Churchill and the Admirals,* 126.

101. These quotations are from Churchill minutes, 10 March, 28 April, and 28 June 1941, *GA,* 744–45, 760, 776.

102. Churchill to first lord, 3 April 1941, ibid., 131.

103. Roosevelt to Churchill, 1 May 1941, in Loewenheim and Langley, *Churchill and Roosevelt,* 138–39.

104. *GA,* 357.

105. Churchill to Roosevelt, 15 June 1941, ibid., 369.

106. Colville diary, 21–22 June 1941, quoted in ibid., 370.

107. Churchill speech, 22 June 1941, ibid., 372.

Let me, however, make this clear, in case there should be any mistake about it in any quarter. We mean to hold our own. I have not become the King's First Minister in order to preside over the liquidation of the British Empire.

—WINSTON CHURCHILL
10 November 1942

Chapter Three

We Mean To Hold Our Own

The German invasion of Russia changed not only the course of the Second World War but Churchill's position as well. For one year he had dominated the war against Germany. Although he had worked for steadily deeper American involvement and hoped for a Russo-German rift, he had not yet known the constraint imposed by powerful allies. The leaders of the dominions were not equals, nor were the heads of the various governments in exile that dwelt under British protection in London and Cairo. Stalin, however, was a different proposition. The Australian government could be bluntly reminded that Britain bore the weight of the war and would therefore make the crucial strategic decisions. The Russians, absorbing the impact of 170 German and satellite divisions, could not be dealt with in quite the same way. Moreover, the United States, although still not in the war, was also expressing views on strategy, as unwelcome to Churchill as the Russian demand for an immediate second front. Yet the Americans too had to be taken seriously. June 1941 marked the opening of a struggle by Churchill to maintain a strategy designed not only to defeat Germany but also to keep intact the fundamental elements of British power. For nearly two years Churchill enjoyed a remarkable degree of success; thereafter, he was driven inexorably into retreat.

The constraints imposed by stronger allies were not the sole reason Churchill's position began to alter. The palpable danger of defeat and national extinction had undeniably produced both unity and a curious exhilaration during the intense summer days of 1940. By mid-1941, however, the heady excitement of "Spitfire summer" had been replaced by the consciousness that a long, grinding slog lay ahead, while the prospect of imminent defeat had faded. Domestic politics again reared its head. Although Churchill's position was safe as long as the Labour leadership stood firm, he could not ignore the home front as much as he wished to at the time, and as he did in his memoirs. Finally, the advent of powerful allies in June and December may have made victory over Hitler certain, but that event also complicated enormously the maintenance of Britain's imperial authority, a definite war aim of both the prime minister and the party he led. Indeed the cumulative impact of wartime strain and successive defeats at German and Japanese hands made the year following the German attack on Russia one of prolonged imperial crisis, culminating in a widespread revolt in India. The empire weathered that crisis but at a cost which Churchill never completely understood. If the events of the twelve months after the opening of Barbarossa made a British victory certain, they made equally inevitable an imperial defeat.

For the moment, however, the sense of relief in Britain as the Wehrmacht plunged into Russia was enormous, although tinged with pessimism about Russia's chances of survival. The prime minister immediately grasped both the strategic and psychological advantages to Britain of prolonged Soviet resistance. "A premature peace by Russia would be a terrible disappointment to great masses of people in our country," he minuted on 10 July, adding: "As long as they go on it does not matter much where the front line lies."[1] To assist the Russians to "go on" as long as possible, Churchill offered them as much as he could, in many cases more than his advisers deemed wise. In late June he overruled "C"—Sir Stewart Menzies, head of the Secret Intelligence Service—and ordered that the product of Britain's most valuable and sensitive of intelligence sources, Ultra, be made available to the Russians, "provided no risks are run."[2] Suitably disguised as information from British agents, the relevant portions of Bletchley Park's daily haul were passed to the Russians via the British Military Mission in Moscow.*

The prime minister also urged the Admiralty to explore operations in the Arctic, as much for the morale value he believed it would have for the Russians as for any damage it would do the Germans. The diversion of war material from British factories, as well as from American production earmarked for Britain, provided

---

*There is no way to know either the impact of this intelligence on Russian planning or whether the Russians deduced its real source. At any rate the story that the British used the Swiss-based Russian espionage apparatus known as the "Lucy ring" to pass Ultra intelligence to the Russians in a suitably disguised form seems, on present evidence, rather fanciful.

a more substantial aid proffered at great cost with results impossible to assess. But the sort of help the Russians really wanted was made plain in Stalin's first message to Churchill: "A front against Hitler in the West."[3] Perhaps anticipating what was to become the staple of strategic exchanges between Russia and its Western allies, Churchill, in his initial message to Stalin, placed great stress upon the one direct assault the British were capable of mounting against Germany: "On Saturday night over two hundred heavy bombers attacked German towns, some carrying three tons apiece, and last night nearly two hundred and fifty heavy bombers were operating. This will go on."[4] What the Russians made of this is uncertain, but it was perhaps fortunate for Bomber Command that it had suddenly acquired a role in alliance politics, because its actual performance had begun to raise serious questions about its contribution to British strategy.

Even as Churchill held out to Stalin the promise of a steadily mounting bomber offensive inflicting such damage on Germany that it would force a defensive redeployment of German air power, D. M. Butt of Lord Cherwell's Cabinet Office Statistical Section, was conducting an examination of "about 650 photographs taken during night bombing operations between 2 June and 25 July." The outgrowth of Cherwell's growing doubts about Bomber Command's actual achievements, Butt's conclusions were devastating: "Of those aircraft recorded as attacking their target, only one in three got within five miles . . . of the total sorties only one in five get within five miles of the target, i.e., within the 75 square miles surrounding the target."[5] Even with a remarkably generous definition of "target"—one that foreshadowed the "city-busting" strategies—Bomber Command could do little damage to the enemy in return for the enormous demands it was making on Britain's war production and skilled manpower. Neither the army nor the Admiralty was satisfied with the degree of support they were receiving from the Royal Air Force. Uncertainties about the wisdom of the bombing offensive were becoming widespread in Whitehall, yet Bomber Command weathered the crisis of confidence that began with the Butt report and did so primarily because of the prime minister's continuing support.

Churchill had always had doubts about the strategic bombing thesis, going back to its birth in the waning days of World War I. He had embraced the bomber offensive in 1940 only because it offered the sole possibility of striking at the German homeland. Now Britain was no longer alone. Russia was in the war, with America drawing steadily closer. Bomber Command clearly had not lived up to the claims made by Lord Trenchard and his disciples, but it remained a way to damage Germany. Direct assault on the enemy, Churchill knew, had its value both as a stimulant to domestic morale and a makeweight in alliance politics. Therefore when Chief of Air Staff Sir Charles Portal sent the prime minister a paper on 7 October that, perhaps with the dictum in mind that a good offense is the best defense, restated the pure Trenchardian gospel and argued that 4,000 heavy bombers would produce "decisive" results against German morale within six months, Churchill served notice that he had reverted to his original doubts about strategic bombing and that he would nonetheless continue to support Bomber Command: "We all hope that the air offensive against Germany will realize the expectations of the Air Staff. . . . I deprecate however placing unbounded confidence in this means of attack . . . he is an unwise man who thinks there is any *certain* method of winning this war, or indeed any other war between equals in strength. The only plan is to persevere."[6] Thereafter Churchill sustained Bomber Command, for the damage it could do and the political and psychological dividends it would yield. In his memoirs though he would distance himself as much as possible from what by then had become one of the most controversial aspects of British wartime strategy.[7]

Blockade, bombing, and subversion were the three long-range strategies which the chiefs of staff had pointed to in May 1940 as answers to German domination of Europe. The first had been crippled by the extent of Hitler's conquests; the second by mid-1941 was revealed to be a seriously flawed weapon. The whole approach to subversion adopted by SOE also had come under critical scrutiny, and major changes impended there as well. SOE had been born of Churchill's impulse to "set Europe ablaze," but during the first year of its existence, the dominant strain in SOE thinking was the preparation of "secret armies" in occupied France that would act as "detonators," setting off a massive uprising when the moment came for British armies to reenter Europe. This inevitably postponed their utilization to the distant future, when Germany would have been weakened by the other pressures of bombing and the blockade. Not only did the secret army concept mean passivity in the present, but it also would make enormous demands on long-range aircraft to carry the necessary supplies to the growing underground armies.

Russian entry into the war may have suggested to some SOE policymakers that the largest but most distant of the secret armies, those in Poland and Czechoslovakia, would operate in an area of

Russian influence.[8] There can be no certainty about the last, but it is clear that in the two months following the German attack on Russia, a Whitehall debate on SOE's future direction culminated in the abandonment of the secret army concept, with no demur from Churchill. From being, at least in the imaginations of British planners, the primary mover in a European-wide network of powerful underground organizations, circumstances were now pushing SOE inexorably in the direction of what became its principal activity: supplying and advising resistance movements springing up as a result of the impact of defeat and occupation on European societies.* In any case this was more congenial to the prime minister's romantic activism. As early as July reports of resistance in Yugoslavia reached London. In September Churchill asked Hugh Dalton what contacts SOE had with Balkan guerrillas and suggested that favorable press coverage of their activities should be arranged.[9] It was the beginning of a long and convoluted story.

With the blockade weakened, bombing a disappointment, and subversion reduced from "the Fourth Arm" to an ancillary role, what remained of the strategy the British had shaped in the aftermath of the French collapse? Very little except the war in the Mediterranean. This, the only theater where British troops were actively engaged, had been the scene of an uninterrupted series of reverses from April until Wavell's relief in June, counterpointed solely by British success in crushing both the Iraqi rebellion and the Vichy garrison in Syria. American doubts about the wisdom of the intense British commitment in the area had been voiced for the first time during this run of disasters. Yet the pressures that had first committed the British to the Mediterranean struggle not only remained but also had intensified.

Oil, the importance of the Middle East to Britain's world power, and the simple fact that only in that theater could Britain engage the enemy on land were all factors present when the decision not to abandon the area had been taken in June 1940. Now, with Russia in the war and pressing for an impossible second front, it was even less likely that the British could or would slacken their commitment in the one theater where they were engaging at least a small part of the German army. Furthermore, if Russia should be overrun, as nearly everyone expected, the British position in the Middle East would be at risk from the north, which made the

---

*Without Britain's continued resistance and the German attack on Russia, there would have been little incentive for even the most Germanophobe in the occupied countries to risk active resistance. Britain—and Barbarossa—were the detonators of European resistance.

destruction of Rommel's threat from the west doubly important. Finally, the prime minister had made plain in April that the British position in the Middle East was to be defended at all costs, so great would be the ramifications, strategic and political, of its loss. General Sir Claude Auchinleck therefore had barely taken over from Wavell before he was being queried about his offensive plans. Through the month of July cables flashed between Cairo and Whitehall as Churchill sought to probe the new commander in chief's intentions, an exercise that culminated in Auchinleck's being invited to London late in the month.

Out of these meetings came a November date for "Crusader," an offensive both to relieve Tobruk and to destroy Rommel's German-Italian forces. The argument between Cairo and London, between Auchinleck and Churchill, was due in part to the commander in chief's cautious insistence on adequate time to prepare, an insistence based on an appreciation of how far behind the Wehrmacht in tactical skills his forces actually were. There was also a very real difference in perspective, however. Ultra provided a great deal of information about German supply traffic and logistic problems but none on German strategic intentions in the Middle East. Churchill assumed Rommel was still relatively weak and Germany preoccupied with Russia; Auchinleck was more concerned with the weaknesses of his own force and the vulnerability of his northern flank. If Russia collapsed, might he not face a German thrust through Anatolia more serious than anything Rommel could develop from Libya? This difference in outlook, inescapable under the circumstances, colored all of Auchinleck's strategic arguments with London during his year in Cairo.

The July exchanges also brought out another aspect of Churchill's attitude toward the forthcoming offensive. It had to be not only a victory but also one that bore, to the greatest degree possible, a British label, since victory in the desert was not only a matter of strategy but of alliance politics as well. Britain's manpower, stretched by the demands of industry, the world's largest navy, and the huge bomber force which the Royal Air Force was creating, simply could not support a large army as well. As a result, although many of the troops in the Middle East were British, the bulk of the divisional formations engaged in battle had been imperial and dominion forces—Indian, Australian, and New Zealand formations. India was not self-governing, and its forces in the Middle East were drawn from the prewar, long service professional army that had nurtured Auchinleck. The Pacific dominions, however, were independent Commonwealth partners, their armies made up of volunteers. There already had been dominion criticism of British handling of the campaign in Greece and the fighting on Crete. Shortly after Auchinleck took over he was confronted with a demand by the Australians that their 7th Division, which had been besieged in Tobruk since April, be relieved, a demand from which the Australian government refused to recede despite pressure from both the prime minister and the commander in chief. "I was sensitive to the hostile propaganda which asserted that it was British policy to fight with any other troops but our own and thus avoid the shedding of United Kingdom blood," Churchill wrote in 1950. He further added: "British casualties in the Middle East, including Greece and Crete, had in fact been greater than those of all our other forces put together, but the nomenclature that was customary gave a false impression of the facts. . . . This was not a trifle. The fact that 'British' troops were rarely mentioned in any reports of the fighting provoked unfavorable comment not only in the United States but in Australia."[10]

When Auchinleck, convinced that his northern flank was the most sensitive, put the newly arrived 50th British Division into Cyprus, far from the scene of actual fighting, the prime minister was particularly distressed. In his memoirs he referred to Auchinleck's "disproportionate concern" for the northern flank, an assessment perhaps easier to make in London than in Cairo, where the weaknesses of Britain's sprawling Middle East imperium were vividly realized. (Indeed, constant admonitions to stand ready to send aid to the Turks, if they could be enticed into the war, must have reinforced Auchinleck's concern with his northern flank.)* "Decisive action" in the western desert was what Churchill wanted, for decisive action that produced a British victory would not only yield strategic advantages but also still questions at home, satisfy the dominions, and perhaps more importantly offer a possibility of enticing America to commit itself across the Atlantic.

When exactly Churchill first began to think of French North Africa as the scene of a joint Anglo-American effort is not certain. Perhaps he sensed Roosevelt's concern about this area during the exchanges over naval aid in the summer of 1940. Certainly by the autumn of 1941 he was positive about American interest, telling

*British concern with Turkey, a concern to which at various times Churchill gave high priority, should be viewed in light of pre-1939 British thinking on the defense of the Middle East, which saw Turkey as a barrier to Germany's southeastern drive. With vivid memories of Turkish fighting qualities in the First World War, the British seem to have overestimated the utility of the obsolete Turkish forces; they certainly overestimated their own persuasiveness with the Turks.

the chiefs of staff three weeks before Crusader that "our friends in the United States are much attracted by the idea of American intervention in Morocco.[11] Frank Knox, Roosevelt's secretary of the navy, had talked to Halifax about 150,000 American troops landing there. The possibility that a decisive success in Crusader might unleash a sequence of events that would open the Mediterranean and draw America more actively into the conflict made Churchill all the more eager for the operation. He was anxious because his careful courtship of the United States and its leader, while it yielded important dividends, had so far been barren of any U.S. commitment to intervene actively. American participation would be welcome not only in Europe but also, it was assumed, would ease the most pressing of British strategic anxieties in the Far East, where Britain's vulnerability to Japan could not be limited by any substantial redisposition of its own resources.

The strategy for the defense of Britain's eastern interests and possessions against Japan had rested, from its inception in 1919–21, upon the shakiest of foundations: the assumption that the Royal Navy would be free to shift its weight eastward when the need arose. German rearmament and Italian hostility had eroded that assumption well before the war began; the fall of France finally toppled it. The substitute devised in the hectic summer of 1940—the use of air power to keep the Japanese at bay—was never implemented. The demands of the war in the Mediterranean and the diversion of equipment to Russia simply made it impossible to meet the target of 336 modern first-line aircraft set for the Far East.* The prime minister stood firmly behind the order of priorities that starved Malaya of aircraft. He also went a step further and did his best to keep the number of troops there to a minimum. It was a calculated risk based on a clear-sighted realization that Britain had to concentrate its limited resources on Germany. This policy rested as well on two assumptions and one hope. The first was that the Japanese would prudently calculate their chances, that is, would not take the gamble they in fact took. Second, that, if they nonetheless did attack, they would be considerably less formidable than any Western opponent. Finally, Churchill hoped that the United States would deter a Japanese attack, or absorb the worst of it if one came. These ideas, assumptions, and

---

*By the early autumn of 1941 the Air Ministry's estimate of the cost of what already had been sent or promised to Russia was twenty squadrons of medium and heavy bombers and fifteen each of light bombers and fighters. The light bomber and fighter squadrons had been earmarked for India and the Far East. When Japan struck there were 188 British aircraft in Malaya. None of them were modern.

hopes were by no means original to the prime minister. They were a stock accumulated by a generation of British policymakers since 1919, a stock on whose basis alone the British could pretend that they had a coherent defense policy for the Far East. Churchill, however, had to face the consequences as these beliefs collided with reality.

Nowhere were the potential problems more embarrassing or explosive than in Britain's relations with Australia, already bruised by Mediterranean events. Australia—and New Zealand—had committed the bulk of their armed forces to the struggle in Europe, on the assumption that they had a firm British promise to defend them against Japan. In fact, that commitment, part of the Singapore-based strategy, had been qualified increasingly since 1938. Here again the prime minister inherited a policy of not being completely frank with the Pacific dominions, which for their part never pushed embarrassing questions too hard. Before the war Churchill had urged a policy of plain speaking with the Australians, writing in March 1939:

> If Japan joins the hostile combination, which is by no means certain . . . we must bear the losses and punishment, awaiting the final result of the struggle. . . . I am aware of the promise we made to send a strong fleet to the Pacific, but this would be folly in the opening stages of the war, and I am sure that if the strategic argument is laid before the Australian Commonwealth, they will play the game by us as they have always done.[12]

However, once in office, he was no more open with the Pacific dominions than his predecessors had been, and for the same reason. To admit that Britain could do almost nothing by itself against Japan would be to forfeit dominion aid in Europe and to fatally weaken Commonwealth ties.

In another respect as well the prime minister continued pre-war Far Eastern policy. From the mid-1930s, when the British began actively to solicit American aid in the Far East, they had been much more open about their own weakness there with Washington than they had ever been with the Pacific dominions. When in February 1941 intelligence indications seemed to point to an imminent Japanese move, the prime minister sent a message to Roosevelt, stating that the British could not cope with a Japanese attack.[13] If, however, the British were not to face military defeat and imperial bankruptcy at the hands of Japan, it was essential to persuade the United States to play the deterrent role for which the

British had long cast it in the Pacific. Moreover, the Americans had to be persuaded, if possible, to commit themselves to treat a Japanese attack on Britain as an assault on themselves. The Japanese move into southern Indochina in late July, leading to the freezing of their assets and an oil embargo by the United States— actions the British hastened, perforce, to emulate—made the Far East a matter of urgency. Against this background the "Atlantic Conference," the first encounter between the president and the prime minister, took place aboard warships anchored in Argentia Bay, Newfoundland.

A personal meeting between the two men was inevitable and had been discussed since the beginning of the year. The impending crisis with Japan made the occasion timely, but the variety of pressures acting upon Churchill is aptly illustrated by the fact that, before his departure for Scapa Flow and the battleship that would carry him west, his days were filled with meetings on the progress of the plans for an autumn offensive against Rommel. Auchinleck, home for consultations, was cross-examined about the three-month delay on which he had insisted. He carried his point but also resolved to avoid future journeys home to explain his policy. The defense of the northern flank of the Middle East was also discussed, as, with German armor rolling forward apparently irresistibly toward the Black Sea and the Caucasus, it had to be. At Chequers on 2 August, Churchill told Auchinleck that aid to Turkey came second in priority only to defeating Rommel, and that he should be prepared to send 100 3.7-inch antiaircraft guns to the Turks if necessary. (At that moment Malaya had less than half its approved scale of AA guns.) The next day the prime minister began his journey west.

Perhaps the most important fact about the Atlantic meeting was simply that it took place. The president and prime minister had an opportunity to assess one another, as did members of their respective parties. In the case of General George C. Marshall and Sir John Dill, this would prove to be of great importance. This feeling-out process brought to the surface a number of areas where the partners to the incipient alliance disagreed. These disagreements on the proper method of defeating Germany, on planning strategy in the Far East, and on shaping the postwar world, while tentative at Argentia, would run thematically through the wartime relationship, as they continue to run through the writing of its history. The Anglo-American wartime partnership between two sovereign nations of uneven strength and divergent interests always contained an element, however muted it might at times be, of competition and wariness.

American doubts about the primacy the British accorded the Middle East came as no surprise to Churchill. Roosevelt's confidant, Harry Hopkins, had displayed great interest in the issue when he came to London in January, and, in a message to the prime minister at the time of the British withdrawal from Greece, the president had indicated that he did not regard retention of the Middle East as crucial to ultimate victory, drawing a sharp response from Churchill. The question was raised again in London in July by an American delegation that once more included Hopkins.

American reservations about the Middle East were almost as complex as the roots of British involvement there. Historically suspicious of European imperialisms, especially the British variety, Americans saw in the eastern Mediterranean and the Middle East a British fief whose holders had every intention of retaining, perhaps even of enlarging, their sphere of control. Up to a point this was perfectly true since the maintenance of an imperial structure, of which the Middle East was a vital part, did represent a British objective. The American view, however, failed to realize the pull of circumstances that had made the area the focus of Britain's war effort, or the degree to which a collapse there would have affected both Britain's will and its ability to fight. Above all, perhaps, it completely ignored the fact that, having committed itself to fight there, the successful prosecution of the war in the Middle East had become politically essential to the Churchill coalition. It was easier to overlook this since U.S. Army planners had a clear vision of how Germany was to be beaten, and it did not include the Middle East.

As Marshall conferred at Argentia a War Department planner, Major Albert Wedemeyer, a graduate of the German *Kriegsakademie*, was drawing up a paper that came to be known as the Victory Program, the American specifications for the total defeat of Germany. Wedemeyer projected a 200-division army of over 8 million men, a force that could only be employed in a massive confrontation with the German army, to grip it in battle, wear it down, and destroy it. To this American approach, an amalgam of the strategic legacy of Ulysses S. Grant and German doctrine, the British strategy, born of limited resources and options, seemed not merely politically inspired but militarily irrelevant. Since no immediate operations by U.S. troops were in contemplation in August 1941, the differences over the place of the Middle East in what was becoming alliance strategy were only touched upon rather than confronted. The British thought they had made the Americans aware of the significance of the area. In fact, beneath surface harmony, the Americans retained their fundamental views unaltered.*

The same was true in the case of Japan. A crisis obviously loomed in the Pacific. Roosevelt told Churchill he hoped to buy three months' time by holding talks with the Japanese. If after that war came, how was the British position in the Far East to be safeguarded? Singapore always had been the key in British eyes, and if they could no longer find the fleet to use the great base, then perhaps the Americans could. In his first message to Roosevelt after becoming prime minister, Churchill had offered the use of Singapore to the U.S. Navy. It was a theme to which he returned repeatedly without any success. The staff discussions in Washington that produced ABC-1 went no further than to agree that the American Asiatic fleet, a small force based at Manila, could come under British operational direction in the event of war. All attempts to follow this up with detailed plans, as at an American-British-Dutch conference at Singapore in April, broke down on American reluctance to become involved in the defense of Singapore, to which they attached much lower priority than did the British. Before the Atlantic meeting even the concession that the Asiatic fleet might move to Singapore had been canceled. During the discussions between the service chiefs at Argentia, Admiral Harold Stark, the American chief of Naval Operations, revealed the extent of the difference between British and American perceptions of Singapore's significance, when he inquired whether the British could not find alternative sources that would allow them to do without the raw materials they drew from the Far East.

Knowing that much more than economic loss was at stake in the Far East, and that British defenses there were and would remain scanty, Churchill had reason to press Roosevelt very hard for assurances that the United States would treat a Japanese attack on the British, or the Dutch, as an assault upon itself. When the president agreed to give the Japanese a stiff warning that further southward moves would involve Japan with the United States, the prime

---

*It is interesting that Churchill in *The Grand Alliance* begins his account of the Atlantic meeting by recounting the discussions between Dill and himself in the spring over the priority to be given the Middle East, followed by an account of the explanation of Britain's Middle East strategy to an American military mission headed by Admiral Robert L. Ghormley in July. The implication is that the meeting offered him a chance to explain and defend personally the focus of British strategy.

minister could relax, at least temporarily. He had always thought of America as the prime deterrent to a Japanese attack that would confront Britain with imperial catastrophe. Now, after many false starts, that deterrent seemed about to become operational. In retrospect, the failure to appreciate that the expansionists in Tokyo were unlikely to be put off by a policy of gestures and protests seems a major failure in understanding on Churchill's part. While made easier by an underestimation of Japanese abilities, together with an assumption that they would behave "rationally" (as defined in the West) and not a little wishful thinking, it was, given Britain's weakness, the only basis left on which to build a strategy for dealing with Japan.

Neither Japan nor questions of basic strategy for the defeat of Germany, however, are most commonly associated with the Argentia meeting but rather the writing of the Atlantic Charter. The British saw this as both reinforcing America's commitment to them and particularly as underlining for the Japanese the meaning of the warning that Roosevelt would deliver. It may well be that the prime minister viewed it primarily in that light. He certainly did not arrive at Argentia with any wish to make a declaration about war aims, fearing that fissures would thereby open up in the facade of anti-German unity. After dining with the president aboard the U.S.S. *Augusta* on the evening of 9 August, however, Churchill returned to H.M.S. *Prince of Wales* impressed by Roosevelt's desire for a joint declaration of principles. The following morning, aided by the permanent undersecretary at the Foreign Office, Sir Alexander Cadogan, he put together the first draft of what became the Atlantic Charter. The document and the attitudes of the president and prime minister toward it and one another provide an insight into the nature of the Anglo-American alliance.

Roosevelt and Churchill had encountered one another only once before August 1941—at a dinner at Gray's Inn in London shortly after the end of the First World War. Of that first encounter Churchill later wrote: "I had been struck by his magnificent presence in all his youth and strength. There had been no opportunity for anything but salutations."[14] In fact, Churchill did not recall the meeting at all, which irritated Roosevelt when he discovered it. The apparently pointless, if harmless, lie written after Roosevelt's death reveals a great deal about the relationship. From the moment he became prime minister, Churchill clearly saw that survival perhaps, and ultimate victory certainly, depended on drawing an increasing measure of support, moral and material, from the United States.

He therefore set himself single-mindedly to woo and cajole the Americans. He also tried consistently to present the Anglo-American alliance as one that transcended the normal in annals of sovereign states—a "special relationship." In the same way, he set about to win Roosevelt's friendship and esteem. A sentimental and impulsive man, there is no doubt that he succeeded in convincing himself that he and the president were warm friends, although there also can be little doubt that there was more warmth on Churchill's side than on that of the complex Roosevelt.

Churchill, however, was remarkably successful in imposing his idea of the Anglo-American alliance, of which his relations with the president were a crucial element, on accounts of the war that leaned heavily on his own massive memoirs. The rewriting of his first encounter with Roosevelt was part of the process of shaping an image of a noble wartime companionship in arms which he hoped would help to buttress Britain's position in the postwar world vis à vis a supremely powerful and self-confident America. This presentation tends to obscure the intricate mixture of friendship and wariness, cooperation and competition, that characterized the partnership.

The Atlantic Charter (the British preferred the less emotional label "joint declaration") is a good case in point. Churchill, proud as he was of his American antecedents and convinced as he was that the two nations together could bring about a *pax anglo-saxonia,* nonetheless was determined to defend British national interests. He insisted on modifications to a clause that otherwise would have threatened the sterling bloc created by the Ottawa agreements of 1932, and he would strongly deny, shortly after the charter was issued, that its endorsement of self-determination had anything to do with India. Roosevelt, a Wilsonian in his early years, wanted his principal ally to endorse his vision of the world the war was being fought to create, a vision, as Churchill could not help but notice, that did not include the great imperial agglomerations of which Britain's was the most striking. At Argentia both sides got some of what they wanted, but Roosevelt got more. An American vision of the future had been endorsed, albeit with mostly unvoiced reservations, while the British successes at the conference proved illusory. The public restatement of American commitment to Britain was a clear gain, but the British had not really dented their ally's scepticism about the Middle East, and the president's promise to deliver a blunt warning to Japan evaporated once he was back in Washington and exposed to the full force of State Department reservations. For the prime minister this was a particularly bitter pill, for it brought him face to face with the problem of potential disaster, military and imperial, in the Far East.

When Roosevelt's promised stern admonition turned into an anodyne statement to the Japanese ambassador, Churchill's response was to declare in a radio address that, if war came to the Pacific, Great Britain would stand beside the United States. The real question was: If Japan struck at Britain, or the Dutch who were dependent on the British, would the United States take the same position? Roosevelt, at a post-Argentia news conference, had denied the existence of any commitment to join in the war, a statement that produced widespread disappointment among the British public. But, if the United States had no formal commitment to Britain, the British had more than enough to their smaller allies. The Dutch had pressed the British for over a year for a promise to help if the East Indies were attacked by Japan, a promise the British had evaded as consistently as the Americans had evaded Britain's pressure. The Australians, however, were not so easily put off.

With three divisions in the Middle East, along with a large proportion of its warships and air squadrons, the Commonwealth of Australia believed that in the western desert, Greece, Crete, and Syria it had borne a considerable part of the imperial war effort—and casualties—in the theater. There already had been complaints of a lack of consultation over strategy as well as about British generalship. The Australians were soon to send their one remaining division to Malaya. If Japan attacked they would expect British help; failure to send it might well break up the Commonwealth. But Britain could not adequately defend against Japan its own interests, much less those of Australia.

An American guarantee would have been an exit from this dilemma, but Roosevelt, cautious as always of isolationist sentiments, drew back from offering, or even appearing to offer, one. Churchill therefore was driven to a policy of symbolic gestures. This, like many of the prime minister's wartime policies, had pre-war roots. As the prospect of sending the main fleet to Singapore faded in the later 1930s, the idea of sending a smaller force of capital ships to play a deterrent role began to find some support, although less among the Naval Staff than in the Foreign Office. Anthony Eden, for instance, told an American diplomat in November 1937 that "the moving around of a few ships would have a good effect on our efforts for a peaceful solution."[15] The belief that the movement of British battleships might affect Japanese calculations was one that also occurred readily to Churchill, born into an era when such gestures gave pause to chancelleries in Europe. Thus, out of misunderstood Japanese attitudes and political realities, underestimation of Japanese efficiency, and the need to redeem twenty years of promises to the Pacific dominions, was born the doomed voyage of *Prince of Wales* and *Repulse* to Singapore.

There can be no doubt of the extent to which this expedition was Churchill's personal decision, although strongly seconded by Eden. Shortly after the Atlantic meeting, the prime minister took up with the Admiralty the question of sending a small force of modern ships to Singapore. In addition to the deterrent argument, Churchill developed another, based on a misleading analogy with the situation in the North Atlantic. There, the small German surface fleet, especially the battleship *Tirpitz,* tied down a disproportionate share of Britain's capital ships. The Naval Staff was hostile to the prime minister's proposals, hoping to be able to build up a larger fleet of older ships in the Indian Ocean by the spring of 1942, keeping the newer battleships like *Prince of Wales* in the Atlantic. Churchill's relationship with Admiral Sir Dudley Pound was a complex one, its nature still controversial.* The first sea lord stalled the prime minister's proposal in the late summer, but by autumn, as tension mounted in the Far East, Churchill brought the idea up again and put all his force behind it. On 20 October 1941 the Defense Committee ruled that political considerations were paramount and therefore *Prince of Wales* would sail for the east, joining the older battlecruiser *Repulse* in the Indian Ocean. The Japanese decision for war, taken before *Prince of Wales* left England, was confirmed to the Japanese armed forces while the ship was still in Atlantic waters.

Despite the momentous consequences of Churchill's decision to risk sending a deterrent force to Singapore, it must be remembered that the focus of his attention and that of the chiefs' of staff in the late summer and autumn of 1941 was not the Far East, except intermittently, but the war that was actually taking place. The Russians were still holding out, and by late summer the Joint Intelligence Committee, on the basis of Ultra information, had become convinced that the Germans would not be able to finish off the Soviet Union in time for major operations elsewhere in 1941. This respite made the prime minister all the more anxious to make the greatest possible gains in the Mediterranean theater while the Germans were engaged in Russia. If Rommel could be beaten, several possibilities seemed to offer themselves: rallying French

*See above, p. 74, fn.

North Africa, opening the Mediterranean, or even crossing it to Sicily. If the war swung against Germany and Italy, the Turks might be induced to abandon their cautious neutrality. If they did, a solid northern flank could be organized to protect the vulnerable British position in the Middle East against the arrival of the Wehrmacht in force if 1942 brought it final victory in Russia. Churchill's sweeping vision was one of his greatest assets, and his artist's imagination must have painted this scene for him in vivid colors. It is therefore not surprising that he concentrated his energies on Crusader and its aftermath, only turning intermittently to concern himself with an area where war, if likely, did not yet seem certain and where only the Americans could seriously influence matters.

The buildup before Crusader was impressive. British forces had suffered heavy losses in the spring and early summer fighting, and many of the 770 tanks, 3,400 trucks, 900 mortars, and 600 field, 240 antiaircraft, and 200 antitank guns that reached Middle East command between July and October went to replace that wastage. Nevertheless, backed by fifty-two squadrons of aircraft, the command's three armored and thirteen infantry divisions, plus numerous brigades and battalions not incorporated into divisional formations, constituted a force formidable in numbers and equipment, and one from which the prime minister had great expectations. Even before Crusader finally began, his mind was leaping westward toward Tripoli, French North Africa (where possible American intervention was an added attraction), and across the Sicilian narrows to the Italian homeland. This, in fact, was the shape the war in the Mediterranean eventually took, and it is important to note that it was not merely Churchill's personal strategy but one to which the British were wedded both by resources and past choices. Aware of the particularly close identification with the war in the Mediterranean his role as the articulator of the British position had given him in American eyes, Churchill asked rhetorically in his memoirs: "What other plan of active offensive warfare was open to Britain and the Empire by themselves in 1942?"[16] Limited resources and past choices had established constraints from which escape was not possible by late 1941. But before victory could yield any fruits, "Rommel . . . and his small audacious army" had first to be beaten.[17] Here was the crux of the problem, and its solution would evade the British for nearly another year.

The enormous literature that has grown up around the desert war makes clear two salient facts: German equipment generally was better than that of their opponents, but this advantage in weaponry was less important than that conferred by superior technique.* Time and again the British were simply outgeneraled, a situation Churchill understood at the time and stated quite bluntly later, writing of one of Rommel's successful counterattacks: "Nor should the British nation, in probing these matters, be misled into thinking that the technical inferiority of our tanks was the only reason for this considerable and far-reaching reverse."[18] This crucial British weakness at the top was compounded by the loss in an air crash of Lieutenant General Vyvyan Pope, who was to have commanded the British armor in Crusader. A serious student of mobile warfare, Pope could ill be spared in an army struggling to make up ground lost in the twenty years before 1939. Auchinleck, a tough and capable commander, remained in Cairo, supervising his vast theater and watching the northern flank. The newly christened Eighth Army was taken into its first battle by Lieutenant General Sir Alan Cunningham, a cautious infantryman, while the armor was commanded by Lieutenant General Willoughby Norrie who had never handled a large armored formation in battle, let alone a corps.

Crusader, freighted with so many of Churchill's hopes, began on 18 November. Three weeks of fighting produced a victory of sorts. Tobruk was relieved and Rommel's forces withdrew westward, battered but intact. Auchinleck had intervened at a crucial moment to prevent Cunningham from breaking off the attack, a decision that made possible ultimate British success. Then, distracted by the duties that his position as Britain's military viceroy in the Middle East entailed, he returned to Cairo, leaving as the new Eighth Army commander his former chief of staff, Major General Neil Ritchie, an officer untried in high command, inexperienced in handling armor, and junior to many of his subordinates. Despite Ritchie's appointment (perhaps Auchinleck's greatest error as commander in chief) and Norrie's hesitant command of the armor, Crusader was nevertheless a victory, the first over the German army since the war's beginning. It was, however, immediately overshadowed by a much greater defeat that began to unfold.

Early on the morning of 7 December (December the 8th in Malaya on the other side of the international date line), the Japanese struck. Churchill was spending a weekend at Chequers,

---

*However good individual German weapons such as the 88mm dual purpose gun might be the Germans had fewer of them than did their opponents, and they were further handicapped by the periodic near severance of their supply lines.

and there he learned from the radio that American entry into the war, so long sought and hoped for, was at last a reality. "We are all in the same boat now," Roosevelt told the prime minister when Churchill spoke to him on transatlantic telephone. "Being saturated and satiated with emotion and sensation, I went to bed and slept the sleep of the saved and thankful," Churchill recalled.[19] The note of relief is unmistakable, a relief so intense that it can still be felt in words written nearly a decade later. But for that relief there was a price. American entry into the war was accompanied by a series of disasters in the Far East that touched off a complicated imperial crisis. That crisis in turn made it virtually certain that the 1939 empire and the world role derived from it would not survive into the postwar era. Moreover, American entry made it certain that alliance strategy would sooner or later be shaped by American perceptions which, the British already had reason to apprehend, were fundamentally different from theirs. It is doubtful whether Churchill sensed any of this at the time. He was momentarily swept away by one overwhelming emotion: "We had won the war."[20]

Exultation was not, however, destined to last long. In the last hours before Japan struck, Roosevelt had finally given the assurance the prime minister had so long sought, remarking casually to the British ambassador that a Japanese attack on Britain would bring America into the war. This and the certainty that Japan was about to attack turned his attention toward the *Prince of Wales* and *Repulse*. The general sentiment among the prime minister's advisers was that they had best get out of harm's way. Churchill recorded in his memoirs a meeting late in the evening of 9 December where the consensus was that the ships "must go to sea and vanish among the innumerable islands."[21] A final decision on their ultimate destination was postponed until the next day. Even as the prime minister and his advisers deliberated, "Force Z" sortied to attack the Japanese landings in northern Malaya. Caught in broad daylight the next day by Japanese naval airmen, both ships were sunk, a more impressive Japanese feat than the destruction of the stationary and unprepared American battleships at Pearl Harbor.

The news reached Churchill shortly after he awoke on 10 December, and he later confessed that he had writhed in agony. He bore the principal responsibility for sending the ships to the Far East, and the memory of it haunted him for years afterward. It was only the beginning of the chain of disasters that would culminate in the fall of Singapore.* But the prime minister had little time to mourn; Auchinleck had to be urged on even as he was told that men and equipment destined for him must now go to the Far East. Above all, Churchill bent himself to arrange the first wartime summit meeting with the Americans, and as quickly as possible, lest under the impact of Pearl Harbor the agreed strategic priorities be set aside and American energies concentrated on the Pacific war. Roosevelt, amidst the sudden pressures of war, was reluctant, but the prime minister was insistent and for the second time in five months a new battleship bore Churchill westward.

On the voyage he took advantage of his partial isolation from the daily rush of business to prepare three remarkable papers on the form and sequence of the war. The first two, "The Atlantic Front" and "The Campaign of 1943," set out the case for what became alliance strategy in the eighteen months after Pearl Harbor: clearing North Africa and opening the Mediterranean, all the while hammering at Germany from the air. The third, "Notes on the Pacific," was only completed after Churchill reached Washington.** The order of composition is revealing. Even the Japanese attack, the shock caused by the sinking of *Prince of Wales* and *Repulse*, and the steadily mounting tale of defeat and retreat in Malaya did not shake the prime minister's conviction that it was the war in Europe that really counted.

Because they represent Churchill's vision of the war at the climactic moment of American entry, these three memoranda deserve close scrutiny. He was quite certain in his mind about the immediate steps that the Anglo-American alliance needed to take: safeguard the Atlantic lifeline to Britain, and as its first joint offensive, clear North Africa and open the Mediterranean. What would follow this was less sharply delineated. "The war can only be ended through the defeat in Europe of the German armies," the prime minister wrote. But how to accomplish this? Possibly the bombing offensive, economic dislocation, and the attrition of prolonged war would lead to collapse as in 1918. However, Churchill no longer expected this to be the case, for he immediately offered a different scenario:

---

*It is interesting that Churchill's instincts counseled him that a rapid retreat from northern Malaya by the dispersed imperial forces there was necessary to concentrate them on the defense of southern Malaya and Singapore. By the time he sent a message to that effect on 15 December, it was too late. The defeat in detail of the ill-positioned forces in Malaya had begun. *GA*, 636–38.

**These three papers—Churchill's strategic vision at its most characteristic—can be found in *GA*, 646–58.

If adequate and suitably equipped forces were landed [in occupied Europe] the German garrisons would prove insufficient to cope both with the strength of the liberating forces and the fury of the revolting peoples. . . . The landings should be made by armoured and mechanized forces. . . . It need not be assumed that great numbers of men are required. If the incursion of the armoured formations is successful, the uprising of the local population, for whom weapons must be brought, will supply the corpus of the liberating offensive.[22]

This romantic notion of a tormented continent rising in fury to wreak vengeance on its oppressors is, in fact, an artist's version of SOE's detonator idea, the concept that had given birth to the secret army scheme. SOE itself had been moving away from this for some months, but the idea still held attractions for the prime minister. For one thing, it brought the cost of liberating Europe within range of what Britain could afford to pay. The most striking feature about Churchill's paper on 1942, however, is what is absent, namely, the further development of the Mediterranean campaign after the clearance of North Africa into an assault on Italy. In fact, although British planners had already sketched out an attack on Sicily, the shape of the final offensive against Germany was not yet clear in Churchill's mind. Only the events of the next twelve months would convince British war planners, and then the prime minister, that great strategic dividends awaited further development of the Mediterranean war.

Churchill's final note on the Pacific was more vague than either of his European papers. There were some shrewd guesses, such as the prediction that aircraft carriers would be the key to Pacific fighting, but the general impression left is that the entire theater of the Japanese war was far less real to the prime minister than was Europe and the Middle East. There, American entry made final victory certain, and this was for him perhaps the most important single fact about the Japanese attack. Writing nearly two years later, Churchill commented tartly upon the final dispatch submitted by Sir Robert Craigie, British ambassador in Tokyo when war came:

He writes of the breach with Japan as if it were an unmitigated disaster. . . . It was however a blessing that Japan attacked the United States and thus brought America whole-heartedly into the war. Greater good fortune has rarely happened to the British Empire than this event which . . . may lead, through the merciless crushing of Japan, to a new relationship of immense benefit to the English-speaking countries and to the whole world.[23]

The assumption in that statement that partnership with America in total war against Germany and Japan could be made compatible with the survival of British world power represented the most fundamental of all the prime minister's errors.

By late December 1941, however, Churchill was in a total war against two major opponents and in active partnership with the United States. Long-range problems had, perforce, to take second place to managing the difficulties at hand. Viewed from this perspective, the Arcadia Conference represented a considerable British success. The "Germany first" principle was reaffirmed.* Churchill made considerable progress in selling the concept of a joint North African venture to the Americans, and the key institution in the Anglo-American alliance, the Combined Chiefs of Staff, took shape.** Finally, in considering Churchill's success at Arcadia it is important to note that during the conference Churchill apparently capped the structure of Anglo-American cooperation in intelligence matters that had gradually taken shape over the past year by revealing to Roosevelt the full dimensions of Ultra, which could only have strengthened his hand in the discussions.

The full extent of the stresses borne by the prime minister became physically apparent in Washington when he suffered a mild heart attack, a fact concealed from him by his doctor Sir Charles Wilson (who in 1943 became Lord Moran). Churchill completed a heavy program of activities and then, after a brief working vacation in Florida, decided on a hazardous flight home rather than the slower and safer battleship that awaited him at Bermuda. This sense of urgency was not misplaced. He had been away for a month, and while his negotiations with the Americans had been very successful, the steadily mounting tale of disaster in the Far East was

---

*The United States, in fact, put as much effort into the Pacific theater as into the Atlantic for some eighteen months after Pearl Harbor, a reflection both of the need to stabilize the situation there and of the U.S. Navy's overriding concern with the Pacific. If it had not been possible to ignore in practice during these months, the priority for the German war might have been harder to maintain in theory.

**Here the element of chance played a role. Just before Pearl Harbor, Dill, exhausted by his eighteen months as chief of the Imperial General Staff and his credibility with Churchill gone, was replaced by the commander in chief (Home Forces), General Sir Alan Brooke. Churchill, who had intended to send Dill into honorable rustication as a field marshal and governor of Bombay, took him to Washington since he had already met General Marshall and because Brooke was still "settling in." Dill remained in America as the British representative on the Combined Chiefs of Staff, where his tact, ability, and an increasingly intimate relationship with Marshall played a key role in the structure of alliance cooperation until his death in November 1944.

producing stresses both in Parliament and in Britain's imperial structure that could only be dealt with by the prime minister in person.

As the British position in Malaya crumbled, relations with Australia became steadily more tense. Three of Australia's four divisions available for overseas service were in the Middle East; the fourth was in Malaya. Scraping up emergency reinforcements for the latter temporarily exhausted what Australia had available to send overseas. Looking at the apparently unstoppable Japanese advance and informed in no uncertain terms by V. G. Bowden, its representative in Singapore, of the full dimensions of the military rout occurring in Malaya, the Australian government took the extraordinary step of announcing in the newspapers its disillusionment with Britain and its choice of an alternate great power protector. On Christmas day Bowden told his government that the fall of Singapore was only a matter of weeks. Two days later a letter, signed by the Australian prime minister, John Curtin, appeared on the first page of the Melbourne *Herald*:

> We refuse to accept the dictum that the Pacific struggle must be treated as a subordinate aspect of the general conflict. . . . The Australian government, therefore, regards the Pacific struggle as primarily one in which the United States and Australia must have the fullest say in the direction of the democracies' fighting plan. Without any inhibitions of any kind, I make it quite clear that Australia looks to America, free of any pangs as to our traditional links or kinship with the United Kingdom. We know the problems the United Kingdom faces. . . . But we know, too, that Australia can go and Britain can still hold on. We are, therefore, determined that Australia shall not go.[24]

To have this printed while the prime minister was in Washington was painfully embarrassing, and, while Churchill quickly and wisely set aside his first angry impulse to broadcast an appeal to the Australian public over the head of its government, he arrived back in London vividly aware of both the damage already done to Commonwealth relations and the need to make the level of British support far more visible to the Australians.

Shortly after his return Churchill seems to have finally accepted that the situation in Malaya was desperate. The critical piece of information was a cable from General Sir Archibald Wavell, recently translated by the Arcadia Conference from his position as commander in chief (India) to the hopeless job of allied supreme commander, ABDA (American-British-Dutch-Australian)

Command. In answer to a question from Churchill about the length of Singapore's resistance under siege, Wavell pointed out that the "fortress" Churchill imagined simply did not exist. Singapore was a naval base, fortified against attack from the sea but virtually naked on its landward side and dependent on water supplies brought by pipeline from the mainland.* At that point the prime minister began to think about diverting reinforcements destined for Malaya to Rangoon. The most important of these was the British 18th Division, whose convoys had been redirected from Suez to Singapore. The Japanese attack on Burma had just begun in earnest, and holding Burma not only kept a buffer between the Japanese and an increasingly restive India but also would satisfy the American desire to keep up the flow of supplies to China via the Burma Road.

However, when the Australian representative in London informed his government that the British were about to write off Malaya, and with it an Australian division, Curtin furiously argued that such a move was "an inexcusable betrayal."[25] Churchill described the message, with considerable understatement, as "serious and unusual."[26] He went on to deny that the Australian reaction sealed the fate of the 18th Division, but in fact that is exactly what it did. Looking back on it later, Churchill found another rationale, which to him was even more compelling: "The effect that would be produced all over the world, especially in the United States, of a British 'scuttle' while the Americans fought on so stubbornly at Corregidor was terrible to imagine."[27] The East Anglian units of the doomed 18th Division were, like the *Prince of Wales* and *Repulse,* sacrifices to the policy of trying to sustain an imperial position on inadequate resources. And, even as this sacrifice was being made, another aspect of the complicated imperial crisis, precipitated by the Japanese attack, was unfolding in the Middle East.

Auchinleck had ensured the success of Crusader by his personal intervention, but the tactical skills of his subordinates were not equal to the task of turning Rommel's defeat into his destruction. The Desert Fox had gotten his battered German forces away, much to the prime minister's sorrow. Then the pressure on Rommel's

---

*The legend that Singapore's guns "pointed the wrong way" and could only be aimed seaward may be symbolically correct but is factually untrue. What is of much greater interest is the question of why Churchill's repeated statements (over a period of fifteen months prior to the Japanese attack) of his assumption that Singapore was a fortress capable of standing a lengthy siege went uncorrected by his advisers, unless they were equally ill-informed about Malayan realities.

supplies relaxed as he fell back toward Tripoli and a sequence of losses crippled British sea power in the central Mediterranean, while the arrival in Sicily of a *Fliegerkorps* from Russia sharply increased pressure on Malta. As a resupplied Afrika Korps began to revive, the British, their pursuit stalled at El Argheila, withdrew battle weary but experienced formations for a rest and replaced them with the newly arrived 1st Armored Division. It was an uncanny repetition of what had happened in April 1941. The British, forced to pause in their advance, assumed their opponent equally incapable of forward movement. When Rommel confounded their expectations, he met once again in his path raw troops, poorly disposed and led with a singular lack of tactical flair. By early February, Auchinleck had stabilized his front just west of Tobruk, the gains of Crusader gone and the 1st Armored Division temporarily erased as a fighting formation.

This setback angered Churchill perhaps more deeply than anything that had yet happened in the Middle East. Eight years later, in *The Hinge of Fate,* his outrage was still palpable. "The ineffective use made of the [1st Armored] division remains unexplained," he declared and then quoted Auchinleck's dispatch in which inexperienced troops and poor quality tanks were cited as primary causes, an explanation against which Churchill deployed his heavy verbal artillery:

> All these statements require careful scrutiny. The 1st Armoured Division was one of the finest we had. It consisted largely of men who had more than two years training and represented as high a standard of efficiency as any to be found in our Regular forces. . . . Yet, without having been committed deeply into action this fine division lost over a hundred of its tanks. The very considerable petrol supplies which had been brought forward were abandoned in its precipitate retreat, and many of its tanks were left behind because they ran out of fuel. . . . When we remember the cost, time and labour the creation of an entity like an armoured division, with all its experts and trained men, involves, the effort required to transport it around the Cape, the many preparations made to bring it into battle, it is indeed grievous to see the result squandered by such mismanagement. Still more are these reflections painful when our failure is contrasted with what the Germans accomplished. . . . Nor should the British nation in probing these matters, be misled into thinking that the technical inferiority of our tanks was the only reason for this considerable and far-reaching reverse.[28]

In fact, deep suspicions about the battle worthiness of the British army and the quality of its leadership were taking shape in the prime minister's mind by the beginning of 1942 and would affect his calculations for months to come.* His anger over the setback in the desert also was sharpened by the fact that a full-dress parliamentary debate on the conduct of the war opened as Auchinleck retreated, the first serious challenge to Churchill's position since May 1940.** It also came as Nationalist discontent in the Middle East, quiet since the suppression of the Iraqi revolt, boiled ominously again, this time in Britain's critical Egyptian base.

Many Egyptian Nationalist leaders doubted whether Britain would win, uncertainties that seemed well founded in early February 1942. Sirry Pasha, whose conduct as prime minister the British had found satisfactory, resigned on 2 February. A major crisis then erupted, with university students shouting "long live Rommel" and King Farouk showing no disposition to accept British advice to appoint another "reliable" figure, Nahas Pasha, in Sirry's place. British Ambassador Sir Miles Lampson was a massive, jovial-looking figure with an implacable determination to preserve British control of Egypt. New Zealand troops were brought in to patrol Cairo's streets, and preceded into the courtyard of the Abdin Palace by three light tanks of the New Zealand divisional cavalry, Lampson, accompanied by "an impressive array of specially picked stalwart military officers armed to the teeth," forced himself into the king's presence. An instrument of abdication, drawn up by the ambassador, was handed to Farouk for signature. The "completely cowed" monarch capitulated, Nahas became prime minister and British authority in Cairo was again secure until the next defeat.[29] This episode, which finds no place in Churchill's memoirs but which certainly did in the contemporary British press, had lasting consequences.†

The memory of the humiliation inflicted by Lampson became one of the most powerful spurs in urging postwar Egyptian Nationalists on to the final elimination of the British presence. It also exposed a major contradiction. The wartime ideals, strongly felt in both Britain and the United States and embodied in the Atlantic

---

*The evidence for this must be drawn from many scattered sources. Joseph Strange, in a suggestive article, has done so in "The British Rejection of Sledgehammer: An Alternative Interpretation," *Military Affairs* (February 1982): 6–14.

**See below, pp. 182–83.

†Lampson became Baron Killearn in the 1943 New York's Honors Lists. Churchill may have found it expedient to omit this episode from his memoirs, but there is no doubt of his wholehearted approval of Lampson's methods.

Charter, confronted the realities of an imperial position, whose maintenance was not only crucial to the British war effort but also one of the objectives for which Churchill and the imperialist minority in Britain were waging the war. On both counts its omission from the prime minister's memoirs is not surprising. The same pressure for a radically altered postwar world straining against the creaking framework of the old order is observable in the political crisis that was coming to a head in Britain simultaneously with the crises in the desert, in Cairo, and in Malaya.

The unity that mortal peril created in 1940 could not last, although the British preserved a remarkable degree of domestic consensus until war's end. The foundation of Churchill's coalition was the loyalty of the Labour leadership, plus his own growing dominance over the Conservatives as it became clear that the events of 1940 had given the prime minister a stature that no other political figure could hope to approach. However, this did not mean that there was perfect unity. The press and political debate were remarkably free for a society under such pressure, and the ambitious, idealistic, or discontented—whatever their political labels—retained a considerable freedom of maneuver.

As the fear of invasion faded, to be replaced by the prospect of a long, weary struggle, and with final victory nowhere in sight, discontent came to focus on two issues. Was the war being prosecuted efficiently? What would British society look like when it was over? If the first were capable of intermittently causing serious problems to Churchill, the second was the more worrisome, for it touched upon the crucial question of Labour party loyalty to his government. If the two fused together, a major crisis could occur, and this is precisely what happened at the beginning of 1942. Repeated British defeats since Norway convinced some critics that British army training and equipment, along with British war direction, were in need of major changes. This overlapped feeling that the root of the problem was the continued control of so much of British life by the "old gang"—"the Establishment"—who apparently feared change that would threaten their dominance more than they feared defeat. Critics who thought this way found a symbol of the complex of attitudes they were attacking in the alleged failure to aid Russia more effectively.

Finally there was a growing impatience to see the social goals for which the war was being fought, the blueprint for the rebuilding of Britain on a fairer basis, made plain. Most of Churchill's assorted opponents throughout the war held some or all of these views. Some of these opinions were unfair, or missed the point. British central war direction was, in fact, more efficient than that of either Germany or the United States. The prime minister was more aware than any of his critics of the shortcomings in British military equipment and leadership, although neither was as easy to remedy as the critics supposed. But on one point they were certainly on the mark; the heart of the opposition to spelling out a program for postwar reconstruction was Churchill.

The prime minister's reasons for this stand were complex. His own past record was far from hostile to social reform. He had, however, concentrated his enormous energies on the business of managing Britain's war and resented distractions. Perhaps more importantly, he realized that an open debate on the future direction of British society would not only distract attention and energy from the war effort but also would imperil the solidity of the coalition upon which his government depended. He had seen enough from 1914 to 1922 to know how fragile coalitions could be once basic issues affecting the distribution of political power were raised. Churchill's technique for dealing with any challenge, whatever the premise of the opponent, was in keeping with his basic approach to life. He confronted the challenger head-on, secure in the knowledge that public opinion cherished him both as a war leader and as a symbol of national determination. After the withdrawal from Greece in May 1941, this technique had brought a 477 to 1 vote of confidence and a rousing ovation from the House. Similar robust tactics squelched grumbling in June after the fall of Crete. In the opening months of 1942, however, in the depths of the war's third winter, the discontent aroused by successive disasters was far too great for the prime minister to brush aside easily. This was particularly the case since a figure suddenly appeared from the wings who could provide a focus for the opinion that major changes were necessary if Britain was to both win the war and build a more just society in its aftermath. That figure was Sir Stafford Cripps, a left-wing Labour leader (indeed, the party had expelled him for heresy before the war) and until recently ambassador to Russia.

In his memoirs Churchill generally strove to depict the British war effort against a background of political consensus, but the events of early 1942 defeated him. He did, however, do his best to minimize them, discussing the vote of confidence that took place on 29 January largely in the context of the defeats in the desert and Malaya. He won it as overwhelmingly as he had in May (464 to 1), making it clear on the opening day of a three-day debate that he would not remain as prime minister if deprived of effective power as minister of defense. Since even his harshest critics could think of no substitute for him as national leader, the opposition immediately crumbled. "One can actually feel the wind of opposition dropping sentence by sentence," one member of Parliament, summarizing the impact of the prime minister's speech, recorded in his diary.[30]

Discomfiting his opponents in the House was not the end of the story. Sir Stafford, wealthy barrister, puritan socialist, and a curious repository of many hopes for a more efficient war and a more egalitarian society, remained to be dealt with. Cripps refused Churchill's first offer of a cabinet-rank office but without a war cabinet seat. The prime minister knew that the forces Cripps represented would have to be appeased and that his parliamentary triumph had by no means restored his position entirely, especially as the war news became worse in February. In that month he reconstructed his government on a major scale for the first time. Chamberlainite relics like Maurice Hankey and Secretary of State for War David Margesson, formerly Conservative chief whip, went and Cripps came in, with a seat in the war cabinet.* His arrival signaled the increasing salience of postwar issues as well as the mounting impatience for an end to military disaster. The former Churchill tried to contain during the remainder of the war and largely ignored in his memoirs. The latter, a growing threat to the prime minister, was unrelieved until El Alamein ten months later. Churchill was fortunate that the two issues never fused again, prior to Montgomery's victory, in quite the way they had in January and February.

February 1942 saw a cascade of defeats at the hands of Germany and Japan that not only weakened Churchill's domestic position but also touched off another imperial crisis, this time in India, the most sensitive of places. After his realization that it was politically impossible to cut British losses in Malaya and concentrate on Burma, there was little Churchill could do except wait for the inevitable defeat. He did, however, apply himself to urging on Wavell a last-ditch defense on Singapore Island. The prime minister made no secret of his hope that honor would be saved by such a defense and that British credibility with Russia and the United

---

*Lord Beaverbrook, personally cherished by the prime minister but politically always an equivocal friend, also departed in February, although Churchill brought him back later in a minor office. Beaverbrook also had sought to play the Russian card, perhaps in the hope of capitalizing on public enthusiasm for the Red Army's feats and acquiring a popular following of his own, to what end it is hard to say. In any case, the vaguely unsavory Anglo-Canadian newspaper mogul and backstairs operator was literally incredible as an embodiment of the hopes that came to focus on Cripps.

States would be enhanced as well. On an inquiry from the hapless GOC* Malaya, Lieutenant General A. E. Percival, about the destruction of reserve ammunition stocks as the end drew near, Churchill minuted that the best method would be to fire the shells at the enemy. His messages in the last days before Singapore's fall have a savage quality that reflects not only the strain under which he found himself but also a deep fear that there were fundamental flaws in the British army, a fear that had been building for months. Lady Violet Bonham Carter, Asquith's daughter and a lifelong friend of Churchill's, found him deeply depressed, a prey to fears that the British soldier and the society that bred him were no longer as tough and enduring as they had been in the First World War: "We have so many men in Singapore, so many men—they should have done better."[31] The prime minister, who by his own admission was poorly informed of the state of affairs in Malaya, was unrealistic about the possibilities of prolonged defense on Singapore Island and unfair to the troops involved, but the anger and the concern remained in his mind to influence decisions for a long time. "I cannot get over Singapore," he remarked dejectedly to his doctor months later.[32]

Simultaneously with Percival's surrender on 15 February, and to some extent blanketing it, came a far less significant but immensely embarrassing setback on Britain's doorstep. For several months a considerable portion of the German surface fleet—the battlecruisers *Scharnhorst* and *Gneisenau,* together with the heavy cruiser *Prinz Eugen*—had been at Brest, periodically attacked by the Royal Air Force. A bold German decision to bring them back to home waters by the most direct route, up the English Channel, together with meticulous preparation on their part and a series of errors and mischances on the British side, led to the ships' successful passage of the Channel on 11–12 February, an event that provoked widespread public outrage. Known through Ultra, the extent of the damage the battlecruisers sustained in their dash—*Gneisenau* was never repaired—could not be made public, and the emotional reaction of a nation that believed deeply and instinctively in its superiority at sea was intense. The perceptive Harold Nicolson noted in his diary on 16 February: "I find that people are more distressed about the escape of the *Scharnhorst* and *Gneisenau* than they are even by the loss of Singapore. . . . They cannot bear the thought that the Germans sailed by our front door. Winston will have to face a

*General Officer Commanding

bad situation in the House tomorrow." The House lived up to Nicolson's expectations, while the prime minister's performance, after six unremitting weeks of pressure, depressed him. "Winston made his statement this afternoon. It started all right but when people asked questions, he became irritable and rather reckless. . . . He was not at his best."[33] Only victory would relieve the nearly intolerable strain, and that was nowhere in sight. On 8 March Rangoon fell, and as Japanese troops, preceded by a flood of Indian refugees fleeing Burma, approached the borders of the raj, they touched off the war's climactic imperial crisis and the one that Churchill was perhaps least suited to handle.

One of the most durable of Churchill's beliefs was his intense feeling about British rule in India. He had consistently opposed devolution of power there, most spectacularly in his struggle against Stanley Baldwin's India Bill. When he became prime minister, however, it was the consequences of that legislation that provided the starting point for his own policy. His first act was the intervention that transformed what Leo Amery had envisioned as a dramatic gesture to break the Indian political logjam into the toothless August offer.* This he intended to be Britain's final word for the duration of the war. Shortly after the August offer was made the prime minister told the House of Commons that "the right to guide the course of history is the noblest prize of victory."[34]

One of the channels into which he hoped to guide history was indicated in October when he told the Conservative meeting that chose him as a party leader in succession to Chamberlain that he had always served two "supreme" causes: "the enduring greatness of Britain and her Empire and the historical continuity of our island life."[35] Yet the very magnitude of the Indian war effort, crucial to British strategy, was cutting the ground from under Churchill's feet, even if thirty years of political concession had not already done so. Expanding the Indian Army meant "Indianizing" its officer corps, while massive recruitment ended the isolation from political currents that had made its rank and file such a reliable prop of imperial rule. The cost of India's war effort, debited to London eventually at the rate of 1 million pounds a day, was reversing the economic relationship of the two countries. The yearning in Britain for the reconstruction of society on a different and more equitable basis meant fewer would thrill to the imperial bugle call that never failed to stir Churchill. None of this made any difference to the

*See above, pp. 114–17.

prime minister. India was essential to British power, and he meant to preserve that power; therefore, he would not yield on India. In that syllogism the prime minister placed his belief from beginning to end.

For over one year after the August offer his policy seemed to be working. Recruits poured in and the Indian Army grew steadily, while the political scene remained quiescent. Shortly after his return from the Atlantic meeting with Roosevelt, Churchill reiterated his policy in the House of Commons, stressing that the self-determination, of which the Atlantic Charter spoke, did not apply to India. It was after this statement that Ernest Bevin, perhaps the most crucial Labour minister in the coalition, told Amery privately that the idea of waiting until after the war to deal with Indian problems frightened him. He did not, however, confront the prime minister on the issue. Just after Pearl Harbor at the Arcadia Conference, an even more important ally did. The reaction Roosevelt got from Churchill on that occasion was such that the president never again raised the issue directly with the prime minister.* At the same time, Churchill brushed aside an appeal from a distinguished Indian moderate, Sir T. B. Sapru, for a stroke of "enlightened statesmanship" to galvanize the Indian war effort. His rationale, as he reported it to the war cabinet, was that the approach of the war to India's frontiers made political discussion inopportune. More remarkably, he assured his colleagues that American opinion would cause no difficulties over India. Events however did what colleagues and allies had been unable to do and, by threatening the unity of his coalition, forced the prime minister's hand on India.

When Churchill returned to London after Arcadia, he quickly discovered that the political price of holding the line on India was liable to be unacceptably high. "There is a lot of opinion here which we cannot ignore which is not satisfied that there is nothing to be done but to sit tight on the declaration of August 1940. This opinion exists in your party as well as in mine," Clement Attlee wrote to Amery on 24 January.[36] Churchill did not respond immediately to this indication that India might be the final straw for his beleaguered coalition. On 2 February, just after winning the confidence vote, he minuted to Ismay that defeats at Japanese hands made it necessary to increase the number of British troops in India as a safeguard against possible revolt. Three days later, amid the welter

---

*Even in his memoirs the anger Churchill felt on that occasion still showed: "States which have no overseas colonies or possessions are capable of rising to moods of great detachment about the affairs of those who have." *HF*, 209.

of pressures that, despite his victory in the House, had not dissipated but rather acquired in Cripps a focus, the prime minister found himself confronted by a revolt on India policy in the war cabinet. The cabinet's minutes for 5 February record agreement that "it was dangerous to stand on the present position without making every effort to see whether some way out of the constitutional deadlock cannot be found."[37]

It was at this point that Churchill changed his tactics. Some gesture was necessary, as much to Labour colleagues like Bevin and Attlee, useful allies against Cripps, as to Indian opinion; Churchill resolved to make an arresting one. He startled his war cabinet by proposing a "Defence of India Council" which would nominate an Indian representative to the war cabinet, name Indian delegates to the postwar peace conference, and after victory become the constituent assembly with which Britain would negotiate any changes in the 1935 act. The prime minister wanted to inaugurate the scheme with a broadcast appeal to India, and at one moment he even contemplated flying out to launch the idea in person. He was talked out of both ideas (although it is intriguing to think of Churchill tête-à-tête with Gandhi). However, the entire plan served its purpose. It gave the illusion of movement on Indian constitutional affairs without conceding what Churchill saw as the substance: continued British control of executive power by the viceroy and of the Indian Army by the commander in chief. The creation of a war cabinet India Committee, chaired by Attlee, to handle the details of the new British initiative further defused the issue. In fact, Churchill found in the question of India a means of defusing Cripps as well, powerfully aided, to be sure, by Sir Stafford.

Before the war Cripps had developed ties with Indian Nationalist leaders like Nehru, and in the February discussions volunteered himself as an emissary to bear the war cabinet's new offer to India. Since the "Cripps offer"—in fact, a war cabinet proposal heavily weighted to the prime minister's point of view—was form without much substance, Churchill had little to lose if Sir Stafford negotiated its acceptance and a great deal to gain if he failed.* Having conceded the point that a gesture should be made to Indian nationalism, Churchill held the war cabinet firm behind what, to him, was the key point in the Cripps offer: "During the critical period which now faces India, . . . His Majesty's Government must

---

*It offered the calling of a constituent assembly "immediately upon the cessation of hostilities," but it also reiterated the provisions of the August 1940 statement that gave the Muslims a veto.

inevitably bear the responsibility for and retain control and direction of the defence as part of their world war effort. . . ."[38]

Cripps was involved in weeks of hectic negotiations in Delhi,
negotiations that finally collapsed in a welter of semantic confusion
and mutual distrust, a fact the prime minister greeted with considerable equanimity. "You have . . . proved how great was the
British desire to reach a settlement," he cabled Cripps. "The effect
throughout Britain and the United States has been wholly bene-
ficial," he added, indicating, perhaps without intending to, the real
motivations behind his surprising conversion to an activist policy
in India.[39] The negotiations Cripps had undertaken did not fail
merely because of Churchill's insistence on continued imperial control of India's war-making potential. Linlithgow and Wavell were
every bit as firm on that point, as were the serried ranks of officialdom in Whitehall and India.* But Churchill certainly was unin-
terested in their success; to him easing the strain in his coalition
and placating American opinion were the primary objects. That
Sir Stafford was removed temporarily from the British scene and
noticeably unsuccessful on the Indian, seemed to be a nice bonus.
In fact, the failure of the Cripps mission and the steady advance
of the Japanese in Burma were paving the way for the largest
explosion of Indian hostility to British rule in nearly a century.
Indian affairs, however, faded rapidly from the forefront of
Churchill's mind in the spring of 1942, so much so that Wavell,
desperate for reinforcements and supplies, fired off an angry cable
asking whether the war cabinet seriously meant to defend India.
With the domestic political crisis and the imperial crisis abating,
the prime minister immediately plunged into a sharp tussle with
his American allies over the future course of the war.

The design for the conduct of the war that emerged from the
reevaluation after the fall of France had undergone various modifications under the pressure of circumstances, and the relative
importance of its component parts had changed. But its outline
was still that of British strategy, as Churchill's papers, prepared
for the Arcadia meeting, made plain. The disappointments that by
late summer 1941 had left the Mediterranean war the mainstay
of British offensive strategy have already been discussed.** Those
disappointments had intensified as autumn deepened into winter.

---

*After the Japanese advance overran the ABDA area, Wavell reverted to his position
as commander in chief, India.

**See above, pp. 157–59.

Bomber Command's losses had mounted, even as the Butt report undermined its claims. Losses in September-November had equaled the command's front line strength. Throughout 1941 one bomber and its crew had been lost for every ten tons of bombs dropped. In November the offensive was shut down for the balance of the winter and Air Chief Marshal Sir Richard Pierse, the AOC (air officer commanding), replaced.

Similarly SOE, having abandoned secret armies had, as yet, little to show in their place, and in February 1942 the prime minister was even thinking of dividing its functions between the chiefs of staff and the Foreign Office, both of which had long eyed the brash upstart with suspicion. In fact, Bomber Command and SOE were on the brink of a fresh lease on life. New electronic target-finding aids, new four-engine bombers, a dynamic new commander in chief, Sir Arthur Harris, and a novel concept—area bombing of German cities, powerfully supported by Cherwell—were about to restore Bomber Command's credibility. Patiently laying the groundwork for extensive intelligence and sabotage networks in western Europe, SOE was soon to assume a major role in advising and supplying the burgeoning Balkan resistance. In the late winter of 1942, however, only the Mediterranean theater still seemed promising; indeed, a victory there was becoming an imperative for Churchill's coalition. Thus the prime minister, while urging Auchinleck on to a new offensive, bent his massive energies toward persuading the Americans to mount a North African landing that would transform the situation in the theater.

The domestic pressure that the disasters of early 1942 generated would be relieved by a victory, but there were other pressing reasons as well for resuming the offensive in North Africa. Malta, battered into near torpor by the *Luftwaffe*, had to be resupplied, and only by pushing Rommel westward could air bases be acquired from which the Royal Air Force could cover the approach of a convoy to the beleaguered island. The spring also would bring other perils. The opening of the campaigning season in Russia meant the renewal of both the German offensive there and of anxiety in Cairo and London over the Middle East's northern flank. To these concerns, alliance politics added their pressures. The Russians had never ceased to clamor for a second front, and British admirers of Russian valor (a more numerous group than the small band of British Communists) added their voices, demanding a "Second Front Now," at which point domestic and alliance politics interlocked. The final twist in this strategic Gordian knot was added by the Americans.

Roosevelt had responded encouragingly at Arcadia to Churchill's suggestion that the British westward drive in exploitation of Crusader, christened "Gymnast," should be joined by an American descent upon Morocco, the whole combined endeavor to be called "Super-Gymnast." Events had killed the operation but not the idea. The prime minister remained convinced that only such an offensive was within the reach of the alliance in 1942. Here he came up against what was to be the most enduring obstacle to British strategic ideas for the remainder of the war—the formidable chief of staff of the U.S. Army, General George C. Marshall. A member of General John J. Pershing's American Expeditionary Force staff in 1917–18, Marshall had vivid memories of Anglo-French pressures to use American units to reinforce their own crumbling fronts and was determined that in this war the U.S. Army would be employed only in accordance with American strategic concepts, which ironically owed a great deal to German military doctrine. The vast army rapidly coming into being in the United States was designed to confront the German army head-on and defeat it by mass and firepower. British ideas of finishing the war in the Mediterranean struck Marshall and his planners as a strategically unsound use of alliance forces, dispersing them away from the main arena—northwest Europe—where alone decisive results could be expected.

Furthermore, there was widespread suspicion in Washington that the strategy Churchill advocated was designed more to secure postwar British interests in the Mediterranean than to expedite the defeat of Germany, a belief that owed more to memories of Britain's past than to acute analysis of its present situation. American perceptions were doubtless strengthened by the vibrant intensity of Churchill's commitment to the maintenance of Britain's world role, which meant the survival of empire. And a guaranteed future for imperial Britain was not among the war aims of the Roosevelt administration. Both British needs and resources pointed to the Mediterranean as the theater of operations for 1942. Marshall was determined to avert this if possible. Since Roosevelt rarely dissented from his chief of staff's military guidance, the stage was set for the first Anglo-American strategic debate of the war. It came to focus on the inaptly christened "Operation Sledgehammer."

Sledgehammer was a scheme to land an Allied, in fact largely British, force on the French coast in 1942. Its rationale changed over the course of the argument from the acquisition of a bridgehead to be held until the Allies were in a position to break out (which might not be until 1943) to an admittedly sacrificial gambit to take the pressure off the Russians. Throughout the argument there hovered in the background the possibility that the Americans would take a flat British refusal to go across the channel in 1942 as a breach of the basic strategic agreements going back to ABC-1 and so would hold themselves free to reverse priorities and concentrate on the Pacific.* Roosevelt remained in the background during the debate, letting Marshall fight the battle with the British, which he did not only through the combined chiefs of staff machinery but also in two personal visits to London in April and July.

That the resulting strains on the alliance were not greater than they were is largely due to the evolving personal bond between Dill and Marshall. Roosevelt complicated matters by allowing the Russian foreign minister, Vyacheslav M. Molotov, to leave Washington after a visit in May, under the impression that a second front would definitely be opened in 1942. And the Russians consistently defined second front as a landing in France, taking in this case the same view of continental warfare as did the Americans. It was the president, however, who finally broke the deadlock by instructing Marshall to put American forces into action somewhere against Germany in 1942. If the British would not agree to a cross-channel operation, this left only the North African option, rechristened "Operation Torch." Churchill described this entire process in his memoirs as "strategic natural selection," but that was not how it seemed to most of the Americans involved.**

Here we come to one of the major, and perhaps unshakable, legends about the conduct of World War II: Churchill, incurably addicted to "sideshows," led alliance strategy astray in 1942 and prevented an invasion of western Europe until 1944. The first point to be made against this is also the most obvious. The policy for which Churchill argued was not his alone but that of the British chiefs of staff and their advisers. Churchill took the lead in articulating it at the time and defending it subsequently. But, as in the arguments over strategic alternatives in 1915 or the limits of intervention in Russia in 1919, the position he took was not solely his. This is no proof that he was correct; it might simply prove that he erred in company. However, no critic has yet constructed a plausible scenario by which the British and American armies, with the

*For nearly two years after Pearl Harbor as much American effort went into the Pacific war as into the European, exemplifying the constraints that circumstances placed upon strategy, a fact American planners found so difficult to accept in relation to the British in the Mediterranean.

**Eisenhower, who would have commanded it, admitted later that Sledgehammer would have been in a major error.

forces then available, could cross the channel in 1942 and stay there. A failed invasion almost certainly would have ruled out another attempt for a very long time, perhaps forever. And here a second point must be made. The argument that the decision for Torch precluded a cross-channel invasion in 1943 is only true upon two assumptions: 1) that Torch had to develop in the way that it did, and 2) that the British never were serious about a cross-channel operation and always intended to keep the war's focus in the Mediterranean. The former is by no means an unarguable assumption, while against the latter must stand the fact that neither Churchill nor the British chiefs of staff had a fully blown "Mediterranean strategy" in mind at the time the decision for Torch was taken. That developed slowly under the impact of the Torch operations. Finally, there is no question that Churchill had reservations about the ability of the British army, given the state of its training and the quality of its leadership, to confront the Wehrmacht en masse. He was not the only one to think so. Past performance argued the case powerfully, and in the last weeks of the prolonged argument that led to the adoption of the strategy he had long espoused, the British army underlined the point by a series of disastrous reverses at Rommel's hands.*

A protracted argument between London and Cairo over the timing of a renewed desert offensive ended with a virtual ultimatum from the prime minister to Auchinleck: attack or be replaced. Auchinleck, who had intensified Churchill's irritation by refusing to return to London for consultations, agreed. Rommel, however, his supplies flowing relatively freely as a result of the battering Malta was taking, struck first. The German-Italian plan was to drive the Eighth Army back into Egypt, halt while an operation to take Malta was mounted, and then push ahead for Cairo and the Suez Canal. The first stage, the Battle of Gazala, saw British generalship reach its nadir. Combined arms tactics, at which the Germans excelled, were virtually nonexistent on the British side of the battle line. Ritchie acted as an amiable board chairman rather than an army commander, while Norrie demonstrated once again his lack of skill as an armored corps commander. The three German divisions of Rommel's Afrika Korps, in nearly a month of confused fighting, defeated a much larger British force and crowned their achievement on 21 June by capturing Tobruk with 33,000 defenders

---

*The U.S. Army was not any better prepared to meet battle-hardened German troops, a fact that became painfully apparent at the first confrontation. For a good succinct analysis see Martin Blumenson, "Kasserine," *American First Battles* (forthcoming).

and mountains of stores. As a result of the victory, Rommel was made a field marshal, and Churchill was brought face to face with a crisis almost as intense as that generated by the events of January.*

The prime minister received the news of Tobruk in Washington. He had flown the Atlantic to press his case for a combined attack on North Africa, and it was in the president's White House study on the morning of 21 June that Churchill was told by Roosevelt that Tobruk had fallen. The prime minister at first refused to believe the news and sent Ismay out to call London for confirmation. Not only was Tobruk's capitulation true, Ismay reported, but the commander in chief (Mediterranean) was evacuating the Royal Navy's base at Alexandria four hundred miles to the east. Although Churchill wrote the following nine years after the event, there is little doubt that it represents his feelings at that moment:

> This was one of the heaviest blows I can recall during the war. Not only were its military effects grievous, but it had affected the reputation of the British armies. At Singapore 85,000 men had surrendered to inferior numbers of Japanese. Now in Tobruk a garrison of 25,000 (actually 33,000) seasoned soldiers had laid down their arms to perhaps one half their number. . . . I did not attempt to hide from the president the shock I had received. It was a bitter moment. Defeat is one thing; disgrace is another.[40]

In December, while the prime minister was residing in the White House, the Australians had virtually repudiated British strategic guidance. Now Tobruk, whose successful eight-month defense against Rommel had been one of the few clear-cut British military successes of the desert war, had collapsed in twenty-four hours.**

The failure at Tobruk, however, highlights Churchill's stubbornness and determination. Despite the embarrassment, he made progress toward persuading his allies of the inevitability of a North African venture if any offensive action were to be taken in 1942. Roosevelt and Marshall also agreed to strip newly issued tanks and self-propelled guns from U.S. Army formations and ship them to Egypt to reequip the Eighth Army, although it was more inferiority of method than inadequacy of equipment that had nearly destroyed

---

*The magnitude of his victory led Rommel, ever the tactical opportunist, to persuade his superiors to cancel the attack on Malta so that air support would be available to cover his pursuit of the beaten Eighth Army, the first step toward his ultimate defeat at El Alamein.

**It is illustrative of the complexity of the "British" war effort that the hardest part of Tobruk's 1941 siege was borne by Australians, while the bulk of the force that surrendered there in 1942 were South Africans and Indians.

that force. The prime minister, as he flew back to England, might have taken comfort in how successful he had been in playing a very weak hand. Undoubtedly, however, what preoccupied him was the knowledge that the debacle in the western desert had unleashed a political tempest at home that was rapidly coming to center on the machinery for the conduct of the war, machinery of which he as minister of defense was both architect and mainspring.

The explosion over the fall of Tobruk is in some ways curious. As far as Britain's power in the world was concerned, the fall of Singapore was a much more devastating blow. The Far East and the war there, however, were as remote to the average Briton as they were to the prime minister. On the other hand, Tobruk had become a symbol, its stubborn defense and subsequent relief the one British victory over the German army since the war began. Its sudden surrender caused frustration to boil over. A variety of angers and pressures suddenly coalesced. Nicolson noted that the news of Tobruk's fall came like a thunderbolt and added: "If there were any alternative to Winston, he might be severely shaken by this event."[41] Three days later in a by-election at Maldon, the government candidate polled only 22 percent of the highest turnout during any wartime by-election.*

Tobruk alone probably does not explain Maldon, but the conjunction of the two heightened the sense of political crisis that faced Churchill as his flying boat touched down in the Clyde on 27 June. A motion of no confidence in the "central direction of the war" had been tabled by Sir John Wardlaw-Milne, an influential Conservative back-bencher. For the first time since 1940, discontent had taken the form of a direct challenge to the prime minister personally. "This seemed to be a bad time," Churchill recalled. He went to bed in his train "and slept for four or five hours till we reached London. What a blessing is the gift of sleep!"[42] He had need of rest, for in the next few days while anxiously watching the progress of the battle in Egypt and continuing his battle with Marshall over the shape of the first Allied offensive, he faced a major parliamentary test.

---

*Part of the coalition agreement was an electoral truce in the constituencies. Maldon had been a Conservative seat. Therefore when it fell vacant the Labour party did not put up a candidate, which should have allowed the Conservatives to retain the seat. However, the truce could not prevent independents, minor parties, or even maverick members of the major parties from contesting a seat. It was an independent, Tom Driberg, standing with the backing of unhappy Conservatives and Labourites, as well as third party support, who won Maldon.

Wardlaw-Milne's opening speech attacked the combination of offices—prime minister and minister of defense—which Churchill had made clear was his condition for holding office. All observers agreed that he was making an impression when "he . . . suddenly suggests that the Duke of Gloucester [brother of King George VI] should be made Commander-in-Chief. A wave of panic embarrassment passes over the house," Nicolson recorded that evening. "For a full minute the buzz goes round, 'But the man must be an ass.' Milne pulls himself together . . . but his idiotic suggestion has shaken the validity of his position and his influence is shattered."[43] It did not help the cause of Churchill's opponents that the next speaker, Admiral of the Fleet Sir Roger Keyes, V.C., arose to complain, not that the prime minister had neglected professional opinion but rather that he had deferred excessively to it. The next day Churchill wound up the debate with a powerful and uncompromising speech, in which he once again declared his unwillingness to continue as prime minister if he were denied the powers of defense minister. Nicolson's observation that there was no real alternative to Churchill as prime minister is reflected in the vote at the end of the debate. Wardlaw-Milne's motion lost 476 to 25, but those 25 were the tip of an iceberg of restiveness. "The impression left is one of dissatisfaction and anxiety," Nicolson noted, "and I do not think it will end there."[44] He was not the only one who felt this way. The prime minister himself was acutely conscious of the need for a clear-cut military victory to allay discontent. "My diary for 1942 has the same backcloth to every scene: Winston's conviction that his life as Prime Minister could only be saved by a victory in the field," his doctor later wrote.[45]*

Such a victory was ironically taking shape even as Wardlaw-Milne called, in effect, for Churchill's resignation. Auchinleck had assumed direct command of the Eighth Army on 25 June and in a series of confused actions during the first days of July, fought along a line of defenses stretching south from the railway halt at El Alamein, brought Panzerarmee Afrika to a halt only forty miles from Alexandria.** As Rommel reluctantly went over to the defensive,

---

*The political crisis that followed Tobruk's fall differed from that in January and February in two ways. Churchill's powers as minister of defense were directly assailed but, at the same time, nothing threatened the unity of the coalition. Since no one had a credible alternative to Churchill, the crisis, if spectacular, was less dangerous.

**After Auchinleck's success in stabilizing the Crusader offensive the previous November, Churchill was convinced that Auchinleck should take command in the field while also remaining theater commander and had pressed him hard to do so before Rommel attacked.

events on another "front" also began to move favorably for the British. An American delegation led by Marshall arrived in London on 18 July. The American chief of staff intended to fight hard for Sledgehammer, but he also was bound by the president's instructions that American troops had to be in action against the Germans sometime in 1942. Therefore, the British had only to keep saying no to Sledgehammer to ensure that alliance strategy moved along the lines they preferred. Churchill played a leading role in this process, thereby reinforcing American beliefs that the war in the Mediterranean was his personal strategy, although the opposition to Sledgehammer was, in fact, solid throughout the British military and political hierarchy.

Once Sledgehammer had been set aside, the North African alternative became the first Allied offensive. The feeling that they had been outmaneuvered by the British, particularly strong in American service circles, and fueling a determination to bend alliance strategy back onto correct, or at least American, lines was the long-term price the British paid for being correct about Sledgehammer. With the main lines of alliance strategy now set for the balance of 1942, the prime minister bent his energies to ensuring that the next British battle was a successful one and to soothing his exigent Russian ally, certain to be furious at the postponement of the second front. Eager as always to be at the center of events, he decided that the best way to do both was to travel to Cairo and then on to Moscow.

Churchill already had made three lengthy trips abroad, apart from his repeated visits to France in May and June 1940. He would make eight more, but none perhaps was as fraught with high drama as "Operation Bracelet." Assembling in Cairo a variety of advisers—Wavell summoned from India, the South African Jan Smuts, as well as Brooke—the prime minister presided over a complete revamping of the British command structure in the Middle East. He was aware, finally, of the burden and distraction of the northern front to a theater commander in Cairo as well as grimly determined that the next encounter with Rommel would be a victorious one: "Rommel, Rommel, Rommel, Rommel, what else matters but beat-

---

The prime minister was correct about Auchinleck's abilities as an army commander but wrong about the feasibility of his wearing two such hats simultaneously. He acknowledged this, at least tacitly, in the new command arrangements made later, after Auchinleck was removed. The arrangement Churchill urged on Auchinleck had similarities to the impossible situation created later in Southeast Asia Command by the multiplicity of commands held by Lieutenant General Joseph W. Stilwell.

ing him!" he declaimed, striding up and down Lampson's air-conditioned bedroom, commandeered for his visit.[46] In view of the parliamentary realities that he could never allow himself to forget, it was less an hyperbole than a statement of a political imperative. Furthermore, with Torch only some two months away, a British victory was important not only for its reaction on French opinion before that operation began but also to maintain British prestige and leverage in an alliance whose center of gravity, once the American war effort began to be felt upon the battlefield, would inexorably tilt in the direction of the United States. The Cairo decisions had to be the correct decisions. The Middle East theater was divided, and a new command, eventually christened Persia and Iraq Command, was given responsibility for the northern front as well as for internal security over that vast area. Middle East Command in Cairo could now focus almost exclusively on the problem of the war in the desert. Auchinleck, upon whose removal from Middle East Command the prime minister quickly decided, was offered but refused the new command which eventually went to one of Churchill's favorite soldiers, General Sir Henry Maitland Wilson.* Auchinleck's removal set off a complicated reshuffle of commands. The new command structure was primarily Churchill's work, but the identity of the new commanders was decided by a more complicated process in which the hand of chance was as important as that of the prime minister.

Churchill and his personal staff and advisers quickly realized that a new atmosphere in Cairo and at Eighth Army was necessary. Auchinleck's great merits unfortunately did not include either good luck or shrewd judgment in the choice of his subordinates.** It was these factors as much as anything that determined Churchill to remove him. In private conversations Lieutenant General Bernard L. Montgomery's name had been mentioned several times to members of Churchill's staff. Brooke, under whom Montgomery had served, also thought he was the logical successor to Ritchie as army commander. Churchill's first choice, however, was Lieutenant

---

*In the long run Auchinleck's refusal was perhaps fortunate. After a period unemployed he became commander in chief (India) in July 1943. His work during the war and the subsequent transfer of power as the Indian Army's last and perhaps greatest British commander in chief was of immense value to both Britain and India.

**This was due to the fact that Auchinleck, as an Indian Army officer, was not familiar with the British army, from among whose officers most of his subordinates came. It did not help that Auchinleck was honorably, but perhaps excessively, loyal to these subordinates.

General W. H. E. "Strafer" Gott, a desert veteran who had served continuously since June 1940 and who nearly everyone else believed was too tired. Gott however was the sort of gallant warrior to whom the prime minister instantly warmed. Gott himself told Churchill he was tired, but also professed to be willing to take on the job. So it appeared settled; Auchinleck was to go, replaced by General Sir Harold Alexander, with Gott as Eighth Army commander. Then fate in the shape of a roving German fighter took a hand and Gott was killed when the transport in which he was returning from the front to Cairo was shot down. Montgomery was promptly summoned. Thus took shape the most famous British command team of the war. Churchill's personal contribution to this is worth analyzing, both because it was characteristic and because he was not again to be in a position to restructure British commands on such a sweeping scale.

The problem of the relationship between Cairo, the western desert, and the northern flank had been present since Germany attacked Russia. The prime minister, although constantly alert to the need to woo the Turks and the accompanying need to be ready to rush to their aid if they requested it, did not apparently fully grasp how this issue had distracted Auchinleck until he was actually on the spot in Cairo. Once seized of the problem, he quickly developed a solution that his unique authority allowed him to impose almost immediately. His instincts served him less well when it came to personnel. He was almost certainly unfair to some of Auchinleck's subordinates, and his romantic admiration for physical courage, but for a random aerial encounter, would have given the Eighth Army a tired, pessimistic commander. Throughout the process he had the advice, not always heeded, of Brooke, whose stature and influence were steadily growing. The relationship between prime minister and the chief of Imperial General Staff was a stormy one and perhaps neither ever fully sorted out his feelings about the other.* Brooke's professionalism and toughness, the success of the Alexander-Montgomery team, and the fact that coalition warfare would be controlled by Allied commands, such as the Anglo-American Torch headquarters even then taking shape in London,

---

*Brooke's published diaries are full of contradictory emotions about Churchill. At the end of the war he told an associate that hate predominated over affection in his attitude toward the prime minister. A tense, controlled, and emotional man, Brooke clearly felt everything with great intensity, and his observations, although not always either fair or accurate, serve to counterpoint the more admiring and uncritical portraits of Churchill painted by some of his staff. Like Montgomery, the prime minister, on a personal level, could be on occasion very unlovable.

meant that in the future the prime minister's freedom to make and remove theater commanders would be sharply reduced. In this, his climactic venture in this area, he made a sound, if belated, organizational decision and a choice of commanders in which luck aided him greatly.

It is a measure of Churchill's preoccupation with the desert war and the overwhelming significance of victory over Rommel that he took relatively little direct part in the handling of the explosion in India that took place while he was in Cairo. After the failure of the Cripps mission, tension built steadily, culminating in the government of India's decision to arrest the Congress party leadership early in August, an action that touched off the "Congress Revolt," the largest uprising against British rule since the 1857 mutiny in the Indian Army. Wavell and Linlithgow had to depend largely on that army and on Indian policemen to suppress the revolt since British troops were scarce in India. They did so successfully, supervised at a distance by Attlee and the war cabinet's India Committee. The prime minister approved, as he approved of Lampson's February coup. However, in August he had to attend to more immediately pressing issues. The command structure in Cairo sorted out, he was about to meet for the first time with Stalin, carrying the unwelcome news that in 1942 there would be no second front, as the Russians defined it. In fact, the Russians already must have been reasonably certain that their allies would not be landing in France that year. When Molotov had passed through London on his return journey from Washington, Churchill had warned him that, whatever the president might have said, a second front in western Europe was by no means a certainty for 1942. But the prime minister realized that the successive disappointments the Russians had suffered, not only no second front but also the suspension of the Arctic convoys following the loss of twenty-three of the thirty-four merchantmen in the July convoy,* might well, with German armies driving for the Volga and the Caucasus, lead them to become discouraged enough to try to negotiate a separate peace. Churchill remembered Brest-Litovsk and the subsequent near defeat of the western armies by an undistracted Germany. He therefore set himself the task of selling in person the idea that the only feasible

---

*This was PQ 17, one of the most spectacular convoy disasters of the war. The subsequent decision to suspend further convoys until the season of perpetual daylight in the Arctic had passed was inevitable. Then the naval demands of Torch intervened and only two more convoys made the journey to Murmansk in 1942, although material continued to flow in along the "Persian Corridor" route.

western offensive was also one calculated to damage Germany enough to give Russia some relief.

The first meeting between Stalin and Churchill was one of the strangest of the twentieth century, bringing together the Georgian revolutionary who had become the most terrible of czars and the scion of a ducal family intent on preserving as much as possible of Britain's Victorian heritage, both political and imperial. Moreover, Churchill had been one of the most prominent advocates of intervention in 1919–20. Seldom has politics made stranger bedfellows. Stalin pushed Churchill very hard over the issue of the second front, appearing to question the willingness of the British to fight the Germans, a taunt that brought from the prime minister a volcanic reaction and from Stalin the remark that, while he did not understand the words, he admired the spirit. Thereafter the meeting went more amiably, with Churchill explaining Torch with the aid of a hastily sketched crocodile, pointing out that the operation would not hit the beast's snout but its "soft underbelly." Since the Russians had no choice, Stalin gave little away when he accorded Torch his blessing. Neither Churchill nor Brooke found out much beyond generalities about Russian dispositions and plans. Nor was much politics discussed.*

What did the prime minister and premier make of one another? Churchill is alleged to have later remarked that he had met Genghis Khan with a telephone, but in fact his reactions were more complex. He hoped to establish some sort of personal relationship with Stalin that would ease the course of Anglo-Soviet relations, and perhaps by the time he left Moscow he believed that he had begun to establish such a connection. Throughout the war he would occasionally speak, after personal contact with Stalin, in terms of admiration or affection. A man for whom the acquisition and wielding of political power was an all-consuming passion, he doubtless appreciated a fellow practitioner. On the other hand, he seldom forgot the very different ends to which Stalin's power was put. On the last night of his visit, Churchill had a lengthy conversation with the premier, accompanied by a "variety of excellent wines." In this relaxed atmosphere the prime minister asked his host about the

---

*Stalin already had made plain to the British, even before the German armies stalled at the gates of Moscow, that the postwar borders of Poland would have to be changed to meet Russian desires. The British also had been pressed by the Russians to conclude a treaty covering postwar frontiers, a move they could not make without deeply angering the Americans. They had substituted instead a twenty-year Anglo-Russian treaty of friendship signed by Molotov in London in May 1942. Stalin may well have believed he had gotten all he could extract from the British in this area, at least temporarily.

collectivization of Soviet agriculture in the 1920s, a struggle whose human cost had been immense. Stalin's answer, Churchill recalled, left him with "the strong impression . . . at the moment of millions of men and women being blotted out or displaced forever." This chilling reminder of the reality behind the power of the short, stocky, soft-voiced, and momentarily affable man, with whom he was sharing such a pleasant evening, was quickly balanced by the reflection that "with the World War going on all around us it seemed vain to moralise aloud."[47] The single-minded concentration on the war, which increasingly put Churchill out of touch with the movement of domestic opinion in Britain, also kept him, at least intermittently, optimistic about Stalin. Not only did such optimism make the waging of coalition war easier, but it also offered the prospect of a new basis for Anglo-Soviet relations after the war when Russian power would be so greatly enhanced by German defeat.

As he flew back from Moscow, carrying with him the knowledge that the Russians planned an autumn counteroffensive, he confronted again the problem of the impact of continual defeat on his political position at home. During a stopover in Cairo, he received news of the disastrous failure of the Dieppe raid on 17 August and the decimation of the 2d Canadian Division, the latest calamity in what Churchill subsequently described as a series of defeats unparalleled in British history. All the prime minister had to offset it was the undoubted success he had enjoyed in maintaining imperial authority against the Congress party in India, telling the House of Commons in September: "I . . . feel entitled to report to the House that the situation in India at this moment gives no occasion for undue despondency and alarm."[48] But this was not the sort of triumph for which the country yearned, and the prime minister knew it:

> It is indeed remarkable that I was not in this bleak lull dismissed from power or confronted with demands for changes in my methods, which it was known I should never accept. I should then have vanished from the scene with a load of calamity on my shoulders, and the harvest, at last to be reaped, would have been ascribed to my belated disappearance.[49]

The lull became bleaker and longer when the new Eighth Army commander, in the aftermath of his success in stopping Rommel's last attack on the El Alamein line at the battle of Alam Halfa (31 August–September 5), announced that he would not be ready to attack until late October. The complexities of mounting Torch also led to postponement, in this case until early November. Nearly two months of waiting lay ahead.

If the desert battlefront was temporarily quiescent, the political scene was not. One of the dominion high commissioners in London circulated a letter, suggesting that effective power over the war effort be taken from the prime minister whose value, the writer implied, was primarily emotional. Lord Trenchard, the father figure of the RAF, wrote "that there should be one brain responsible for the purely military (in its widest sense) strategical conception of the war in Europe . . . one who believes in the power of the air. . . . There are many such." The prime minister replied: "Would it be too much to inquire who you have in mind? . . . I was not aware that the services were so rich in talent. . . ."[50] But the most serious challenge came, as in February, from Cripps. Nicolson, a devoted Churchillian, noted in his diary early in September that Cripps proposed to resign over the question of the conduct of the war, and late in the month recorded a conversation with the charismatic Aneurin Bevan, a left-wing Labour figure of some note: "He bewails the Government and says that we shall lose the war if Churchill stays. This is all very difficult to answer."[51] Cripps, however, had an answer. He proposed to revamp the central machinery of war direction in such a way as to leave Churchill with his title as minister of defense but with his actual power sharply reduced. While recognizing that "severance between him and me during this period of oppressive pause would have created a political crisis," the prime minister was prepared to face such a crisis rather than give in.[52] The breaking point seems to have arrived when Cripps submitted his resignation. However, he was persuaded by Attlee (among others, who had almost as much at stake as Churchill) to delay his departure until the impending offensives were launched. Cripps's agreement, like his offer to go to India in February, showed both disinterestedness and curious political naivete. It was also a quiet but essential victory for the prime minister.

Fifteen minutes before ten o'clock on the night of 23 October 1942, 882 field and medium guns opened up at El Alamein in a barrage such as the British army had not fired since 1918. Twelve days of bitter fighting followed, much like the opening barrage reminiscent of the grinding attrition battles of World War I but conducted with greater care by a survivor of the worst of that war's slaughters. The prime minister watched the progress of the battle, upon which his own fate hinged, in a mood of considerable anxiety. When Montgomery, five days into the battle, began pulling units out to regroup Churchill exploded at Brooke. But Montgomery's cautious tactics and the virtual paralysis of the Afrika Korps supply lines, a result of Malta's survival and Ultra, wore Rommel's forces down, and on 4 November the German-Italian front disintegrated. With it went any danger to Churchill's position for the remainder of the war.* Cripps's resignation letter, now promptly acted upon, made no impact. "Winston is received with prolonged cheers," the admiring Nicolson recorded of the scene in the House of Commons.[53] But if El Alamein made Churchill invulnerable for the rest of the war, it also marked the point where British influence in the anti-German coalition began to decline as a new set of problems began to come sharply into focus.

Four days after Montgomery broke Rommel's line, Torch was launched. The strategy that gave birth to the operation was mostly British, and the advocacy that won American acquiescence largely Churchill's. Most of the assets that made it possible were also British, but the command structure for the operation was headed by an American, Dwight D. Eisenhower, and the American troops coming ashore in Morocco and Algeria were the vanguard of an army of 8 million being raised by a nation whose industrial mobilization had yet to reach its maximum. Henceforth, Roosevelt and his generals would play the preponderant role in shaping how the alliance waged its war, even if for a while longer they were confined in grooves cut by the British. Ten days after Torch came the opening of the Russian winter offensive, of which Stalin had told Churchill in August. El Alamein had the greatest emotional significance for the British and their leader, but Stalingrad and Torch mark the beginnings of the movement of the two superpowers from their peripheral position to their confrontation in the heart of Europe.

Brooding as he waited for the battle that one of his closest associates, Brendan Bracken, admitted meant victory or dismissal for the prime minister, Churchill sensed the looming shape of events. Writing to Eden about a Foreign Office paper on the postwar period only forty-eight hours before Montgomery's guns opened up, he reiterated his theme that "the war has prior claim on your attention and mine." But he also offered some views on the postwar world: "Of course we shall have to work with the Americans in many ways, and in the greatest ways," although he expressed concern

*Alexander signaled Churchill "ring out the bells" on 6 November. Suddenly as cautious as Montgomery and his generals following up the retreating Afrika Korps, the prime minister decided to wait until Torch was successfully launched before celebrating the first unequivocal British victory of the war over the German army.

about an American attempt "to liquidate the British overseas Empire." He went on to say that "I must admit . . . that my thoughts rest primarily, in Europe—the revival of the glory of Europe, the parent continent of the modern nations and of civilisation. It would be a measureless disaster if Russian barbarism overlaid the culture and independence of the ancient states of Europe."[54] At a luncheon party at Number 10 a few days after El Alamein, the prime minister told his guests that after Germany was beaten it would take two more years to beat Japan, and he intended to fling all available British resources into that struggle because it would constitute a continuing bond with the United States during the difficult postwar settlement of Europe. His European concerns did not drive away his fears for the future of Britain's world power. In the full tide of jubilation after El Alamein, he made it clear, in the words that stand at the head of this chapter, that the victory he sought would be an imperial victory.

Even as he spoke the words, however, the ground was shifting under his feet. On the evening that Montgomery attacked, Nicolson dined with Harold Macmillan, who predicted that the principal concern of the British public would be security and employment and they would judge parties accordingly: "If the present system can give [it to] them . . . they will support it; but if we fail to do so, we shall be swept away, politely but firmly."[55] Cripps's last official act as lord privy seal, leader of the House, and war cabinet member was to introduce a report on postwar social services that spoke directly to the concerns Macmillan identified. The Beveridge report, named for the economist and civil servant who drafted it, was a domestic counterpart to El Alamein, a turning point in the war. Henceforth, the prime minister, his strategic, European, and imperial concerns uppermost, would gradually lose a sense of the mood of the country, a sense he had expressed so brilliantly in 1940.

The Beveridge report and its handling by Churchill indicates how very perceptive Macmillan was about the future. An outgrowth of studies on postwar social planning long germinating within the government machine, it was immediately seized upon as the blueprint for a better postwar world. Churchill, deeply preoccupied with the war, mishandled the issue. The report was published in November 1942, but over two months passed before the government offered any commentary of its own. When the report was finally debated in the House of Commons the government spokesmen, Sir John Anderson, a glacial administrator, and Sir Kingsley Wood, the most prominent surviving Chamberlainite, were seemingly calculated to chill the hearts of those who thought of "Beveridge" as the embodiment of their hopes for the future. The government line was equally disappointing: the report was accepted "in principle" and as a basis for further planning studies, but no commitment was made that any of it would be enacted into law.

The debate on the Beveridge report produced considerable tension between the Labour back-benchers in the House and Churchill's Labour ministers, many of whom, like Bevin, had accepted the prime minister's argument that the war had priority. Churchill himself took no part in the debate. Only after it was over and the damage done did he broadcast to the nation on 21 March on the subject of planning for the postwar period. He never mentioned the Beveridge report and spoke in generalities about the need to avert unemployment and extend the field of government intervention. He added, however, that it was still necessary to concentrate upon winning the war. The prime minister's handling of the Beveridge report was the point at which most Labourites and many progressive Tories accepted that Churchill, immovable and irreplaceable until hostilities ended, would make no contribution to shaping the postwar world toward which British minds increasingly turned.

Churchill's treatment of the Beveridge report, precisely because it was a quiet but immensely important turning point on the British home front, requires some analysis. The prime minister was busy with the political, diplomatic, and strategic aftermath of Torch and from 12 January to 7 February was out of the country. Within a few days of his return, on the eve of the House debate on the Beveridge report, he came down with pneumonia.* But preoccupation and illness are not the full explanation. Churchill had, in fact, a good record on social reform, going back to his days as a minister under Asquith (1908 to 1911). Even if his views on social reform never advanced much beyond those of Edwardian liberalism, he was neither a reactionary nor a devotee of right-wing Conservative attitudes on domestic issues, and when he remarked, as he did in his March broadcast, that there was no finer investment

---

*The question of the prime minister's health in the second half of the war is an interesting and controversial subject, sparked by the publication of Lord Moran's diaries. That period was certainly a time of intermittent ill health for the prime minister. His brush with pneumonia in February 1943 was followed at the end of the year by a much more serious bout which, but for antibiotics, might well have been fatal. There is no question that by 1944 Churchill at seventy was a tired man, but there is no way to link this conclusively with any decisions he made and much to show that those decisions conformed to patterns observable earlier in the war, indeed earlier in his career. This is not to brush aside the connection between health, the aging process, and decision making. It is only to say that in Churchill's case the links have yet to be firmly made for the war years.

for a society than putting milk in its babies, he spoke from heartfelt conviction.

Churchill, however, was apprehensive about the dissolvent effect on both national unity and his coalition, its political embodiment, of an open debate over postwar social policy and so strove to avert one. He also was concerned that commitments for expensive social services would greatly exceed what an economically weakened postwar Britain would be able to afford, leading the public to feel cheated by false expectations. Cherwell reinforced his doubts by advising him that American financial aid, so necessary to British reconstruction, might be endangered if the Americans thought they were being asked to fund British social services. However, the prime minister would have done well to have heeded his deputy, Attlee, who warned him that the war itself was making irreversible changes in British society and that the consequences had to be faced before the war ended.

The one major exception to Churchill's decision to defer social legislation to war's end was the 1944 Education Act, usually called the Butler Act after R. A. Butler, a very bright junior Chamberlainite who had come to rest as president of the Board of Education. Like the Beveridge report, the act was the result of a long process of gestation within the bureaucracy. The prime minister's interest in it, Butler recalled, was "slight, intermittent and decidedly idiosyncratic."[56] The first two adjectives are fair enough; the third rather misleading. Churchill knew that education raised divisive sectarian issues, and divisiveness of any kind was what he did not want. He expressed this forcefully to Butler at an early stage:

> It would be a great mistake to raise the 1902 controversy during the war, and I certainly cannot contemplate a new Education Bill.* I think it would also be a great mistake to stir up the public schools question at the present time. No one can possibly tell what the financial and economic position of the country will be when the war is over. . . . We cannot have party politics in wartime.[57]

Nevertheless, Churchill eventually accepted Butler's proposals when they finally emerged in 1944 and during their passage into law intervened only once, but with dramatic effect, to reverse a relatively

---

*The 1902 Education Act, the work of a Conservative government, aroused deep anger because it was deemed too favorable to the Church of England schools and was considered one of the principal contributory factors in the 1905 Conservative electoral debacle. The episode made a strong impression on Churchill, then a newly elected Tory member for a constituency with a sizable bloc of non-Anglican Conservative voters.

minor government defeat on an amendment. Churchill did this less from any concern with the issue involved than to assert his coalition's solidarity and mastery of the House.

The prime minister's insistence that there could be no party politics in wartime was plausible in the grim circumstances of 1940–41. It became increasingly unrealistic after the tide turned in the autumn of 1942 and particularly after the enthusiasm that focused on Cripps and the publication of the Beveridge report had made it impossible, as Attlee clearly saw, to evade postwar issues. Splendid as he had been in the darkest days of the war, the sense that Churchill was becoming irrelevant to the deep concerns many Britons felt about what would happen afterward was obvious to many observers as the war entered its final stages. Nicolson noted in his diary early in 1944 a friend's comments on the mood in the army: "He says that most of the men who come back from the front state openly that once Germany is beaten, they will refuse to do any more. They are not revolutionary but believe that they have been fighting for a better Britain and identify that with the Beveridge Report."[58] One week later Nicolson recorded another indicator of the mood in the services:

> In the station lavatory at Blackheath last week I found scrawled up, 'Winston Churchill is a bastard.' I pointed it out to the Wing Commander who was with me. 'Yes,' he said, 'the tide has turned. We find it everywhere.' 'But how foul,' I said. 'How Bloody foul.' 'Well, you see, if I may say so, the men hate politicians.'[59]

With the opinion polls consistently showing Churchill's approval rating at 85 percent or higher from El Alamein to war's end, such feelings are hard to reconcile except upon the assumption that public opinion remained committed to Churchill only for the duration of the war, a fact that the prime minister did not fully grasp prior to the shock administered by the electorate in 1945.

If the tide was quietly turning against Churchill on the home front, he was more than holding his own in defense of Britain's imperial interests, as he conceived them, even if shifting moods at home and Britain's weakened postwar situation eventually rendered these successes illusory. Once again India illustrates both the prime minister's domination of policy and the weakness of his approach. The suppression of the August 1942 uprising and the imprisonment of most of the Congress leadership seemed to have left the initiative, at least for the duration of the war, in British hands. Churchill had always claimed that Congress was unrepresentative, a mask for the

"Hindu priesthood machine" which he regarded with ill-concealed distaste. But when events put the Congress party temporarily out of action, he had no Indian policy of his own beyond the negative aim of keeping things quiet on the subcontinent. The 1935 act remained the basis of British policy, and Churchill's government had twice affirmed that it would be open to renegotiation after the war. In fact, it is interesting to note how mild the aftermath of the August 1942 revolt really was. In 1916 a much less threatening upheaval in Dublin had resulted in the rapid execution, after summary courts martial, of all the surviving leaders. In 1942 a far more dangerous rebellion simply led to the internment of Gandhi, Nehru, and the rest of the Congress high command, in Gandhi's case in the home of one of his wealthy supporters. For all his imperial enthusiasm, Churchill never suggested that any of the Congress leaders be tried for treason. American and Labour party opinion ruled out any such course.* Many years later, looking back at the dissolution of the empire, Nicolson wrote: "The moment one is not prepared to shoot people for disobedience, one simply has to let them have their independence."[60] The British had shot people for disobedience in 1942, but in doing so they had drawn on the last reserves of loyalty available to the raj.** The survival of the Congress party indicated that the British would not—indeed, could no longer—take repression to its logical conclusion and that the assertion of imperial authority in August 1942 was the last act in a long-running drama.

The prime minister did not accept this reasoning. He clung to the belief that the situation could be frozen for the remainder of the war and then, reinvigorated by victory, Britain could deal with Indian nationalism from a position of strength. But he never gave any indication of how he expected to do so, ignoring, as he did in domestic policy, the fact that unless preparations were made beforehand there would be no way to capitalize on victory, no matter how complete. It is more than doubtful that Churchill could have reversed a generation of British policy, even if he had tried, but his failure to articulate any policy of his own, together with his refusal to sanction any revival of discussions with Indian nationalism, merely left a vacuum in India for the rest of the war. "There could hardly be a less suitable time for raising again the political agitation

---

*Gandhi was eventually released on grounds of ill health in 1944, to the accompaniment of much grumbling by the prime minister.

.**It is difficult to establish exactly what the casualty figures were, but Churchill's summation that the revolt "fizzled out in a few months with hardly any loss of life" is clearly an example of excessive understatement. *HF*, 509.

on its old and well known lines," he wrote in an October 1943 paper for the war cabinet. "We shall certainly not be in a worse position to deal with the constitutional position in India after we have beaten Germany and Japan, and have revived the prestige of our arms in Burma and Malaya . . . victory is the best foundation for great constitutional departures."[61]

When Lord Linlithgow stepped down in 1943, the prime minister replaced him with Wavell. The new viceroy confided to his journal that Churchill had chosen him to keep India quiet during the war. The prime minister's directive to Wavell put it in a more orotund fashion. After making a bow to Indian independence as "our inflexible goal," it went on to tell the new viceroy, "you will beware above all things lest the achievement of victory and the ending of the miseries of war should be retarded by undue concentration on political issues while the enemy is at the gate."[62] It was an imperial version of his injunction to Butler—no politics in wartime—and was no more attainable in India than at home. Wavell quickly realized this but ran into a stone wall in London and filled his private journal with complaints about the refusal even to attend to, much less sympathetically consider, his communications. Eventually, by traveling to London in the spring of 1945, he won grudging permission from the prime minister to open discussions with Indian political leaders. The resulting Simla Conference, the last British political initiative with any possibility of maintaining a united India, met in July and quickly failed. By that time, Churchill was no longer prime minister and his former Labour colleagues had to find a new basis for Indian policy.

Churchill's wartime record over India, while predictable in terms of his past views and actions, is nevertheless a melancholy one. He had only negatives to offer. Perhaps in his heart he sensed that the raj was in a terminal state and sought only to postpone the inevitable. In any case, the vacuum that the prime minister created in India had the side effect of strengthening the Muslim League and thus the forces that made for partition, thereby undoing the unified subcontinent that had been one of imperial Britain's greatest achievements.

Churchill's Indian policy did show, however, his ability to impose his views. In other areas of imperial policy that same capacity was also manifest, although more intermittently. The opening of the British government's records has made plain just how much was brought to bear upon Britain's imperial position by the United States. The height of the tension came in 1942 when the British collapse in Southeast Asia seemed to confirm what Americans had always believed about imperialism, especially the British variety. Churchill had resisted this pressure, especially over India, with vehemence, and his ringing public declaration of imperial resolve after El Alamein was aimed directly at his American allies. Although the confrontation over imperial issues was never again as intense as in 1942, it remained one of the important themes in the alliance relationship. Churchill brushed aside Roosevelt's suggestion that the British hand Hong Kong back to China (privately, he was always scornful of what seemed to him the perversely high regard in which many Americans held Chiang Kai-shek's regime). He resisted suggestions that European colonial territories should become trusteeships under the auspices of the new United Nations organization. In British discussions the prime minister made no secret of his feeling that much American opinion on colonial issues was naive sentimentalism and some of it hypocritical, since the United States wanted special arrangements for the Pacific islands it proposed to take from Japan. In March 1945, Churchill gave the American ambassador to China a dressing down, in which he reprised a theme from which he had never budged as prime minister or during his entire political life. "I took him up with violence about Hong Kong," Churchill recorded, "and said that never would we yield an inch of the territory that was under the British flag."[63]

In the short term Churchill's position was vindicated, and the British returned to all the territory from which they had been expelled by the Japanese. But despite the prime minister, fundamental shifts were taking place in attitudes even within the Colonial Office where ideas of trusteeship for dependent peoples, economic development, and social justice were replacing the older, more limited view of the ends of colonial policy, a view most aptly summarized by one of its bitterest critics: "To do justice and keep the peace."* Even more important was the shifting mood among the electorate, so acutely diagnosed by Macmillan on the eve of Torch. Domestic reconstruction meant much more than empire to the public that was sustaining the war effort. A. J. P. Taylor recently observed that the British public did not relinquish its empire by accident but simply ceased to believe in it.[64] Nicolson noted the spreading fear of just such a development in the spring of 1944: "The upper classes fear that all this sacrifice and suffering will only mean that the proletariat will deprive them of all their comforts and influence,

---

*E. M. Forster in his *A Passage to India* puts the words into the mouth of one of his less sympathetic characters. Yet there is no doubt that Forster, who had spent some time in India, accurately caught in that phrase the guiding spirit of Victorian imperial administration, to which one would only have to add "and to collect the taxes that pay for the whole process."

and then proceed to render this country and Empire a third-class State."[65] The prime minister, concentrating his energies on the war, failed to notice this change in public attitudes. In the autumn of 1940 one of his most consistent critics, the Welsh radical Bevan, wrote of him that his ear was attuned to the bugle of history but deaf to the clamor of contemporary life. It was, however, that din which was drowning the imperial trumpets to which Churchill still responded so vigorously.

It is ironic that, in the one area of imperial policy where Churchill looked forward rather than backward, his initiative was frustrated, although only after a four-year struggle. For nearly a quarter century he had been one of Britain's "gentile Zionists," a supporter of the dream of the Jewish National Home in Palestine. He had been colonial secretary when the British pledge to Zionism—the 1917 Balfour Declaration—had been transformed into a concrete administrative act, the Palestine Mandate, with the promise of an eventual national home written into its title deeds. Churchill always held himself to be as bound by that pledge as by his commitment to maintain British imperial grandeur. To him the Jewish National Home was compatible with a British imperial presence, since the former always would be dependent on some great power supporter and the British empire was the logical candidate for that role. His long-time contacts with a generation of Anglophile Zionist leaders like Chaim Weizmann hid from him the growth of very different sentiments among the Jews actually living in Palestine. His pledge to Zionism had placed him in the position of leading the parliamentary opposition to the Chamberlain government when it set out to placate Arab nationalism in the later 1930s. When he returned to office in 1939, he rapidly made it plain that he no more considered himself bound by the Chamberlain White Paper policy than he did by Baldwin's assessment of the future of the raj.

Churchill's dissent from official policy, which was backed not only by the bulk of his own party and the powerful bureaucracies of the Foreign and Colonial offices but also by much military opinion, took several forms. He consistently resisted what he regarded as pro-Arab biases among British officialdom and threw his weight on the side of leniency in interpreting the 1939 White Paper rules governing Jewish immigration into Palestine.* From the moment he became prime minister, he conducted a long, stubborn fight with

*On those occasions when his attention was drawn to the problem of Jewish refugees from Nazi Europe trying to reach Palestine, the basic humanity and decency with which Churchill reacted contrasts sharply with the callous lack of imagination shown by most British officials. It is also very different from some of his own rather obtuse commentary on India.

the War Office over a Jewish fighting contingent for the Allied war effort. His determination finally bore fruit as a Jewish brigade group with the Eighth Army in Italy in the autumn of 1944. But the main thrust of the prime minister's efforts where Palestine was concerned was to reverse the tendency of official policy since the mid-1930s and bring into existence a Jewish state on the territory of the mandate.

One of Churchill's first actions in the field of colonial policy during the fraught summer of 1940 was to prevent the Foreign and Colonial offices from settling the future of Palestine by taking the first, and under the circumstances irrevocable, step toward creating an Arab-controlled state there.* Matters remained in uneasy balance until after El Alamein when the debate over future policy revived. Churchill preferred a partition of Palestine that would produce at least a small Jewish state. In July 1943, when the war cabinet established a cabinet-level committee to study the entire issue, Churchill set the terms of reference and saw that the Foreign Office representatives on the committee were balanced by fellow gentile Zionists—Sir Archibald Sinclair and Amery. The committee duly reported in favor of partition. The Foreign Office, however, was not so easily beaten. Eden was Churchill's designated heir and on this issue closer to the mainstream of party opinion than the prime minister. He was as well head of one of Whitehall's most powerful ministries. In January 1944 the Foreign Office won a delay in the final adoption of the committee's report as official policy and managed to protract the delay until the autumn of 1944. By that time a lot had happened.

The prime minister was a much more tired man in the war's last winter, and problems crowded upon him from every quarter, many of higher urgency. He also had lost his zest for the fight over Palestine. The increasing radicalization of Jewish opinion there, fueled by knowledge of what was happening to European Jewry, as well as by the realization that the war could not now go against the Allies, had produced an upsurge of Jewish terrorism. One such terrorist group assassinated the war cabinet's resident minister in Cairo, Lord Moyne, on 6 November 1944. Moyne, a supporter of the White Paper policy, had spoken in callous terms against Jewish immigration, terms that to Zionist ears were anti-Semitic. But the assassins killed more than they knew. As Walter Edward Guinness, Moyne had long been a close friend of both the prime minister and

*The quid pro quo was Churchill's acceptance of the 1939 immigration policy, which he thereafter occasionally would insist on bending.

his wife. The struggle against the main currents of party and official opinion suddenly became too much. Churchill complained bitterly to Weizmann that gangster tactics were killing the noble dream he had always supported. Unwittingly aided by its bitterest foes, the Foreign Office won its fight to keep the issue open. It was still open when Churchill left office. In view of subsequent history, it is intriguing, if futile, to speculate on the consequences if Churchill had successfully imposed his policy on Palestine.

When he wrote in 1950–51 about the post-El Alamein years, Churchill did not discuss domestic issues, Palestine, or even India but almost exclusively alliance politics and strategy as well as the first stages of the western confrontation with Russia which had become the dominant international issue by that time.* Where he led, subsequent historical commentary followed. Anglo-American arguments over strategy, together with the question of the degree to which Churchill was more perceptive than Roosevelt about the menace of Russian expansionism, are the highlights in most portraits of the prime minister from 1943 to 1945. Yet even here the European emphasis in *Closing the Ring* and *Triumph and Tragedy*, where only four of the seventy-three chapters deal with the war against Japan, gives a misleading impression. What happened in the Far East concerned the prime minister greatly, for it affected the future of British world power.

The loss of Burma to the Japanese cut the last overland link between China and its allies. Americans based in northeastern India quickly improvised an airlift over the Himalayas. The cargo planes struggling over the mountains could not, however, carry enough to permit the full development of the military potential American planners believed China to have. A restoration of land communication with China was necessary, and the only way to bring this about was to reconquer Burma. Thus Burma became the pivot of Anglo-American strategic arguments in the eastern theater of war because for the prime minister the reconquest of Burma was largely irrelevant. India's eastern frontier once secured, he dreamed of sweeping amphibious operations retaking Rangoon, moving on to northern Sumatra, and finally reclaiming Singapore. Churchill realized full well that how Britain contributed to the defeat of Japan would determine the degree to which the empire's lost prestige would be restored, and in this case he encountered no

---

*In the collections of personal minutes that are appended to each volume of his memoirs, some trace of Churchill's domestic and imperial concerns do appear but without the context that alone would give them much significance.

dissent from the Foreign Office. However, Britain lacked the resources to mount the sort of campaigns the prime minister had in mind, at least until after the defeat of Germany. The Americans, who had the resources, were certainly not going to make them available so that the British could pursue a strategy of no interest to the United States. Doing nothing in the Asian theater until after the end of the war in Europe was not an option either as, given American enthusiasm for bringing large-scale aid to China, obstruction by the British in Asia would carry a high cost elsewhere. Therefore, the British were pinned to Burma.

At Casablanca early in 1943 the British showed their willingness to accommodate American views by agreeing to a program of operations in Burma.* Events in the theater, however, were raising the question of whether the British could even hold their own there, much less go over to the offensive. The Indian Army, having expanded too rapidly to meet the demands of the Middle East and trained exclusively for that theater, was only at the beginning of a painful process of retraining for a new war when it was launched into a premature offensive aimed at securing air bases along Burma's Arakan coast to cover a later attack on Rangoon. Badly managed, the offensive collapsed in a rout when the Japanese counterattacked in February. The debacle was as bad as anything that had happened in Malaya or Burma the previous year, and only its small scale prevented it from being as widely noticed. At the same time a raid into Burma, led by a highly eccentric protégé of Wavell's, Orde Wingate, produced the first success the British had enjoyed against the Japanese. Publicity machines in London and Delhi seized upon Wingate's "Chindits" with avidity, and Churchill's imagination was caught by Wingate himself. Eager to use, but fundamentally distrustful of, the Indian Army, the prime minister began to think that the Chindit leader might be the man to cut through the "welter of lassitude and inefficiency" in India. At the Trident Conference held in Washington in May, the British had recommitted themselves to a campaign to clear north Burma so that American engineers could drive a road through to China. Perhaps Wingate could do what the Indian Army's generals could not and finally make a success of operations in a theater where success was becoming a necessity of alliance politics.

---

*One of the motivations for Churchill's ready assent to the best remembered part of the Casablanca Conference decisions—Roosevelt's controversial "unconditional surrender" declaration—was the alleviation of American suspicion that the British meant to allow the United States to carry the burden of the war against Japan once Germany was beaten.

This line of thinking produced startling results. At the Quadrant Conference held in Quebec in August 1943, the command structure for the British war effort against Japan was rearranged. Southeast Asia Command (SEAC) was created, severing operational control from the Indian Army's now suspect headquarters in Delhi. Churchill named Lord Louis Mountbatten, chief of Combined Operations and cousin of the king, a substantive captain but acting vice-admiral, air marshal, and lieutenant general as SEAC's commander.* Mountbatten's deputy would be the acidulous Lieutenant General Joseph W. Stilwell, who also acted as Chiang's chief of staff and commander of the American CBI (China-Burma-India) theater. This organizational nightmare reflected the highly specific American needs in the area of the new command and the determination to keep control of the means to attain them. The most important of these were the transport aircraft that Wingate's raid had shown to be the key to campaigning in Burma. Wingate himself, produced at Quebec by Churchill as an earnest of British intentions to make good in Burma, impressed the U.S. chiefs of staff enough to acquire both their backing for much-expanded Chindit operations to facilitate clearing north Burma in 1943–44 and a very large increase in American air strength in SEAC to support them.

By a series of ironic twists, the prime minister and his chiefs of staff were now committed to the sort of campaign in north Burma that they had always hoped to avoid. The Japanese gave the Burma kaleidoscope a new shake when, stung by Wingate's earlier raid and hoping to preempt further British attacks, they launched a major offensive (February–March 1944) against British positions in the hilly Burma-India frontier region simultaneously with the inception of Wingate's massive Chindit II operation. Wingate perished in an air crash early in the ensuing campaign. The use, or misuse, of the Chindits thereafter is still bitterly controversial, as is their overall contribution to the defeat of the Japanese in Burma. In three months of bitter fighting the Japanese Fifteenth Army was smashed by the resuscitated Indian Army commanded by the best British general of the war, Sir William Slim. Sustained at critical moments by air supply, based largely on American transport aircraft, Slim had turned the tide in Burma. Pressing ahead through the wreckage of the retreating Japanese army, Slim, campaigning right through the monsoon, laid the foundation for his remarkable reconquest of Burma the following year.

---

*Brooke chose an orthodox soldier, Lieutenant General Sir Henry Pownall, as SEAC chief of staff, with the mission of keeping the charismatic Mountbatten "on the rails."

Churchill's reaction, both at the time and later, is interesting. He supported Mountbatten's pleas for the use of American aircraft, as well as his action in diverting some to Slim's use without permission, but his attention was really elsewhere, and his account of the fighting in his memoirs is rather detached. Events in the Mediterranean and the preparations for Overlord are part of the explanation, but such time and attention as he had to spare for the war in the east were, in fact, concentrated not on the campaign in Burma he had never wanted to fight but on an amphibious sweep across the Indian Ocean to redeem Singapore and the empire's prestige.*

Throughout the late winter, spring, and early summer of 1944, while Slim broke the Japanese Fifteenth Army, Rome fell, and Overlord was successfully launched, the prime minister engaged in a prolonged and bitter contest with the British chiefs of staff over the shape of Britain's contribution to the defeat of Japan. Churchill described this quarrel in his memoirs as the only major disagreement he ever had with the chiefs of staff, a verdict the official history of British strategy later endorsed. The apparent exaggeration of both these claims vanishes when several points are remembered. However furious the clashes in 1941–42 they took place within a general British consensus on strategy, but the arguments over Britain's role in the war against Japan revealed that where the war in the east was concerned no consensus existed. On the one hand, Churchill's personal design, christened "Culverin," was an amphibious operation aimed at the northern tip of Sumatra as the first stop on the road back to Singapore. The chiefs of staff, on the other hand, wanted to build up a major force based on Australia to operate in the Southwest Pacific on the flank of the twin American thrusts, to be directed by Admiral Chester Nimitz and General Douglas MacArthur. Churchill met this head on in a major paper circulated to the Defense Committee of the war cabinet on 3 March 1944:

> A decision to act as a subsidiary force under the Americans in the Pacific raises difficult political questions about the future of our Malayan possessions. If the Japanese should withdraw from them or make peace as the result of the main American thrust, the United States Government would, after the victory,

---

*Ironically, Burma was declining in importance in American eyes at precisely the moment when its reconquest finally became feasible. The acceleration of the advance across the Pacific in 1944 and greater realism about Chiang's regime downgraded the importance of China to American planners. In the last stages of Slim's campaign in the spring of 1945, Burma had come to seem so irrelevant that American transport planes were nearly pulled out, a momentum-wrecking event averted only by a personal appeal from Churchill to General Marshall.

feel greatly strengthened in its view that all possessions in the East India Archipelago should be placed under some international body upon which the United States would exercise a decisive control. They would feel with conviction: 'We won the victory and liberated these places and we must have the dominating say in their future and derive full profit from their produce, especially oil.'[66]

At the time, however, all the tensions between Britain and America over the future of British power failed to move the chiefs of staff, and the argument, conducted by tired men, dragged on, becoming more rancorous and personal and filling the Whitehall air by midsummer with threats of resignation. Eden noted in his diary on 6 July that it was "a really ghastly Defence Committee nominally on Far Eastern strategy," and he characterized the discussion as "meaningless when it was not explosive."[67] But gradually accumulating facts began to impose a solution. By themselves the British lacked the resources to mount Culverin. As for the chiefs' of staff preferred strategy, it became apparent that the resources to build up a huge base area in Australia were not available, and the Australians in any case unenthusiastic. Moreover, the Americans neither needed nor wanted a major British contribution to "their" war. Indeed, the U.S. Navy wanted no British contribution at all, a point made very plain by Admiral Ernest King, chief of Naval Operations.

By the time the Octagon Conference met in Quebec in September 1944, the prime minister and the chiefs of staff had hammered out a compromise, embodied in a note Churchill wrote before the first plenary session:

> . . . our policy should be to give naval assistance on the largest scale to the main American operations, but to keep our own thrust for Rangoon as a preliminary operation, or one of the preliminary operations, to a major attack upon Singapore. Here is the supreme British objective in the whole of the Indian and Far Eastern theatres. It is the only prize that will restore British prestige in this region.[68]

Lacking the ability to develop either of their competing strategies, Churchill and the chiefs of staff had fallen back on the campaign of Slim's Fourteenth Army, which neither had ever really wanted, as the empire's major offensive against Japan. Although the British had scaled down their prospective role in the Pacific, they had a sharp fight ahead of them in order to be allowed to make even a token contribution. It was a fight Churchill was determined to win, for he was alarmed about the future of Britain's lost eastern possessions if the victory over Japan were perceived as an exclusively American affair. He expressed it somewhat differently in his opening remarks at the first plenary meeting on 13 September:

> For the sake of good relations, on which so much depended in the future, it was of vital importance that the British should be given their fair share in the main operations against Japan. The United States had given us the most handsome assistance in the fight against Germany. It was only to be expected that the British Empire in return should wish to give the United States all the help in their power toward defeating Japan.[69]

The prime minister was making the best of a weak hand, and Roosevelt was willing to concede at least a symbolic British presence in the Pacific by overruling a grumbling King.

The last months of the war against Japan were, for Churchill, an anticlimax, almost an irrelevance. Slim's brilliant campaign resulted in the reconquest of Burma in the spring of 1945, by which time Admiral Sir Bruce Fraser's British Pacific fleet was doing valuable, but scarcely crucial, work as part of the vast American armada closing in on Japan.* The British were told about, and assented to, American plans to use the atomic bomb, but they were frozen out of planning for the invasion and occupation of the Japanese home islands. Churchill's long-awaited return to Malaya took place as an unopposed landing a week after the Japanese surrendered on the quarterdeck of an American battleship in Tokyo Bay. By that time, Churchill was out of office. A few years later in his memoirs he was to adopt a remote, detached tone in his sparse commentary on the British war with Japan, whose conclusion and aftermath had so belied his hopes. Yet it remains true that it is in the strategy he outlined for that war and fought so hard to impose that the clearest correlation can be observed between Churchill's war aims and strategic ideas. To him the entire war effort in the east only made sense if it led to a restoration of British prestige and power. In contrast, the policy advocated by the chiefs of staff, that of playing auxiliary to the Americans, was not one with any discernible political end. Churchill's aim was unattainable; there was no rebirth awaiting the raj. He had never accepted that, however, and given his premises, his strategy came closer to fulfilling

---

*Fraser's presence, however, did mean that there were British forces on the spot to reoccupy Hong Kong rapidly when Japan surrendered, which may have saved the crown colony for Britain.

the Clausewitzian precept than did that of his opponents. By contrast to the Far East, the links between policy and strategy are more complex in the Mediterranean, the theater usually associated with the prime minister as strategist.

Of the courses of action outlined to the prime minister by the chiefs of staff in May 1940, only the Mediterranean offered the British room for maneuver by 1943. The bombing offensive, resuscitated by new technology and Harris's determined leadership, and reinforced by American strategic bombers, had developed a momentum of its own, one that would carry it through to the end of the war. Churchill long ago had moderated his expectations where Bomber Command was concerned, but the pulverization of Germany's cities still had its attractions and would continue to do so until the war's end. SOE also had declined in the significance the prime minister ascribed to it. In 1940, seen as a potential "Fourth Arm," its secret armies of patriots still figured importantly as late as the Arcadia Conference, at least in the prime minister's imagination. Thereafter, SOE's activities were increasingly seen as ancillary to the more orthodox military operations against Germany now becoming possible with American entry into the war. In fact, SOE's success, especially in the Balkans, had begun to yield considerable military dividends as well as to involve political complications that led to repeated interventions by Churchill, accompanied by sharp outbursts of anger, often unjustified, at SOE. Like Bomber Command, SOE would enjoy the prime minister's support until war's end, but like Harris's fiefdom, SOE was no longer central to his vision of how the conflict would be brought to a victorious conclusion.

The Mediterranean theater was a different matter. Prior to El Alamein and Torch, the British had conducted their only major campaign in that theater because first circumstance, then survival, compelled them to do so. After the Allied success at both ends of the inland sea in November 1942, it became possible to look ahead, especially to the relationship between the war in the Mediterranean and the cross-channel operation which, even if postponed, remained the priority operation of the European war for the Americans. In the months after El Alamein, Brooke became convinced that great opportunities beckoned the alliance if the conclusion of the campaign in North Africa were followed up by crossing the Mediterranean and knocking Italy out of the war, a resurrection in light of the new circumstances of the Anglo-French scheme of 1939.

At first Churchill was reluctant to accept that Torch and the protracted Tunisian campaign had actually ruled out a 1943 Roundup, but once convinced, he became the most articulate exponent of the case, both before the skeptical American chiefs of staff during the war and before posterity in his memoirs. The argument was simple: if Italy were forced out of the war Germany would be compelled to accept extensive commitments along the Mediterranean from southern France to the Balkans. This preliminary process of attrition would weaken the German armies and take some pressure off the Russians. The development of the North African campaign into an assault on the Italian mainland was the policy Churchill and his chiefs of staff brought to Casablanca in January 1943 for the war's third Anglo-American summit. Dill had warned Brooke and the prime minister of rising American suspicion and impatience over what was seen as British domination of alliance strategy, and the bargaining at Casablanca was the most difficult yet. But once again the British emerged with nearly all they wanted: an agreement to cross the central Mediterranean narrows to Sicily once Tunisia was cleared.

The future cross-channel operation, however, was reaffirmed by the appointment of a planning staff to begin shaping its outline. When Churchill and Roosevelt met again in May at the Trident Conference, American resistance to further Mediterranean commitments was even more intense. Agreed before the conference, "Husky," the attack on Sicily, remained at its conclusion the only firmly scheduled operation. On the other hand, the Americans got a firm commitment to a May 1944 date for the attack across the channel, and to underline that, agreement that several of the best divisions in the Mediterranean would return to the United Kingdom beginning in November 1943 to prepare for the spring assault. In August, a few months after the Trident meeting, the Quadrant Conference finally agreed to operations on the Italian mainland. Mussolini had fallen in July, and the new Italian government of Marshal Pietro Badoglio was busily negotiating itself out of the war even as Roosevelt and Churchill conferred. Eisenhower's Anglo-American headquarters had planned and prepared for an invasion of Italy. The armies of the alliance finally had the momentum of victory behind them. But shadows and undercurrents were present at this climactic moment. For nine months Churchill and Brooke had argued for maximum development of Mediterranean possibilities against a mounting American resistance fueled by the belief that the British would like to avoid, if possible, a head-on clash with the German army while bending alliance strategy to the support of British national or, even more suspect, imperial interests.

Thus every step forward in the Mediterranean had to be matched by British concessions and commitments elsewhere: a timetable and planning structure for the cross-channel attack as well as unwanted operations in Burma. All the while deep-rooted American feeling that clever Europeans would try to manipulate them and equally deep-seated ambivalences about Britain and the British were being aroused. Churchill himself excited mixed feelings. Admiration for his courage and determination mingled uneasily with doubts about his judgment, based as much on his stubborn advocacy of projects such as "Jupiter," a landing in Norway in which virtually no one except the prime minister could see any merit, as on legends about the Dardanelles. In the early autumn of 1943 these factors came to a head in a way that made the Italian surrender and its immediate aftermath not only the climax of the Mediterranean war but also a turning point in the Anglo-American alliance.

Exploitation of the Italian collapse by taking the Italian-garrisoned Aegean Islands, then using the resulting impression of an inexorable Allied advance to bring Turkey into the war, was a policy that the prime minister threw himself into with great energy. Churchill's concern with Turkey, although it had roots in prewar British strategic planning, became very much his own policy. He had argued strenuously with the Americans about the great benefits that Turkish belligerency would bring and immediately after the Casablanca Conference had flown off to confer with Turkish leaders at Adana in the hope of persuading them to take the plunge. His concern with Turkey and the Aegean simply reinforced American suspicions that the prime minister wanted to lure them into southeastern Europe, although there is no evidence that Churchill ever seriously contemplated a major campaign in the Balkans. Rather he seems to have appreciated that the foodstuffs and raw materials of the area would impose on Germany a major commitment to hold on there if Turkish belligerency and Allied aid to Balkan guerrillas posed a major threat to German control of the region. The Turks, however, had no intention of becoming involved until it was absolutely safe, a fact Churchill was remarkably slow to recognize. He was equally slow to sense the mounting irritation and impatience of his American allies, among whom feelings were becoming intense that no agreement with the British would survive very long before the prime minister would try to revise it. While not entirely fair, this mood, together with mounting American resources and an alliance command structure that made it impossible for the British to move independently, produced a minor tragedy in the autumn of 1943.

Determined to make the most of the fleeting opportunity presented by the Italian collapse, Churchill responded to suggestions from General Wilson by urging him to "improvise and dare" in the Aegean.* Wilson, drawing on British forces from within his own command, was able to rush small parties into a number of islands, but when the Germans reacted strongly, lacked the resources to sustain them. With no air cover the Royal Navy was heavily punished while trying to sustain islands that the Germans mopped up one by one, winning their last victory over the British. The resources needed to support the Aegean operations were available but only within the framework of Eisenhower's command, from which they could not be removed without American consent, which was not forthcoming despite a direct personal appeal from Churchill to Roosevelt. The doomed British garrison of Leros was a sacrifice, both to the attempt to do too much with too little and to the American determination to gain effective control over alliance strategy.

Leros fell on 17 November, its garrison, in part composed of units that had weathered the siege of Malta, becoming prisoners of war. "I feel like I have been fighting with my hands tied behind my back," Churchill told Wilson the following day, adding: "I hope to have better arrangements made as a result of 'Sextant.'"[70] In this respect, however, no better arrangements were possible. Growing American preponderance in the alliance and the integration of British forces in Anglo-American theater commands meant that British ability to launch on their own major operations, or even medium-sized expeditions like that into the Aegean, had come to an end, and with it Churchill's ability as well as Brooke's to shape alliance strategy.

Henceforth, the ability to vary the basic alliance plan, settled on at Washington in May 1943, would depend on the prime minister's persuasiveness with his American allies, a situation that declined as the British military contribution to the alliance was overshadowed by that of the United States. "It is my opinion that no diversion of forces or equipment should prejudice 'Overlord' as planned. The American Chiefs of Staff agree," Roosevelt replied to an anguished appeal from the prime minister for support in the Aegean.[71] That refrain, repeated ever more loudly and impatiently, was the basic American response to British attempts to retain at least some strategic flexibility from the autumn of 1943 until D-day and afterward. That the Aegean was almost certainly a blind alley does not mean that the British restiveness, articulated most

---

*Wilson, who had run Persia and Iraq Command, became Middle East commander in chief when Alexander was translated after Casablanca to the position of allied land forces commander under Eisenhower in North Africa.

sharply by the prime minister, over American insistence that Overlord's priority be treated as absolute was always as groundless.

At the Sextant Conference at Tehran in late November, Churchill discovered that not only was greater flexibility to exploit fleeting opportunity not going to be available to him and the British chiefs of staff but also that the Russians were absolutely firm on Overlord and a companion operation aimed at the south of France. The Russians insisted that only the designation of a commander would indicate real commitment on the part of their allies. The decline in Britain's proportional contribution to the alliance meant that the commander for the cross-channel attack would have to be an American. At Quebec, Churchill already had told Brooke, to whom he had promised the command when an earlier and largely British operation had been under discussion, that this would be the case.* The choice lay between Marshall and Eisenhower. Roosevelt would only name the former if his command included the Mediterranean. Churchill refused, using his remaining leverage in the alliance—British preponderance in that theater. Eisenhower became the commander for Overlord, and General Wilson replaced him in the Mediterranean. From that point on the prime minister watched over the fortunes of the Italian campaign with a passionate interest, and not just because he remained convinced that the vigorous prosecution of the campaign would yield strategic dividends. In the complicated calculus of alliance politics, the Italian campaign, to which the empire's largest and most famous field army was committed, involved issues of status and prestige that to Churchill, intent on safeguarding British power, were matters of major concern.

From this perspective the situation on the Italian front in midwinter, as Wilson took over, was a depressing one. The Allies had been stopped south of Rome by carefully sited and stubbornly defended German positions, the most famous of which was the mountain massif of Monte Cassino, crowned by an ancient and famous Benedictine monastery. While convalescing in North Africa from pneumonia, Churchill bent his energies toward breaking the deadlock and capturing Rome. It is a measure of both his resilience and determination that, while physically at his lowest ebb of the war, he nonetheless played the critical role in finding, in a theater already losing its best divisions and much of its amphibious troop lift to the demands of Overlord, the resources for an amphibious

---

*Ironically, Brooke's ambitions for command in the field fell victim to the success with which he had argued for a Mediterranean emphasis in Allied strategy for 1943.

end run to break the stalemate. In January 1944 the "cat's claw" landing at Anzio, christened "Avalanche," produced disappointing results: a beachhead sealed off and besieged by the Germans until relieved in May by the main armies whose advance it was originally supposed to facilitate. The disappointment elicited the prime minister's much-quoted remark that he thought he was flinging ashore a wildcat, only to discover that he had a stranded whale on his hands.

The story of the Anzio landing has certain eerie resemblances to Gallipoli. Both were conceived as a way to break an apparently unresolvable stalemate. Churchill, a prime mover in 1915, was the principal advocate in 1944. Both operations failed because the commanders made errors of judgment that are still the subject of intense argument. There is, however, one considerable difference. If successful, the Dardanelles-Gallipoli operations might have changed, in a significant way, the course of World War I. Even if the initial success at Anzio had been more vigorously exploited, it is difficult to make this argument about Avalanche. The Italian theater was, and would remain, a secondary theater because the Americans would veto any further augmentation of alliance resources committed to it. Even after the deadlock at Monte Cassino was broken, the German front breached, and Rome taken in May-June 1944, the pursuit of the temporarily disorganized German forces was arrested by American insistence that earlier agreements to mount "Operation Anvil"—the attack on southern France—had to be honored. This could only be done by taking resources from Wilson's Fifteenth Army Group commanded by Alexander. The prime minister, who had been reluctant even to divert aircraft from Italy to sustain Slim's campaign, fought bitterly to prevent Anvil. His direct appeals to Roosevelt met with as little response as the British chiefs of staff received from their American counterparts.

The launching of the attack on southern France in mid-August, by which time its original relationship to Overlord had long since vanished, was a major defeat for the prime minister, underlining the now complete U.S. dominance over alliance strategy. On only one occasion after the autumn of 1943 was Churchill able to order and sustain an operation in defiance of American wishes. That was the decision to commit British troops to Greece in December 1944 to defeat an attempt by the Communist-led guerrilla organization, ELAS (National Popular Army of Liberation), to seize Athens. That operation had nothing to do with the defeat of Germany but rather with the complexion of the Europe that would emerge from the ruins of Hitler's empire, a subject that demanded more and more of the prime minister's time and attention in the last eighteen months of the war.*

The shape of a post-Hitler Europe was not a new source of concern in London in 1943. The Foreign Office had concerned itself continuously with this issue from the beginning of the conflict. The prime minister, however, with his remarkable facility for concentrating intently upon the problem at hand, consistently refused to worry about it during the stressful days of 1940–42. As late as the eve of El Alamein he was brushing aside Foreign Office speculation, with the admonition that the war required all available energy. Shortly after the climactic events of November 1942, however, a change occurred. Churchill realized that, in a military sense at least, the war could not now be won by the Germans. Even his cabinet could carry on to victory, he remarked sarcastically to one of his staff shortly after Casablanca. In his emerging view of the most desirable configuration for the postwar world, two separate but related aspects have to be considered: British relations with a reconstructed Europe and with the emerging East-West superpowers.

Churchill expected a world organization to emerge but assumed that the key relationships would continue to be between the great powers, in whose ranks he firmly intended that Britain would remain. Therefore, a fundamental feature of his assumptions about the postwar world was his conviction that the empire-Commonwealth would emerge intact, both in spirit and territory because Britain's world position alone would enable it to continue to address its wartime coalition partners on an approximate equal basis. Here again, as in so many cases, the prime minister's ideas drew upon concepts long familiar to those concerned with Britain's world position. As far back as 1885 the Cambridge historian, Sir John Seeley, in a set of published lectures entitled *The Expansion of England,* had pointed out that, while the rise of German power was the most immediate challenge on the international horizon, in the twentieth century the great issue for Britain would be the rise of Russian and American power.

Entering politics at the time when the United States first began to make a decided impact upon the world scene, Churchill had witnessed, and in many cases taken part in, the adjustments in British policy and outlook that that impact required. By the time he became prime minister, his views were fixed. American pressure on Britain's imperial position had to be carefully watched and

*See postscript, pp. 239–41.

sternly resisted. Subject to that, however, the closest possible Anglo-American relations were critical for victory as well as for Britain's future. Indeed, given that the war was eroding British strength while it accelerated the growth of American power, such an intimate relationship enabling Britain to influence American policy might be the only way for Britain to safeguard its future position among the ranks of the major powers. Early one February morning in 1943, prior to his barren meeting with the Turkish leadership at Adana, the prime minister lay in bed dictating a paper entitled "Morning Thoughts." In it he gave voice to his concerns about the postwar power balance in Europe:

> Britain will certainly do her utmost to organize a coalition resistance to any act of aggression committed by any Power and it is believed that the United States will cooperate with her, and even possibly take the lead of the world, on account of her numbers and strength, in the good work of preventing such tendencies to aggression before they break into open war.[72]

Churchill was never as blunt as Macmillan about his expectations that British experience and leadership skills would powerfully affect the policy of any Anglo-American alliance, but the spirit of Macmillan's oft-quoted remark that the British must play the role of the Greeks in America's Roman empire, was implicit in much that Churchill did and said from 1943 on. Given the paramount importance that the prime minister ascribed to Anglo-American relations, he had no intention of allowing the susceptibilities of any of the exile governments of Britain's European allies to interfere with transatlantic harmony. Since the most important of the European nations that would reemerge from the German flood, at least for Britain, would be France, represented not by a formal government in exile but by the ambiguous Gaullist movement deeply disliked by Roosevelt and the State Department, the prime minister's American concerns inevitably entailed a clash with Gaullism.

To a greater extent than his pride would ever allow him to acknowledge, Charles de Gaulle was, if not a creation of the British, at least a major—perhaps the major—beneficiary of their desperate need for allies of any sort in 1940. De Gaulle left Bordeaux with the aid of Churchill's representative, Sir Edward Spears, and was personally welcomed on arrival in London by the prime minister, who had noted him down as a determined fighter during his last chaotic meetings with the French government, of which the newly promoted Brigadier General De Gaulle was a junior member. In the atmosphere of June 1940 the refugee governments crowding into London were valued both for what they could bring—the vast Norwegian merchant fleet and the mineral resources of the Belgian Congo—and for their symbolic value, demonstrating that, as Churchill later wrote, "the flag of Freedom . . . in this fateful hour was the Union Jack."[73]

If De Gaulle could be the means of rallying any of the French overseas empire, support for him would be well worthwhile. The American reaction to the French armistice was to maintain contact with the "legitimate" regime in Vichy, which the British did as well, intermittently and clandestinely. By the time it became apparent that De Gaulle could become a serious problem in Anglo-American relations, the Free French Movement had acquired enough of a life of its own to survive the decline in the prime minister's enthusiasm, particularly since it also had found another strong British supporter in Eden. The Foreign Office consistently took the view that good Anglo-French relations would be as important to Britain after the war as they had been since the rise of Germany had pushed the two nations reluctantly together. Germany would be wrecked and partitioned by the war, but the immense increase in Russian power that would result from the eclipse of Germany would leave Britain more than ever in need of a reliable continental ally.

A reborn France was the only likely candidate. Eden and the Foreign Office therefore struggled to moderate not only the American attitude toward the Free French Movement, which they correctly saw to be the force most likely to emerge dominant in a liberated France, but also to temper the prime minister's frequent inclinations to sacrifice the Gaullists to his American policy.* Over the long term, De Gaulle's remarkable combination of shrewdness and obstinacy, as well as the growing support for him inside France as a symbol of liberation and renewal, carried him and Foreign Office policy to success. With knowledge of the future course of Anglo-French relations, it is easy to convict Churchill's policy of an unrealism second only to that which he displayed over India. Both in fact flowed from the same assumption: Britain had to remain

---

*The clashes were heightened by the sharp personal antipathies of the three principals. Roosevelt consistently disliked De Gaulle, as did Churchill intermittently. Beneath the personal clashes, however, were serious policy issues. Roosevelt regarded France as a spent force, Churchill knew Britain needed America, and the Foreign Office could never lose sight of the historic British interest in a western European power balance. There is a good recent study of the Churchill-De Gaulle relationship, highlighting the personal rather than the policy aspects, by François Kersaudy, *Churchill and De Gaulle* (New York, 1982).

a world power. Indian nationalism posed a threat to this, as did anything that threatened the Anglo-American unity which the prime minister believed essential to Britain's future as one of the great powers.

When he wrote about the war years, in the depths of the Cold War and with De Gaulle in what seemed like final retirement, Churchill said as little as possible about Anglo-American clashes over the future of the British empire and somewhat more about his arguments with De Gaulle. He did, however, place considerable emphasis on the course of British relations with the Soviet Union, thus giving the slightly misleading impression that only Russia was seen as posing a threat to Britain's future as a great power and casting himself as the person who had foreseen the Russian menace as he had foreseen that posed by Hitler. Even before Churchill's volumes were published, this view had appeared in the Australian war correspondent Chester Wilmot's influential account of the final eighteen months of the war, *The Struggle for Europe* (1952). Republican and other enemies of Roosevelt's policies were happy to seize upon the idea of the prescient Churchill thwarted in his attempts to contain Russian expansionism by a Democratic administration that was at best naive and some of whose members might well merit more ominous descriptions.

Thus the question of the prime minister's wartime views on Russia became caught up, first in "cold war history" and then in the revisionist attack upon it. Out of this welter certain facts emerge with reasonable clarity. Churchill's attitudes toward Russia can be examined under two headings: ideological and strategic. The former is dealt with easily. Neither before becoming prime minister nor during the war did Churchill's deep revulsion against Communism abate. However, by the late 1930s the strategist in him saw that only Russian power could contain the eastward expansion of Germany. After May 1940 he hoped for a Russo-German break, and his instincts told him that one was very likely sooner or later. Once Hitler struck at Russia, the prime minister made every effort to give the Soviets not only material assistance but also the impression of British willingness, even at considerable cost, to help their new and desperate ally. At a minimum, Russia could absorb the impact of the Wehrmacht for some months, giving Britain invaluable breathing space. If the Russians could hold out until winter and survive into 1942, any aid from the British would be more than amply repaid. And the list of what Churchill was willing to countenance in order to aid Russia is impressive. War materials, particularly aircraft, of which the Middle East never had enough and

Malaya was virtually denuded, were diverted to Russia, followed by tanks and other equipment. To get it there the Royal Navy assumed the burden of running convoys to the North Russian ports of Murmansk and Archangel, through weather and opposition often equally murderous.*

The prime minister took the initiative in seeing that Ultra, suitably disguised, reached Russia. He also sought for ways in which British troops and planes could appear fighting alongside the Russians. Operations in Norway were explored as, until the Japanese attack aborted it, was the commitment of British troops and air squadrons in the Caucasus, where they would provide an advance bastion for the Middle East. (The Russians, with memories of British intervention there in 1919–20, must have quickly noted this.) However, Churchill would not encourage or placate the Russians in 1941 or later by committing the British army to a unilateral and suicidal assault on western Europe, offering instead Bomber Command's costly efforts against the German homeland. He also would make no commitment to the Soviets that endangered relations with the United States.** Anglo-American solidarity during the war and afterwards was his guiding objective; he would fight the Americans, if necessary, to defend Britain's imperial position but not to please the Russians, or the French.

The successful defense of Moscow, along with America's entry into the war, set in motion a shift in Churchill's attitudes. He remained willing to go to great lengths to sustain, and to be seen as sustaining, the Russian war effort, as the continuation, whenever possible, of the frightfully costly Murmansk convoys demonstrated. However, the postwar expansion of Russian power that the complete defeat of Germany would entail began to figure in his thoughts and minutes. He hoped to find a basis for continuing Anglo-Russian cooperation after the war, a hope that tended to peak after personal meetings with Stalin. Such an understanding was doubly important because not only would victory enhance Russian power, but it also was by no means certain that the prime minister's hope for postwar

---

*A second supply route began to develop when the British occupied Persia in August 1941, thus establishing an overland link with Russia. Short of engineer resources and material, the British could not fully exploit this route, and its complete development had to wait until American resources became available. During Russia's most critical months, outside aid amounted, for all practical purposes, to what the Royal Navy could fight through to North Russia.

**It is difficult to know how the Russians reacted to the British, and later Allied, bombing offensive. Not themselves enthusiasts of the strategic bombing theory, it probably seemed ineffectual to them throughout the war and certainly appears in that light in their post-1945 historical writings.

Anglo-American unity on major issues would be realized. Whether or not it was, the European balance of power would continue to be a British preoccupation. Optimism and pessimism thus alternated in the prime minister's view of Russia during the war, although gradually the pessimism became more pronounced. Central to Churchill's evolving view of the Russian problem was the fate of Poland.

The German attack on Poland had been the proximate cause of Britain's entry into the war, and the contribution of exiled Polish soldiers and airmen to the war effort had strengthened Poland's moral standing in British eyes. Yet it rapidly became apparent to almost everyone soon after the German attack on Russia that the pre-1939 borders of Poland would never again be acceptable to the Soviets. With his armies reeling back in disorder toward Moscow and the survival of his regime in doubt, Stalin said as much to the head of the Polish government in exile, General Wladyslaw Sikorksi. Once the war had swung decisively in favor of the anti-German coalition during the winter of 1942–43, postwar issues pressed upon the prime minister with increasing intensity in both the foreign policy and the domestic spheres. The issue of Poland was critical among the former because on it focused both the question of the dimensions of Russian expansion and the degree to which the Anglo-American alliance would face that problem unitedly.

The critical moment for Churchill seems to have been the late autumn of 1943. British mobilization and strength already had passed their wartime peak. A basically insoluble manpower problem—the dearth of the most fundamental of all the resources needed to wage war—confronted the British. Since May they had been firmly committed to a cross-channel attack in the spring of 1944 that might cost frightful casualties, while the American attitude toward the exploitation of the Italian surrender had starkly revealed the decline of British leverage in the alliance brought about by the changing balance of forces. The Russians with their great victories of 1943 behind them—Stalingrad, Kursk, and their subsequent summer offensive—were becoming increasingly assertive. Against this gloomy background Churchill, fatigued and pessimistic, set out for the first "Big Three" conference at Tehran. On the eve of the meeting the prime minister voiced his growing fears to Macmillan:

> Cromwell was a great man but he had one failing. . . . He had been brought up in the tradition of the Armada to believe that Spain was still a great power. He made the mistake of supporting France against Spain and thereby establishing France

as a Great Power. Do you think that will be said of me? Germany is finished, though it may take some time to clean up the mess. The real problem now is Russia. I *can't* get the Americans to see it.[74]

If he were worried about the American attitude before the Tehran Conference, the president's behavior during it depressed his spirits even further. Although opinions differed among Roosevelt's advisers on the best approach to dealing with the Russians, the president was optimistic about the possibilities of building good relations upon the foundation of a personal relationship with Stalin. He also believed, and his view was widely shared among American policymakers, that British imperial power and policy was as likely to cause trouble in the postwar era as Russian ambitions. Churchill knew he needed American support. Roosevelt, on the other hand, saw the United States keeping a certain distance from Britain, at least where relations with Russia were concerned, and occupying a mediating position. At Tehran the prime minister agreed to a new eastern boundary for Poland, with compensation from German territory in the west, but hoped that within its new frontiers Poland might enjoy some degree of independence. Roosevelt, however, seemed less concerned with the concrete question of Poland's future boundaries than with convincing Stalin of American goodwill. The revelation that, on the emerging issue of postwar Russian power, he and the president would not operate as one was perhaps the most significant conclusion Churchill carried away from the conference.*

After Tehran, Churchill and British policymakers faced a dilemma. A close alliance with the United States, extending into the postwar period, would solve many problems. It was by no means certain that it was attainable, at least at any price the prime minister wanted to pay. On the other hand, Russian power was a palpable fact, becoming more pregnant with meaning for the future with every reverse inflicted on the Wehrmacht in the east. For this reason, Churchill wanted to maintain the alliance with the Russians in the best possible order.

---

*The sense of knowing what should be done, while being unable to ensure that it would be, led Churchill several times to employ privately a zoological metaphor in which the United States and the Soviet Union were great hulking beasts with the British a lesser, but cleverer, animal. This perhaps unconsciously patronizing approach to American policymaking, while not entirely unwarranted, was widespread among the British and was clearly perceived by the Americans, who thereby were not made more amenable to British wisdom.

Toward that end he exerted heavy pressure on the London Poles to accept the inevitable with grace, both to save what could be saved for them and to avoid further complicating British relations with Russia. But the sense of pessimism was growing, and it became dominant in the late summer of 1944. The Polish underground, known as the Home Army, rose in Warsaw as the Russian front approached. The primary aim in the minds of the Polish leadership in both the underground and abroad was to see that the most critical piece of Polish territory was liberated by the Poles themselves. The Russians, who had been broadcasting exhortations to the Poles to strike out at the retreating Germans, stalled on the eastern outskirts of Warsaw. At the end of a lengthy and rapid advance they were at the outer limits of their logistic support, while the Germans, falling back along their lines of communication, were gradually stiffening their resistance, a familiar rhythm on the eastern front and similar to what was happening almost simultaneously in the west as Eisenhower's forces reached the German borders and the limits of their supply system.

What put a much different complexion upon the matter, however, was the adamantine Soviet refusal to help in any way as the Germans inexorably crushed the Home Army. British and American aircraft, near the limit of their operational range in flying supply missions to Warsaw, were denied landing rights at nearby Russian airfields. Churchill contemplated ordering British aircraft to land in Russian-held territory, advising the Russians that if the planes and their crews were not properly received the Arctic convoys would be stopped. Roosevelt declined to support such a drastic step. Early in October Warsaw's resistance collapsed. "Terrible and even humbling submissions have to be made to the general aim," Churchill reflected later, adding that he could remember no occasion in war cabinet discussions "when such deep anger was shown by all our members, Tory, Labour and Liberal, alike."[75] Nicolson noted a similar mood in the House of Commons: "People . . . are really horrified at the collapse of the Resistance in Warsaw, and think that Russia has behaved abominably . . . distrust of the Russians is universal, and by no means confined to people of the right and middle wings."[76] Despite this Churchill refused to deviate from the line of policy he had marked out. For the sake of keeping open the possibility of good postwar Anglo-Russian relations, much could be endured, especially by the Poles, whose stubbornness and unrealistic assessment of their rapidly vanishing leverage on the British made it easy to write them off as hopeless.

At his second bilateral meeting with Stalin in late October, Churchill pressured Sikorski's successor as head of the Polish government in exile, Stanislaw Mikolajczyk, to accept Russian demands over both the frontier question and the inclusion in his government of Polish Communists.* At a time when future American involvement in Europe was uncertain—the war with Japan was expected to last at least eighteen months after the German defeat and Roosevelt had said that American forces would rapidly leave Europe to participate in it—the prime minister may have thought that he had no choice but to do his best with Stalin by accepting what the Poles were bound to lose in any case. But the strain of pessimism in him over the Anglo-Russian relations was now deep, and he began to take damage control measures on his own, to the limited extent that this was still possible.**

At the same October meeting in Moscow, Churchill made his famous "percentage agreement" with Stalin, conceding Russian primacy everywhere in southeastern Europe except Greece, although parity of interest was agreed to in Yugoslavia. It was the culmination of a complex story, many of whose details remain obscure. One fact, however, is clear. At each stage in the story of British involvement in the Balkans, the prime minister had made a significant personal contribution. Yugoslavia, together with Greece and Turkey, had been a key element in Britain's projected Balkan front from the moment the idea was born in 1939. The Belgrade coup of March 1941 for a brief time had seemed to bring the dream to life. Greece, long linked to Britain by ties of sentiment, had won a special place in the affections of Churchill and his countrymen by its stubborn resistance to Italian forces in the autumn and winter of 1940–41. When the German avalanche fell on Yugoslavia and Greece, their royal governments took refuge with the British in Cairo and London. However, ties of sentiment, memories of facing adversity in common, and monarchical forms counted for less in the subsequent development of the prime minister's views than the needs first of wartime strategy and then of postwar British interests.

Despite American fears at the time, Churchill never contemplated a major land campaign in the Balkans, although he was very much alive to the benefits that widespread guerrilla resistance could bring in diverting and tying down Axis forces. And here the problems

---

*Sikorski was killed in an airplane accident in July 1943, a devastating blow to the Polish exile government.

**There is an interesting Polish viewpoint on Churchill and his policies in Jan Nowak, *Courier from Warsaw* (Detroit, 1982).

began. Resistance in Yugoslavia organized around two centers: the conservative, mostly Serb, Chetniks and the partisans, led and dominated by a veteran Communist, Tito. The two movements clashed with one another as well as with the occupiers. Amid the turmoil of conflicting information coming out of Yugoslavia, it was initially difficult to assess who was doing the most damage to the enemy, but gradually the evidence, of which Ultra information was a crucial component, swung in the direction of the partisans. The prime minister then intervened with decisive effect to support the recommendation of the operational chief of SOE's Cairo office, Brigadier C. W. Keble, that the British should make contact with the partisans.*

It is highly unlikely that Churchill ever deceived himself about the political implications of what he was doing. The switch during 1943 of British support from the Chetniks to the partisans, coming at a time when the acquisition of Italian bases made that support of increasing value, amounted to the abandonment of the Royal Yugoslav government, although the prime minister, as in the case of the Poles, made an effort to save something by urging upon Tito a coalition with the king's supporters. However, it was basically the pressures of war—the expectation that the partisans would tie down and burn up more German troops than their rivals—that shaped the prime minister's actions. The parity of influence agreed to at Moscow was a reflection of the British hope that wartime support would produce postwar diplomatic advantage. But Tito's subsequent break with Stalin should not be taken as the validation of a farsighted policy. The decision to support Tito was a wartime decision, taken in the interest of the shortest route to victory. The fact that Yugoslavia became Communist without ceasing to be Nationalist could not have been foreseen.

Greece was another matter. Historically a friendly Greece had been viewed as desirable in view of Britain's extensive eastern Mediterranean interests. The Royal Hellenic government was an ally in a formal sense, which the Yugoslavs were not. Greece was more accessible to the British than Yugoslavia, at least until after the Italian surrender. SOE's operatives reached Greece earlier and in larger numbers than elsewhere in the Balkans, and British money and supplies played a greater role in creating and orchestrating

---

*After the demise of the secret army concept, SOE had gradually concentrated on developing supply, communication, and intelligence links with European resistance groups, as well as providing direction to those amenable to it. The Balkans became its chief field of European operations, and SOE Cairo, which ran Balkan operations, enjoyed a considerable measure of autonomy in the crucial years from 1941 to 1943.

resistance there. However, the largest resistance force, ELAS, was equally Communist dominated and antiroyalist, although far less militarily effective. In Yugoslavia, Churchill accepted the partisans as allies because he had no other choice if he wanted effective resistance. In Greece, the prime minister also wanted military value from the resistance but believed that here he could avoid the political price. A friendly postwar Greece was one in which Britain's prewar friends returned to power. Moreover, Greece was accessible to British sea power, and British military power in the Middle East was still sufficient to mount an expedition to safeguard the return of the exiled government when the Germans withdrew or collapsed. The prime minister had supported SOE Cairo over the question of aid for the Yugoslav partisans. He periodically fulminated against it for the state of affairs in Greece, where he blamed it for calling ELAS into existence. The charge was not fair, as ELAS, like the partisans, had come into being under the impact of defeat and occupation. What SOE had done in both cases was to argue for support for the largest resistance movement without much concern over the long-range implications.

As in the case of Tito, Churchill's stand was crucial. He secured a relatively free hand in Greece from Stalin in October 1944, and when the Germans withdrew from Athens, British forces from the Middle East shepherded the Greek government back, although the king remained outside the country temporarily in deference to the strength of antiroyalist sentiment. When ELAS made an attempt to seize Athens in December 1944, it was the prime minister who insisted on fighting the matter through by withdrawing troops from Italy, thereby facing Labour party anger and open American hostility.* His motivations seem clear. Although he identified Britain's interests in Greece with the king, it was not simply a romantic admiration for monarchy as such.** Rather, Churchill was convinced that in Greece Britain could do something about the emerging configuration of postwar Europe in an area of particular importance. About Poland and Yugoslavia he could do little. In Greece, Britain still had some power to influence events, and the prime minister used it with decisive impact. Without Churchill's

---

*It is, and probably always will be, a matter of controversy, who actually fired the first shot on 3 December 1944, but there can be little doubt that ELAS had decided to strike while it still retained the power to do so.

**Typically insistent upon being on the spot, Churchill flew to Athens in late December 1944. Convinced finally that the stability of the Greek political situation required that the king remain abroad pending a plebiscite on the monarchy, he then took the lead in forcing the king to accept a Council of Regency. A non-Communist government rather than the monarchy was his aim, although he hoped to have both.

insistence, ELAS might well have seized power in Greece in 1944.

Greece, however, was the only success Churchill had to show in his policy of damage control against the westward spreading flood of Russian power in the last months of the war. Because he had little option, at Yalta he accepted a solution to the Polish issue which, if actually put into operation would have saved something, at least nominally, for the London Poles. Unfortunately, it rapidly became evident that the Russians had no intention of treating the agreement as anything but window dressing. In the last week of Roosevelt's life, and in the early days of the Truman administration, the prime minister's mind turned increasingly toward acquiring positions from which the Western allies could bargain with their brutally assertive eastern partners, urging that Eisenhower's forces drive as far eastward as possible in aiming for Berlin and Prague.* His frustration, chronicled for posterity in *Triumph and Tragedy*, was due not only to the different perceptions in London and Washington of the nature of the growing rift with Russia but also to the very structure of the Anglo-American alliance. Except in cases like Greece, where the British could achieve their objectives by drawing upon resources still under their control, Churchill and his advisers were straightjacketed by the machinery of the Combined Chiefs of Staff and the integrated theater commands. Eisenhower's plan for the advance into Germany, like his earlier decisions to assume overall land command and advance on a broad front to the Rhine, could only be altered if Roosevelt and Marshall could be persuaded of the desirability of making changes. Montgomery's Anglo-Canadian 21st Army Group represented a minority, although a substantial one, in Eisenhower's Allied army and could not be ordered to follow a completely independent strategy except at an unthinkable polit- ical cost.** If the Americans could not be persuaded over to the British viewpoint—and in the war's final year they were steadily less malleable—then the prime minister had no recourse but to follow a policy and strategy with which he was steadily more uneasy.

There is, however, another approach to the question of post- war British relations with the Russians. As the German war—the one with which the British public was emotionally involved—drew

---

*In view of what he said and wrote about Roosevelt in his memoirs, Churchill's failure to attend the president's funeral is interesting. Clearly the relationship had cooled by the spring of 1945 as American disregard for British wishes became more pronounced.

**Montgomery could be ordered to make the most of his opportunities within the context of the policy of Supreme Headquarters Allied Expeditionary Forces. This he did, sealing off the Danish peninsula from the advancing Russians by driving to the Baltic.

to a close, what really concerned the British electorate was demobilization and postwar reconstruction. Looking back from the Cold War years, Churchill's concerns seem particularly cogent. In the war's last winter and spring they were another example of the distance that had opened between the prime minister's preoccupations and those of the British public. Accustomed for nearly four years to regarding the Russians as invaluable and heroic allies, most Britons were not ready for the abrupt change that Churchill's policies seemed to imply and that later Cold War polemics treated as an obvious course of action. Domestic issues, which had become increasingly important to everyone except the prime minister from the time of the Cripps phenomenon and Beveridge report episodes of 1942–43, simply could not be denied any longer. Churchill had recognized that the coalition, based on a House of Commons elected in 1935, could not last beyond the end of the German war and had said so publicly in the autumn of 1944. At the last moment he wavered and, impelled both by his fears for the future and a reluctance to lay down the most completely satisfying task he had ever had, suggested the prolongation of the coalition until the end of the war with Japan, then expected to be 1946 or even later.

The momentum for an early election and the beginning of "postwar" was simply too strong. On 23 May 1945, Churchill resigned as coalition prime minister and immediately formed a new Conservative "caretaker" government to manage during the interim before the election. It was the end for him of the position he had always sought above all others, that of a recognized war leader sustained by patriotic men and women of all parties. He awkwardly changed gears to the role of a party leader fighting a general election.* Churchill himself later blamed the Conservative defeat at the polls on the general rustiness of their party machinery due to the absence of so many party workers in the forces. Others blamed it on the bad advice he took from cronies like Beaverbrook and Bracken. Neither explanation can stand up to examination. There is no evidence that the Conservative party organization was in worse shape than that of Labour. The evidence, in fact, indicates the reverse may have been the case. Neither Beaverbrook nor Bracken was as close to the prime minister during the campaign as was alleged. Churchill's worst campaign blunder, a speech in which he

---

*An awkwardness made more pronounced by Churchill's distaste, voiced as early as December 1940, for a postwar confrontation on the hustings with his wartime Labour collaborators.

proclaimed that only some type of "Gestapo" would enable Labour to carry into effect its policies (different more in degree than in kind from those advocated by the Conservatives) was all his own doing.

The real problem was much more basic than organization, choice of counsellors, or rhetorical tone. The tide was flowing strongly against the Conservatives and their beliefs. Since June 1943, shortly after the Beveridge report, the percentage of voters telling British Institute of Public Opinion pollsters that they planned to vote Conservative had steadily declined, until in May 1945 it stood at 24 percent. Labour's share had climbed slightly to 40 percent. Incredibly, the prime minister was unaware of these figures until 1946. However, he should have been aware of the mood in a very important segment of the electorate—the armed forces—because he had had some pungent and informed commentary on it. Home for consultations before moving up from Fourteenth Army to become allied land forces commander, Southeast Asia, Slim was invited to Chequers to meet Churchill for the first time. When the conversation turned to the impending election, Slim, who knew how strongly the morale of his British troops had been affected by the end of the German war, startled the prime minister by predicting that 80 percent would vote Labour, either from conviction or seeing it as a quicker ticket home. When Churchill asked if at least the balance would vote Tory, he was told that the balance would probably not vote at all. The mood in the forces worldwide differed in degree, not kind, from that described by Slim. Churchill had seen the war as a struggle not only for Britain's survival and independence but also for its continued greatness as an imperial power. Much of Britain's middle- and upper-middle class agreed with him, but the rank and file of men and women who had waged the war had other aims. They wanted an end to the mass unemployment, slums, malnourished children, and grossly inequitable distribution of opportunity that had characterized and disfigured the Britain of the 1930s. And they meant to make a beginning in this direction by voting Labour.

This mood was not immediately apparent to Churchill. His victory address to the House of Commons on 10 May struck many of his customary notes, to rapturous applause. Indeed, the next few weeks were one long and, electorally at least, misleading triumph. The enormous cheering crowds that met him everywhere, drowning out the occasional demonstrations of hostility, were cheering the national symbol of unity, defiance, and ultimately victory. In the most profound sense, they were applauding what their efforts had accomplished. It was all too easy, however, to convert those delirious cheers into Conservative votes. Churchill was not the only one to do so. Two days before the results were announced on 26 July, William Jowitt, who would become a Labour cabinet minister within a few days, told Nicolson that it was entirely possible that the Conservatives would have a majority of fifty in the new House of Commons.

Throughout the election campaign Churchill was occupied with the aftermath of the war in Europe. Here he sought vainly to persuade President Harry S Truman to keep the positions that Eisenhower's armies had reached as bargaining assets rather than pulling back to the previously agreed occupation zones. He also was concerned with the continuing war in the Far East, where the invasion of Malaya and redemption of Singapore were scheduled to begin in September. And perhaps most of all he was concerned with the preparations for the last wartime summit, which convened at Potsdam in mid-July. From arguing the problems of Poland's western frontiers and the plans for the final reduction of Japan, and from learning that the atomic bomb worked, Churchill returned to England for the declaration of the election results.* Despite a premonitory dream of defeat, described in his memoirs, both the fact and the dimensions of that defeat came as a crushing blow. Even then he did not completely grasp the degree to which the electorate had passed a final verdict on the cause dearest to him. Wavell, whose viceroyalty had been shaped by Churchill's adamantine negatives, came home quickly for consultations with Attlee's government. After paying a courtesy call on Churchill at his temporary residence at Claridge's Hotel, the viceroy was seen to the elevator by his former chief who, as the door closed, said to him in a remark that summed up so much of what he had fought for, "keep a bit of India."[77]

Postscript

The absence of any discussion of the mounting and launching of Overlord may seem strange. Yet in any assessment of the meaning of Churchill's career it has to be recognized that, from the time the date was chosen and the commanders named, the prime minister

---

*Preliminary work on the military uses of the atom began in Britain before American entry into the war. When that work was subsumed in the American Manhattan project, Churchill had sought to safeguard Britain's interests in a series of agreements, the most important being reached at Roosevelt's Hyde Park home at the time of the August 1943 Quadrant Conference in Quebec. Nonetheless, it is a measure of the auxiliary status to which the British had been reduced by war's end that at Potsdam and after they were informed about American plans for the use of the bomb rather than seriously consulted.

could make little direct personal impact on the operation, however much he may have contributed to the creation of the conditions that permitted its successful mounting. Much the same can be said of the campaign in Northwest Europe that followed. Churchill and the British chiefs of staff could argue issue after issue, but Eisenhower and Marshall were the final arbiters, although when they made their decisions, the desirability of keeping their British partners at least minimally happy was doubtless an important consideration.

This attitude toward the British can be demonstrated by considering several cases. The plan for the isolation of the lodgment area in Normandy from German reinforcements called for heavy air strikes on French road and rail communications in the weeks before D-day. When he saw the first estimates of the French civilian casualties likely to be caused, Churchill balked. British aircraft would have to do much of the work, and the prime minister feared a postwar legacy of bitterness that would poison Anglo-French relations. The argument was long, intense, and complicated, but its essence was simple. Eisenhower, as allied supreme commander, would make the decision. Since he was an allied supreme commander, the British could not give him an order unless it was agreed to by the Americans, and Roosevelt and Marshall declined to interfere with Eisenhower's "military judgment." Fortunately for the French civilians involved, it proved possible to savage German road and rail communications at a much lower cost than originally had been forecast.

Similarly, Anvil, the landing in the south of France, was one that strongly affected the British. The troops, ships, and planes involved were overwhelmingly American and French, but many were drawn from the Italian theater and their departure would remove much of the punch of Alexander's army group thrusting north from Rome toward the Po Valley. Despite Churchill's watchful care over the fortunes of Alexander's command and the suspicion, which now seems to have been well founded, that the whole business had become strategically irrelevant, British pressures did not succeed against Eisenhower's assertion that he needed the great port of Marseilles.

After the breakout from the Normandy bridgehead in late July, and particularly after Eisenhower assumed direct control of his ground forces on 1 September 1944, the British argued ceaselessly for an overall Allied land forces commander between the supreme commander and his three army groups. On the analogy of the arrangements in the Mediterranean theater in 1942–43, that land forces commander would have to be British. Montgomery was out, leaving Alexander. Brooke, who thought little of Eisenhower's skills as a commander, pushed this arrangement strongly with the prime minister's backing. As late as the Malta Conference in January 1945, the British were arguing for an arrangement that would push Eisenhower back into the strategic stratosphere. However, he did not want to go, while Marshall, upon whom Roosevelt was leaning more and more heavily, was adamantly hostile. In the face of this, all British pressure could do was irritate.

Finally, in the war's waning days there is the well-known case of Churchill's pleas to Eisenhower to push for Berlin and Prague. However attractive such advice came to seem in the Cold War years that followed, the key point is that Churchill could only plead; Eisenhower and Marshall decided. Churchill's impact on the war after 6 June 1944 has to be sought in other areas than that of alliance strategy. Insofar as it was not already set, it was shaped by the Americans and, above all, by Marshall. Whether it was correctly shaped is another question entirely, but not one for this book.

Notes

1. Churchill to first lord and first sea lord, 10 July 1941, *GA*, 382.
2. Quoted in F. H. Hinsley et al., *British Intelligence in the Second World War*, 3 vols. (London, 1978–81), 2:59.
3. Joseph Stalin to Churchill, 18 July 1941, *GA*, 383.
4. Churchill to Stalin, 7 July 1941, ibid., 381.
5. The Butt report is printed as Appendix 13 to Sir Charles Webster and Noble Frankland, *The Strategic Air Offensive Against Germany*, 4 vols. (London, 1961), 4:205–13. The quotations come from 205.
6. Churchill to Charles Portal, 7 October 1941, *GA*, 508–09. The entire minute should be read.
7. The best brief assessment of the "crisis of confidence" and the prime minister's role is in Max Hastings, *Bomber Command* (London, 1979), 106–22.
8. This argument is tentatively advanced, due to the continued closure of certain documents, by the most careful student of SOE policy, David Stafford, in his *Britain and European Resistance 1940–1945* (London, 1980), 63–64.
9. Ibid., 73.
10. *GA*, 400.
11. Churchill to chiefs of staff, 28 October 1941, ibid., 552.

12. Churchill memorandum on the naval situation, 25 March 1939, quoted in Paul Haggie, *Britannia at Bay: The Defence of the British Empire Against Japan, 1931–41* (New York, 1981), 140–41.

13. Churchill to Franklin D. Roosevelt, 15 February 1941, in Francis Loewenheim and Harold D. Langley, *Roosevelt and Churchill: Their Secret Wartime Correspondence* (New York, 1975), 129–30.

14. *GS*, 440.

15. Anthony Eden's remark is quoted in Haggie, *Britannia at Bay*, 114.

16. *GA*, 541.

17. Ibid.

18. *HF*, 35.

19. *GA*, 605, 608.

20. Ibid., 607.

21. Ibid., 616.

22. Ibid., 656–57.

23. Churchill to Eden, 19 September 1943, PREM 3, 158/4, Public Record Office (PRO), Kew, London.

24. Quoted in Lionel Wigmore, *The Japanese Thrust* (Canberra, 1957), 183.

25. John Curtin to Churchill, 23 January 1942, *GA*, 57–58.

26. *GA*, 58.

27. Ibid., 58–59.

28. *HF*, 34–35.

29. Trefor Evans, ed., *The Killearn Diaries 1934–1946* (London, 1972), 197–219, recounts the crisis from Lampson's rather smug point of view. The description of the ambassador's military escort is from Lampson's report to the Foreign Office, dictated a few hours after the event, 213.

30. Diary entry, 27 January 1942, in Nigel Nicolson, ed., *The Diaries and Letters of Harold Nicolson*, vol. 2, *The War Years, 1939–45* (New York, 1967), 207.

31. Lady Violet Bonham Carter retold the story to Harold Nicolson the next day. Diary entry, 12 February 1942, ibid., 211.

32. Charles, Lord Moran, *Churchill: The Struggle for Survival 1940–1965* (Boston, 1966), 29. Moran is quoting from his diary but does not provide a date.

33. Diary entry, 7 February 1942, *Nicolson Diaries*, 212.

34. *CCS*, 6:6267–68.

35. Ibid., 6295.

36. Clement Attlee to Leo Amery, 24 January 1942, N. Mansergh and E. W. R. Lumby, eds., *India: The Transfer of Power 1942–1947*, vol. 1, *The Cripps Mission* (London, 1970), doc. no. 35.

37. Ibid., doc. no. 66.

38. Ibid., doc. no. 465. This is the text of the Cripps offer.

39. Ibid., doc. no. 597.

40. *HF*, 383.

41. Diary entry, 22 June 1942, *Nicolson Diaries*, 229.

42. *HF*, 390.
43. Diary entry, 1 July 1942, *Nicolson Diaries*, 231.
44. Diary entry, 2 July 1942, ibid., 232.
45. Moran, *Churchill*, 51.
46. Recorded in the diary kept by Brigadier E. I. C. Jacob of the prime minister's staff, this story has been repeated many times. I am grateful to Lieutenant General Sir Ian Jacob for allowing me to read his entire diary of "Operation Bracelet."
47. *HF*, 499.
48. *CCS*, 6:6675–77.
49. *HF*, 550.
50. Lord Trenchard to Churchill, 29 August 1942; Churchill to Trenchard, 4 September 1942, ibid., 552–53.
51. Diary entry, 29 September 1942, *Nicolson Diaries*, 244.
52. *HF*, 554.
53. Diary entry, 11 November 1942, *Nicolson Diaries*, 262.
54. Churchill to Eden, 21 October 1942, *HF*, 561–62.
55. Diary entry, 23 October 1942, *Nicolson Diaries*, 252.
56. R. A. Butler, *The Art of the Possible: The Memoirs of Lord Butler* (London, 1971), 108.
57. Churchill to Butler, 13 September 1941, quoted in ibid., 94.
58. Diary entry, 31 January 1944, *Nicolson Diaries*, 346.
59. Diary entry, 7 February 1944, ibid., 347.
60. Diary entry, 4 February 1960, in Nigel Nicolson, ed., *The Diaries and Letters of Harold Nicolson*, vol. 3, *The Later Years, 1945–1962* (New York, 1968), 380.
61. WP (43) 445, October 1943. This paper is in the CAB 66 series, PRO.
62. WP (43) 450 (revise), 10 October 1943, CAB 66, PRO.
63. Note by Churchill, 11 April 1945, in William Roger Louis, *Imperialism at Bay: The United States and the Decolonization of the British Empire, 1941–1945* (New York, 1978), 548. Louis is quoting from the Foreign Office file that contains Churchill's record of the conversation.
64. Ibid., viii.
65. Diary entry, 27 March 1944, *Nicolson Diaries*, 356–57.
66. Churchill minute, 3 March 1944, quoted in John Ehrman, *Grand Strategy*, vol. 5, *August 1943–September 1944* (London, 1957), 442.
67. Quoted in Anthony Eden, *The Memoirs of Anthony Eden, Earl of Avon*, vol. 2, *The Reckoning* (Boston, 1965), 461–62.
68. Prime minister to Hastings Ismay for chiefs of staff, 12 September 1944, *TT*, 167.
69. Here Churchill is closely paraphrasing the official transcript of his opening remarks. Ibid., 155.
70. Churchill to Sir Henry Maitland Wilson, 18 November 1943, *Great Britain. Cabinet Office. Cabinet History Series: Principal War Telegrams and Memoranda, 1940–1943* (Nendeln, 1976).
71. Roosevelt to Churchill, 8 October 1943, ibid.

72. *HF*, 712.

73. *FH*, 629.

74. Sir Harold Macmillan told this story to Sir John Wheeler-Bennett in 1964, and it appears in John Wheeler-Bennett and Anthony Nicholls, *A Semblance of Peace: The Political Settlement After the Second World War* (New York, 1972), 290. It is odd that it does not appear in the relevant volume of Macmillan's memoirs, *The Blast of War* (London, 1967).

75. *TT*, 141.

76. Diary entry, 4 October 1944, *Nicolson Diaries*, 404.

77. Penderal Moon, ed., *Wavell: The Viceroy's Journal* (London, 1973), 168.

Chapter Four

Missing the War

Anyone writing about Churchill's post-1945 career is entering a territory that, in comparison with earlier years, is as yet incompletely mapped. No Churchill memoirs and, to date, no volume of the official biography illuminate the last stage of his career, while scholarly writing, based on British government archives, is just beginning. But in many ways this may be one of the two most important parts of his career, second only to 1940. This is so not because of what he did but because of what he wrote. The six volumes of *The Second World War* are a legacy of great significance. Those who would attempt to chart and assess Britain's war, and the view that the British came to have of what they had done during it, are immediately confronted by this remarkable final burst of literary productivity. It put Churchill beyond financial worries, won him a Nobel Prize, and enshrined him where he had always wanted to be, a dramatic and commanding figure at a culminating point in his country's history. In a long perspective on his career, what he wrote during this decade is probably of much more importance than his performance as Conservative party leader, either in opposition (1945–51) or in office (1951–55).

The composition of his war memoirs, although doubtless always one of Churchill's intentions, began in the aftermath of defeat at the polls, as had been the case with *The World Crisis* a quarter century earlier. In September 1945 he flew to Italy to rest and paint, staying at a villa near Lake Como as a guest of Field Marshal Sir Harold Alexander. His doctor noted the beginnings of the memoirs:

2 September 1945

We left Northolt this morning in Alex's Dakota and arrived at Milan after the flight of five and a half hours. All the time

Winston remained buried in a printed copy of the minutes which for five years he had sent out month by month to the Chiefs of Staff and the Cabinet. Even during luncheon he went on reading, only taking his eyes from the script to light a cigar.

4 September 1945

All morning Winston has been immersed in his minutes. He has not looked at them for a long time; now he wants to know how he comes out of it all. . . . He is finding his role of prophet, as painted in these telegrams and minutes, very reassuring and gratifying.[1]

Churchill brushed aside Lord Moran's suggestion that he should give up politics for authorship (although he had once claimed it would be his sole postwar activity), with the remark that he had no intention of writing books because the new Labour government's taxation would prevent him from earning any money. The desire to vindicate his stewardship, however, quickly overcame all else.

A small army of assistants was assembled. F. W. Deakin acted as a general editor; Hastings Ismay helped, as did Churchill's old associate Sir Edward Marsh. Lieutenant General Sir Henry Pownall served as military adviser, and a naval captain, together with an air marshal, rounded out Service representation. There were several stenographers as well as a meticulous professional proofreader, C. C. Wood. Dennis Kelly and Alan Hodge (recommended to Churchill by Brendan Bracken) were responsible for general editorial work, often traveling to the south of France for conferences with Churchill during his frequent stays there. With this much-expanded version of the literary production machine he had developed during the 1930s, *The Second World War* was dictated, typeset, revised, corrected, and ready for publication in a remarkably short time.

In the autumn of 1947, Harold Nicolson wrote for *Life* magazine an introduction to the serialization of the first volume, *The Gathering Storm*, and the book itself appeared in 1948. In quick succession four more followed. The speed was directly related to the improving electoral prospects of the Conservatives. "Pug Ismay told me Winston is in too much of a hurry over his book," Nicolson noted in early 1949:

It may be full of inaccuracies. He has a sailor to do the naval part, and an airman to do the air part and young Deakin to be a sort of general editor. But he expects them all to produce their stuff within twelve hours. Pug thinks it is because Winston is convinced the Tories will get in at the next Election and he wants to finish his book before he is once again Prime Minister.[2]

In September 1951, Churchill signed the preface of *Closing the Ring*, which ends on the eve of D-day with the capture of Rome. His concluding words have a distinctly valedictory ring:

> Here, then, we reach what the Western Powers may justly regard as the supreme climax of the war. Nor, though the road might be long and hard, could we doubt that decisive victory would be gained. . . . The Hitler tyranny was doomed. Here, then, we might pause in thankfulness and take hope, not only for victory on all fronts and in all three elements, but also for a safe and happy future for a tormented mankind.[3]

Within two months he was back at Downing Street.

If Churchill had intended in 1951 to close his story in 1944, there were artistic as well as practical reasons: Britain's declining weight in the alliance after mid-1944 and the demands on his time and energy as prime minister. However, he soon decided to carry the story on to the end of the war. His doctor, who saw more and more of him after his return to office, described the genesis of *Triumph and Tragedy:*

> . . . it was often in his mind—when his record came before posterity they must be fair to him. All this talk about the war having been fought in vain made him angry. At any rate, he was not to blame. To get that quite clear he had added a sixth volume to his book and called it *Triumph and Tragedy*. . . . His publishers tried to persuade him that it was a mistake to bring out another volume. But he would not listen to them. For he was resolved to make it known that he wanted to take precautions against some rather ugly possibilities as early as the spring of 1945, at a time when the Americans were still busy making friends with Stalin and had not woken up to the danger of Communism.[4]

With the publication of the sixth and final volume in September 1953, *The Second World War* was complete. That same year Churchill received the Nobel Prize for literature, in some ways a curious award because *The Second World War* is far from the best written of his books. The Nobel Selection Committee, however, was accurate in its evaluation of their importance. Thirty years later

Churchill's memoirs stand like a rock in the flood of war literature. Assessing Churchill, the writer of history, four years after his death, a distinguished professional historian wrote:

> The phases of the war are the phases into which he divided it. And this will deeply influence, indeed has already deeply influenced, subsequent historians. They move down the broad avenues he drove through the war's confusion and complexity. Hence, Churchill the historian lies at the very heart of all historiography of World War II, and will always remain there.[5]

With the qualification that this applies perhaps with greater force in the English-speaking world than elsewhere, the judgment cannot be faulted. Churchill's unique authority; the documentation he was able to offer years before official histories were completed or archives opened, incomplete and one-sided though it may have been; and the speed with which he placed his arguments before the public all contributed to the powerful impact his memoirs made. That impact was multiplied and brought to bear upon many who would never read Churchill because the massive authority his memoirs acquired shaped many secondary accounts and textbooks as well as the viewpoint of many lecturers.* Thus Churchill's view of the origins and course of the war became something like historical orthodoxy. No comparable American memoir existed, or could exist with Roosevelt dead. The books written by, or ghosted for, generals, diplomats, and civil servants could never have Churchill's authority or reach a fraction of his audience.

Nowhere is the dominance of Churchill's view more apparent than in the history of the appeasement years. Chamberlain and Baldwin were dead, and the party they had led was only too glad to distance itself from their memory.** The enormous success of *Guilty Men* had paved the way for what Churchill would do in *The Gathering Storm*, which was to give shape to a picture of the 1930s, now so widely and firmly held as to be virtually beyond alteration. *The Gathering Storm*, alone among the six volumes, is a narrative unencumbered by the minutes, telegrams, and other documentation that, in many of the succeeding volumes, would often reduce the

---

*The only other book published within a decade of the war's end to have an impact comparable to Churchill's was the Australian war correspondent Chester Wilmot's *The Struggle for Europe* (New York, 1952). Wilmot reinforced the Churchillian interpretation. Indeed, he took it further, arguing for the existence of Balkan opportunities squandered by American refusal to listen to Churchill.

**Perhaps fastening the blame so firmly to Baldwin and Chamberlain helped obscure the degree to which they represented the mainstream of the Conservative party.

narration to little more than linking passages. It also was written, as was its successor, *Their Finest Hour*, before the slow deterioration of Churchill's health, which began with a minor stroke in August 1949. It has a drive and passion reminiscent of the early volumes of *The World Crisis*.

Churchill, as he would do in the rest of the volumes, skated lightly over such episodes as his role in the general strike, the India Bill controversy, and the abdication of Edward VIII. By eliminating these distractions, he overemphasized the consistency of his position on Germany. He also underestimated the constraints upon British governments of the 1930s, that is, public mood, economic weakness, and uncertainty about allies. One crucial question Churchill never addressed and may never have asked himself, although Baldwin and Chamberlain certainly did, was: If Britain's national interest was its survival as a great power, was another major war likely to advance that interest? Churchill approached the problem in another way. Germany was a menace both to the balance of European power and to the values of British life. Nazism had within it an evil dynamism that made negotiations not only fruitless but also dangerous unless undertaken from a position of strength. British governments of the 1930s failed in their most basic duty by not trying to make the British public understand this issue. The vindication that events had accorded Churchill, together with the substantial element of truth in his diagnosis, won his version the widest readership enjoyed by any account of that decade.

The conclusion "appeasement never pays" and the emotive quality of the word "Munich," validated by Churchill, have become part of the frame of reference for judging foreign policy in the English-speaking world, simple concepts often applied in wildly dissimilar situations. Churchill's version of the 1930s also served as a backdrop against which he would depict the British war effort. The British had been foolish—and foolishly led—during these years, but they had not wished for war. When it came, they fought to defeat evil. It was this viewpoint, in which he deeply believed, that made Churchill impatient with any attempt to question the war's value. It may too have helped cushion the sense of loss experienced by those in Britain who saw their privileges and national power eroded by the war and its consequences.

Part Two of *The Gathering Storm* closes with Churchill's reticent account of the political crisis of May 1940, a chapter that serves as an introduction to the key volume of the memoirs. *Their Finest Hour* recounts one of the climactic moments of British history and certainly of Churchill's life. The most concentrated volume of the memoirs, it deals with the period of Britain's maximum peril but displays as well the pattern of reticence already visible in *The Gathering Storm*. The important policy decisions of July-August 1940 on India and the Far East are not discussed by Churchill, although the former was perhaps his most important venture in Indian policy during the war, and the latter a significant milestone on the road to the debacle of February 1942. But possibly the greatest of Churchill's silences, in this and the succeeding volumes, concerns that part of the war not directly associated with strategy and operations. The politics of war, both on the home front and in relation to his American allies, and the course of imperial policy during the war, are subjects only touched on glancingly, if at all.

Churchill wrote to vindicate his wartime leadership and to underline the British contribution to victory. The former, besides staking his claims before history, had current value to a Conservative party leader hoping to return to office; the latter pointed out to the British, amid the greyness of postwar austerity, how great had been their achievement, as well as serving to remind the powerful and self-confident Americans of how much they owed to their British allies. The power of Churchill's narrative, the fame of the narrator, and the lack of access to records that would amplify and alter Churchill's account, for a generation effectively screened off entire areas of the Anglo-American war effort.

Churchill also practiced a great deal of discretion in several areas connected with the war itself. About Ultra, and the closely related subject of strategic deception, he could say nothing; that remained secret until nearly a decade after his death.* About the bomber offensive there was no requirement to be reticent, but there were a variety of practical reasons. His emotions had never been involved with Bomber Command as they had been with the Eighth Army, and the bombing of Germany already had become a controversial issue. Churchill was no stranger to controversy and seldom shrank from it, but on this occasion he preferred to pass over the issue, if not in silence, then with a sense of detachment. SOE and the entire story of British assistance to the European resistance was another area in which discretion prevailed. There were links between this story and Ultra, but the real reason why SOE and its activities are seldom discussed is that resistance was a sensitive topic in countries once occupied and an awkward one where Poland

---

*Comparing Churchill's account of the desert war with the complete picture of the intelligence background now available does not, however, make the prime minister seem less, but rather more, reasonable in his relations with Generals Archibald Wavell and Claude Auchinleck.

and Yugoslavia were concerned. But Churchill's treatment of events is most sharply restrained when writing about the war against Japan. A discussion of the fall of Singapore was unavoidable, but the war in Burma is treated sketchily; indeed, as much space is given to the American campaigns in the Pacific as to one of the most remarkable military achievements in British imperial history. The proportions may conform to the ultimate strategic importance of the Pacific and Southeast Asian theaters, but it was the frustration of his hopes in the latter that surely accounts for the remoteness of Churchill's tone in discussing events there.*

When all is said, however, and the necessary qualifications made, the six volumes of *The Second World War* are a remarkable achievement, giving posterity a sense of how one of the greatest of modern war leaders saw his war—even the reticences and silences become informative from this point of view—as well as establishing for the nation he had led the image of one of the greatest of Britain's national experiences. Churchill's accomplishment becomes more impressive when it is remembered that as he wrote it he continued to be active as a party leader and traveled and spoke frequently in Europe and the United States. He also began to suffer serious health problems, a physical deterioration that would be the background to the remainder of his public life.

Churchill always had benefited from a sturdy physique. He survived a bad bout of pneumonia at his preparatory school and rebounded without lasting ill effects from a serious fall involving internal injuries during adolescence. He dislocated a shoulder in India as a subaltern but continued to play polo, and he fought his losing campaign at Dundee in 1922 while recovering from an appendectomy. He had a mild heart attack in December 1941 and two more attacks of pneumonia in 1943 and 1944. And periodically, when out of office and at bad moments in his career, he suffered from depression. Despite all this he maintained a schedule throughout the war that would have killed many men, even if they had been able to retire for afternoon naps as the prime minister almost invariably did. One member of his staff, with him continually throughout the war, estimated later that Churchill averaged a ninety-hour-work week.[6] By the end of the war there is no doubt that

---

*It is also true that Churchill did not know Sir William Slim and his subordinate commanders as he knew Lieutenant General Bernard Montgomery, Sir Bernard Freyberg, Alexander, and many of the other figures of the desert and Italian campaigns. But while this personal factor was doubtless of some importance, the way Churchill treated Britain's war against Japan was conditioned more by his conception of his memoirs as a success story. The campaigns in SEAC were harder to envision that way, followed as they were almost immediately by the end of British power in India.

Churchill, in his seventy-second year, was a very tired man, but there is little convincing evidence to link important policy decisions to the state of his health. In the late 1940s, however, time finally began to catch up with him. In August 1949, while staying in the south of France, he had a stroke. The following February he had what his doctor called an "arterial spasm." Reflecting on it later, Lord Moran noted:

> Winston was in his seventy-fifth year. The shock of the [1945] election, coming right on top of the strain of the war years, had done him no good. However, as the months passed I think my fears were half forgotten; he seemed to get back his interest in life, vigour returned and he appeared to put the past behind him, so that his stroke took me completely by surprise.[7]

Churchill was finally beginning to be worn down by age and illness when, while finishing his memoirs, he took his party into two back-to-back general elections in 1950–51 and then returned to Downing Street with a slender margin in October 1951.

In 1940, Churchill had become party leader in succession to Chamberlain, in part at least to give himself a secure political base, the lack of which had ruined Lloyd George after 1918. Some regretted his decision to become a party leader instead of remaining a national figure "above politics." Such regrets, however, were unrealistic. The Conservatives were the majority party in the House, and the party still contained far more Chamberlainites than Churchillians. While Churchill did not intend to devote any more than the necessary minimum of attention to domestic politics, he knew the necessity of protecting his flanks and rear, and as the political crisis of 1942 showed, he was not without enemies there. However, the experience of acting as a party leader in the 1945 general election was not a satisfactory one for Churchill. Although his wife and others hoped he would quit politics at that point, the stunning defeat of 1945 almost certainly put an end to any thoughts of retirement he may have had. A political animal all his life, the idea of final separation from Parliament and politics was more than he could bear. Moreover, he now had a defeat to erase.

Leading a party in opposition was a new experience for Churchill, and in some ways he never adjusted to it. The pattern of his parliamentary life was similar to that of the 1930s. He attended the House and spoke on major issues and then departed to other activities. A complaint from rank-and-file Conservatives that the party leader should be more visible in the House was followed shortly by Churchill's departure on a lengthy vacation and speaking tour in the United States. When he did attend the House, or spoke on party topics, particularly in the early days after the 1945 election, he often got the tone wrong. To one of his shadow cabinet ministers he lamented on the changing composition of Parliament, recalling that when he was a young Liberal hard words on the floor of the House or on the hustings seldom compromised personal friendships that, based on common backgrounds, easily crossed party lines. He added that that was no longer the case, thus putting his finger neatly on a crucial factor in the changing social geography of British politics. Yet in these immediate postwar years important changes were set in motion in the Conservative party that reshaped it to face the new world, changes that opened the way for Churchill's return to power in October 1951.

A key question in any assessment of Churchill after 1945 is his relationship to those changes. The critical arena lay within the Conservative party, where organization was being modernized and, even more importantly, a new philosophy was being hammered out. The central figure in this process was R. A. Butler. Never close to Churchill, Butler nonetheless had piloted through the House one of the Churchill coalition's major domestic achievements, the 1944 Education Act. The task of reviving the Conservative Research Department and guiding the effort to work out a positive Conservative response to post-1945 conditions fell naturally to him. He had the advantage of drawing on much new blood flowing into Conservative politics in the postwar years, individuals as varied as Iain Macleod, Reginald Mauldling, and Enoch Powell, all in different ways to make a mark on the future of the party.

A strong minority of progressive Conservatives, of whom Harold Macmillan was the most notable, had long wanted to modernize Tory thinking. Butler, however, with his Chamberlainite background, was a more reassuring figure to the bulk of the party than a longtime maverick like Macmillan would have been. Butler approached the task with the attitude that the party was at a turning point in its fortunes. As in the nineteenth century, the Conservatives, in order to survive, had to accommodate themselves to the coming of a social revolution, which is what the 1945 election represented. The upshot of Butler's labors was the *Industrial Charter* of May 1947. A major transformation of Conservative policy couched in deliberately bland language, its commitment to full employment and the social services of the Welfare State marks one of the turning points in the long history of the Conservative party. Accepting the Welfare State, as Sir Robert Peel had accepted on behalf of the

Tories the great franchise extension act of 1832, Butler and his associates positioned the Conservative party to launch the successful comeback of the 1950s.

What was the party leader's role in this process? In his memoirs Butler remarked that "the constructive part of his mind always dwelt more naturally on the international scene than on bread-and-butter politics."[8] There was a certain measure of detachment reflected in his reception of Butler's work:

> At a dinner party for his senior colleagues at the Savoy, he placed me on his right hand, plied me with cognac, and said several agreeable and no disagreeable things about my work. Emboldened by this prodigality, I gave instructions that the Charter should be published on 12th May, though none of us at the time was one hundred per cent certain whether it was to be regarded as 'official' or even whether it had received the Leader's detailed scrutiny. It was not well designed to captivate his attention.[9]

Yet even if the details passed him by, Churchill contributed something very important to the remaking of the Conservative party, and that was his attitude toward domestic affairs.

During a discussion of the *Industrial Charter*, Churchill described himself to Butler as a Liberal Tory, a label that is a considerable oversimplification. He had certainly never been part of the Conservative mainstream, and for twenty years not even part of the party. His desire to be a national leader supported by a broad consensus had become a reality in 1940, and if he became Conservative leader at the end of that year, it was not from any passion for the party as such. The Labour leaders of 1945–51 had been reliable colleagues in 1940–45 and Churchill, rehearsing Britain's "immortal services to mankind" in his speeches and evolving memoirs could never forget that they had been part of the epic whose Homer he was determined to be. He disliked "socialism" and attacked Labour policies with vehemence, but the Liberal in him espoused many of their goals, and the coalition leader of the war years had accepted the Welfare State, at least in principle. If Butler gave post-1945 and pre-Thatcherite British conservatism its characteristic garb, he was able to do so because the party leader had no fundamental objection to appearing in it, even if he occasionally complained of the fit.

Of the two great issues in British politics after 1945, the creation of the Welfare State evoked a positive Conservative response. In view of his past, Churchill's assent to that response is not really surprising. However, the second issue—managing the demise of empire—was one that, in view of that same past, seemed least likely to draw any constructive reaction from him and most likely to produce a bitter die-hard resistance. Yet, interestingly, little of this materialized. India, as always, provides the touchstone.

Churchill had worked to slow the rate at which India moved toward self-government for a quarter century, and his parting remark to Wavell in 1945 expressed one of his most deeply held beliefs. Yet he made no effort, as party leader, to defeat the Attlee government's India policy that was at all comparable to the furious contest he had waged as an individual to stop the India Bill a decade before.* As suggested earlier, he may have known that the battle was over and lost but simply could not bring himself to approve.† In any case, the post-1945 consensus embodied in Attlee's policies and accepted, however grudgingly, by the Conservatives excluded any commitment to the Indian empire. When Indian independence became a fact, Churchill's speech was more melancholy and elegiac than bitter. He later snubbed Lord Mountbatten for his role as the last viceroy, but even this seems more an emotional gesture than a considered judgment.‡ Churchill's relative calmness about the demise of the raj can be linked to his developing vision of how Britain could best adjust itself to the new shape of the world, especially the new era of American dominance.

In the 1930s, Churchill had fought the India Bill, and his opposition during the war to any diminution of British power had been adamant. The postwar years in opposition, the time to adjust and reflect, were clearly advantageous, given that Churchill was determined to remain in politics. When he returned to office he took up no such die-hard stance on Middle Eastern issues, the next area in which emergent nationalism challenged Britian's position.§ Privately, the whole business of withdrawal from the Canal Zone

---

*From 1930 to 1935, Churchill spoke over eighty times on India and related matters; from 1945 to 1947, only five times, and the predominant tone was not combative. *CCS*, 5, 6, 7, passim.

†Powell, working under Butler in the Conservative Research Department, produced a paper arguing that with ten divisions the British could reconquer India. Butler showed it to Churchill, whose first reaction was to inquire about Powell's sanity. Then he told Butler that it was too late to reconquer India and added that ten divisions would not be enough!

‡He shortly thereafter, when once again prime minister, enabled Mountbatten to fulfill his lifelong ambition of becoming first sea lord. In doing so, Churchill may well have been repaying an old sense of obligation. Mountbatten's father, Admiral Prince Louis of Battenberg, had been driven from his position as first sea lord in the autumn of 1914 by the prevailing anti-German hysteria, an action that Churchill, then first lord, regretted but did not think he could oppose.

§Even as Conservative party leader, Churchill stressed the obligation he personally felt toward the policy of supporting the Jewish National Home, a policy that took shape during his tenure as a Liberal colonial secretary (1921–22), and from which the Conservatives had been distancing themselves since the mid-1930s.

and the Sudan in the early 1950s was distasteful to him, but he yielded far more easily than anyone with a knowledge of his past might have expected. One reason, perhaps the chief reason, is that while out of office his sense of the realities of power had led him to adjust his views on how Britain could best preserve its position in the world. In doing so, he reemphasized themes already sounded: the Anglo-American connection and the importance of unity among the English-speaking nations. Churchill's famous "Iron Curtain" speech at Fulton, Missouri, in March 1946 was as much about the Anglo-American relationship—"the crux of what I have travelled here to say"—as about Russia:

> Neither the sure prevention of war, nor the continuous rise of the world organisation will be gained without what I have called the fraternal association of the English-speaking peoples. This means a special relationship between the British Commonwealth and Empire and the United States.[10]

A few days later, addressing the General Assembly of Virginia in Williamsburg, he returned to the same theme:

> In these last years of my life there is a message of which I conceive myself to be a bearer. It is a very simple message which can well be understood by the people of both our countries. It is that we should stand together. . . . Above all, among the English-speaking peoples, there must be a union of hearts based upon conviction and common ideals. That is what I offer. That is what I seek.[11]

In New York, before embarking for his journey home, he played the tune again, this time with variations to meet the charge that the United States was being invited back into the British Empire:

> Now I turn to . . . the relations between Great Britain and the United States. On these the life and freedom of the world depend. . . . I have never asked for an Anglo-American military alliance or a treaty. I asked for something different, and in a sense I asked for something more. I asked for fraternal association, free, voluntary, fraternal association.[12]

Even as he christened and preached the "special relationship" that was to be one of the principal themes of his remaining years as a politician and publicist, he took another idea to which he had been

devoted and gave it a new twist in the interest of Britain's future
security.

Churchill had always believed in Anglo-French understanding, however much on occasion this had been clouded by his wartime quarrels with De Gaulle. In the face of Stalin's expanding
empire, he saw the need to enlarge this conception and to embrace
a reconstructed Germany within a wider and permanent western
European grouping. When he called for a united Europe, first tentatively at The Hague in May 1946 and then robustly at Zurich in
September, it was this that he had in mind. A loose federal structure
that would contain the Franco-German quarrel and present a coherent European front against Russia was his aim, not the bureaucratic colossus that eventually emerged from the Treaty of Rome.
Like his old associate and antagonist, De Gaulle, Churchill was
committed to the idea that "Europe" was a federation of nation
states that would always retain their unique characteristics.

It is in relation to his vision of a united Europe that the
ambiguity of Churchill's conception of Britain's new role in the
world stands out most clearly. Churchill saw Britain associated
with, but not integral to, a united Europe, a British attitude that
would last for nearly a decade after the establishment of the European Economic Community. During the war he had argued for
regional groupings of powers within the framework of the United
Nations. However, he believed Britain's interests were too broad
for the country to confine itself exclusively to any one grouping.
Europe, the Commonwealth, the United States, and the shrinking
but still extensive empire were all areas in which Britain had important interests and ties, and all had to be nourished. In Churchill's
youth the Cambridge historian, Sir John Seeley, had argued that
Britain could confront the emerging power of Germany, Russia,
and the United States by organizing the vast resources of the Greater
Britain that emigration and imperial expansion had created.*

In his last years in public life, Churchill had given Seeley's
ideas a new shape. To give the lead to a recovering Europe, to
maintain the special relationship with the United States, and to
sustain Commonwealth ties and the remains of imperial authority
where feasible would give Britain a secure place among the powers
in the new world emerging from the wreckage of Hitler's war. "Let
no man underrate the abiding power of the British Empire and
Commonwealth," Churchill told his audience in Fulton.

*Seeley's book, *The Expansion of England*, first published in 1885, remained continuously in print until 1956.

Because you see the 46 millions in our island harassed about their food supply . . . or because we have difficulty in restarting our industries and export trade after six years of passionate war effort, do not suppose that we shall not come through these dark years of privation as we have come through the glorious years of agony, or that, half a century from now, you will not see 70 or 80 millions of Britons spread about the world and united in defence of our traditions, our way of life, and of the world causes which you and we espouse. If the population of the English-speaking Commonwealths be added to that of the United States with all that such co-operation implies . . . there will be an overwhelming assurance of security.[13]

Churchill, as he spoke those ringing words, never questioned that Britain could and should continue to play a great world role. To him, it was part of the natural order of things. His very presence in public life was, for many, an assertion that such a role was still feasible for Britain.

Therefore, in October 1951, when Churchill once again found himself prime minister, he brought with him to Downing Street an unusual combination of strengths and weaknesses. Perhaps his greatest strength was in his past as the most remarkable war leader in Britain's history, a figure already taking on legendary proportions. He perceived clearly the centrality of relations with the United States, but he overestimated, as he had done during the war, both Britain's strength and British ability to shape American policies. He wanted domestic peace and consensus and presided over a Conservative bid, forecast in the *Industrial Charter*, to take over the post-1945 structure of full employment and social legislation and run it more efficiently.

Bored, however, by peacetime administrative minutiae, he left the details of domestic policy to his ministers—Walter Monckton at the Ministry of Labour, Macmillan at Housing, and Butler at the Treasury. A party leader, many of whose followers hoped he would soon step aside, he spent his final three and one-half years at Downing Street conducting a careful and determined rearguard action against the assaults of time. Over all his actions hung the shadow of steadily declining health. He had two strokes while in office, one in July 1952 and the second, much more serious, in June 1953. After the latter his energies sharply diminished. He hung on, partly from reluctance to finally say good-bye and partly from the belief that he had a final contribution to make: to break the rigidities of the Cold War by taking advantage of Stalin's death to achieve some form of détente with Russia.

One of the most interesting aspects of Churchill's last years in office is this careful focusing of effort on a few key matters, in contrast to the lavish expenditure of energy that had characterized him during the war. Seventy-seven and ailing, he established broad guidelines for domestic policy and then let his ministers carry on; the restless urge to probe into every corner was gone. Stung by charges made in 1945 and repeated in the 1950 and 1951 general elections that war was all he understood or cared about, he wanted the last chapter he wrote in history to show him as a peacemaker.* The radical alteration in Britain's military position pushed him in the same direction. In 1914 the fleet could guarantee Britain's safety; in 1940 the Royal Navy, Fighter Command, and radar could again do so. But the V-2 bombardment of London in 1944–45, against which no defense was possible, was the harbinger of things to come. The atomic bombs that ended the Pacific war were even grimmer portents. In an era of missiles and nuclear weapons, Britain was almost impossible to defend against an unacceptable level of damage, except by avoiding nuclear war. Nonetheless, the Attlee government had decided that Britain must develop its own atomic arsenal in order to remain a great power. Churchill would follow this same line of reasoning by deciding that Britain must add thermonuclear weapons.

The impact of the ballistic missile and nuclear weaponry on Churchill, however, was to convince him that future safety for Britain lay in the winding down of the intense levels of hostility between East and West that had characterized the late 1940s. Even the cost of maintaining conventional forces was escalating at a pace that made it steadily more difficult for Britain to maintain its position. The Indian Army, which had reduced the strain on British finances and manpower and provided the strategic reserve for the entire British position from the Middle East to the Malacca Straits, was no more. The burden and cost of residual imperial responsibilities thus became heavier at a time when some economies in defense expenditure seemed increasingly urgent, if only to free resources for the new and costly military technologies necessary if Britain were to remain in the ranks of the major powers. Reduction in overseas responsibilities would come only slowly, but some pressure could be removed if détente with the Russians became a reality.

*In the general election campaign of 1950–51, charges of being antiworking class as well as being a warmonger stung Churchill. Monckton's policy as minister of Labour, which consisted of avoiding major industrial disputes, often at the cost of inflationary wage settlements, was a consequence of Churchill's desire to lay the first charge to rest, as his desire to improve East-West relations doubtless was spurred by the second. In his final years in public life he was trying to remove the last blemishes from his image.

Accomplishing this would depend not only on the Russians but also on Churchill's ability to sway American policymakers.

Here was the heart of the problem. Churchill had made many concessions during the war to cement the Anglo-American tie, too many in the opinion of some of his associates. He had done his best, in what he wrote and said after 1945, to emphasize the conclusion he wanted drawn from the war: together the United States and Britain had nothing to fear. Just as his wartime strategic arguments looked somewhat different when viewed from an American perspective, so his enthusiasm for the special relationship struck American policymakers as yet another attempt to enlist American power for British goals. When Churchill, newly reinstalled at Downing Street, decided on an immediate trip to Washington, the briefing papers prepared by the State Department for President Truman reflected this feeling:

> Churchill . . . hopes to reestablish the intimacy which existed between the two governments during the last war. . . . Among others, his objectives are:
>   To buttress Britain's waning prestige and influence by demonstrating a special relationship between the U.K. and the U.S.

A second paper warned of Churchill's formidable skills as a publicist and negotiator:

> He will almost certainly attempt, by institutional or public means, to make the US-UK relationship more obvious to the world.
>   It should be borne in mind that Mr. Churchill thinks in terms of grand global strategy. He will not be interested in going into details or working out in these meetings specific and detailed solutions to problems. In the 'grand' manner he can be expected to tour the world and make observations on a multitude of questions. All of these random observations, however, are apt to have the objective of pointing towards several specific requests he will make of us.

The State Department officials who drafted these papers also had a response to offer the prime minister when he pressed for a tightening of Anglo-American bonds. "I don't need to tell you," they suggested that Truman should reply,

> that the United States considers its relationship with Great Britain as a cornerstone of U.S. foreign policy. . . . In my view,

however, our relationship is generally most effective when it underlies other multilateral relationships such as NATO, and leads to difficulties if it is too apparent to other friendly powers who are suspicious of an association which they do not quite share.[14]

Churchill tried to cast a glow of romance on the Anglo-American relationship, partly because such an approach came naturally to him, and partly because his purposes could best be accomplished if that relationship were elevated above the competitive arena in which the game of nations was normally played out. The Americans, at the summit of their postwar power, looked upon the entire issue with colder eyes. In the last analysis the special relationship was a one-way street; the British did more to keep it alive simply because they needed it more.*

The prime minister soon realized all this. When his doctor saw him in his bedroom at the British embassy late one January afternoon, after only a few days in Washington, "he was unhappy," Moran recorded. "Once more he spoke of the feeling of inequality; it was a canker in his mind, he grieves that England in her fallen state can no longer address America as an equal, but must come, cap in hand, to do her bidding."[15] Churchill's principal private secretary, John Colville, looking back, commented that "the Americans were on guard," adding that "Truman had wary counsellors who were fearful of the effect the giant from across the Atlantic might have. . . ." But he also noticed the enormous enthusiasm with which Churchill, the symbol and legend, was greeted. "He left Washington with the sure knowledge that whatever reservations the Administration might have, in the eyes of Congress and the press Winston Churchill was still a formidable and deeply loved statesman of much more than purely British significance."[16] This

---

*Perhaps the most clinical dissection of Churchill's dream of an enduring special relationship was done by his old wartime associate, Dwight D. Eisenhower. On 6 January 1953 the president noted in his diary: "Mr. Churchill is as charming and interesting as ever, but he is quite definitely showing the effects of the passing years. He has fixed in his mind a certain international relationship he is trying to create. This is that Britain and the British Commonwealth are not to be treated just as other nations would be treated. . . . On the contrary, he most earnestly hopes and intends that those countries shall enjoy a relationship which he thinks will recognize the special place of partnership they occupied with us during World War II. . . . Winston is trying to relive the days of World War II.

In those days he had the enjoyable feeling that he and our president were sitting on some Olympian platform with respect to the rest of the world and directing world affairs from that point of vantage. Even if this picture were an accurate one of those days, it would have no application to the present. But it was only partially true, even then, as many of us who, in various corners of the world, had to work out solutions for nasty local problems are well aware." Robert H. Ferrell, ed., *The Eisenhower Diaries* (New York, 1981), 222–23.

feeling, that he had become one of Britain's major international assets, doubtless encouraged Churchill in his decision to hang on as prime minister, in the hope that he could turn it to national advantage.*

Whether this hope was realistic or not is another question. The basic determinants of Anglo-American relations were not actually the personal relationships between statesmen—useful though those ties could occasionally be—but the resources and situations of the two nations. Britain's resources were shrinking, while the demands of the British electorate for a larger investment in social programs were rising. The cost of a world role was now beyond the British. America had come out of the war perhaps the only complete victor, with its homeland intact, its wealth vastly increased, and its self-confidence brimming over. To some extent, Churchill's continued presence at the heart of affairs could mask this disparity between the two countries and, perhaps, provide a better hearing in Washington for the British point of view, but he could not alter the fundamental differences in resources and per-spectives that underlay Anglo-American relations. His continued presence also may even have slowed down British realization of the need to adjust to their altered circumstances, a realization that came with such painful suddenness during the Suez crisis within eighteen months of his departure.

Does this mean that Churchill's final years in office were a failure? This view has gained some currency and certainly has a measure of validity. Aging and intermittently ill, Churchill lacked the energy to tackle many issues and, in any case, had never had much enthusiasm for the mundane business of peacetime domestic administration, or at least not since the distant days when he had been a young Liberal building his career before World War I. He could not impose his views of the proper direction for international relations on his American allies, and the contemporary Conser-vative party in Britain, although it may invoke and revere his name, shows little sign of holding some of his more liberal views on domes-tic policy.

Those who regret, however, that he did not take his wife's advice and retire in 1945, ignore the fact that the same character-istics that had made him a dynamic first lord and creative strategic

---

*There is no question that Churchill's international prestige helped him to rationalize his desire to remain in office as long as possible, but the balance between personal inclination and possible British advantage in the prime minister's mind is impossible to assess. He probably made no such careful distinctions on this issue.

thinker in the pre-First World War years from 1911 to 1914, a determined advocate of opposition to Germany in the 1930s, and a great war leader for five years were still present in the man who refused to step aside until finally worn down utterly by time in April 1955. The belief that he had a destiny to fulfill in politics, an iron determination, and a will that overrode bodily weakness and depression, all these Churchill still deployed in his final active years, and they kept him going, as they had so many times before. To the end, he also continued to display the wide-ranging vision that had worried the drafters of the State Department briefing paper for President Truman. The prime minister saw that the consensus of the war years in domestic politics could only be preserved by Conservative adaption to the new world which the war and the Attlee government had shaped. He saw, even if he did not like, the fact that Britain's position in the world was changing and that relations with the United States and with some form of European union had to be constant factors in Britain's future. He realized more rapidly than many, especially in the United States, that the rigidities of East-West relations had to be replaced with less confrontational policies. He saw that nuclear stalemate and Stalin's death provided openings to move in the direction of negotiation and détente.

Churchill's sweeping vision was never more in evidence than when he rose in the House of Commons on 1 March 1955 to deliver his last great speech. His doctor, who had watched the prime minister's mounting nervous anxiety as he prepared for what he knew would be his final performance—and to the end Churchill shaped every word of his own speeches—observed from the Peers Gallery as the prime minister entered the House and made his way slowly, once almost losing his balance, to his place. When he rose to speak, however, the vigor of his delivery and the memorable phrasing evoked once again memories of 1940. The subject was deterrence, specifically the 1955 Statement on Defense which announced the British decision to construct its own hydrogen bomb.

> We live in a period, happily unique in human history, when the whole world is divided intellectually and to a large extent geographically between the creeds of Communist discipline and human freedom, and when, at the same time, this mental and psychological division is accompanied by the possession by both sides of the obliterating weapons of the nuclear age.
>
> We have antagonisms now as deep as those which led to the Thirty Years War. But now they are spread over the whole

world instead of only over a small part of Europe. We have, to some extent, the geographical division of the Mongol invasion in the thirteenth century, only more ruthless and more thorough. We have force and science, hitherto the servants of man, now threatening to become his master.

He then went on, to a House silent and attentive to what all knew was a final performance by a great virtuoso, to develop an argument for a strategy of deterrence. During his speech he hinted that he saw such a strategy as opening the way for disarmament by producing a stalemate in strategic weapons: ". . . it may well be that we shall by a process of sublime irony have reached a stage in this story where safety will be the sturdy child of terror, and survival the twin brother of annihilation." He ended on a note of optimism, asserting his belief that mankind would survive and progress. And then in a final concluding chord of his farewell, he sounded a note that had reverberated through his whole career: "Never flinch, never weary, never despair."[17] In his swan song before the House, Churchill turned in a performance remarkable for both its clarity on a subject soon to be lost in thickets of jargon and its vision of what had to lie beyond deterrence. The significance of a career must surely be assessed not only by what was accomplished but also by what was envisioned and urged. By this measure Churchill, in the twilight of his career, cannot be judged to have failed.

Churchill (Sir Winston from 1953) finally retired from office in April 1955. He retained his seat in the House of Commons until the autumn of 1964, just a few months before his death in January 1965. He spoke very little after he left office, however, and toward the end attended Parliament infrequently and then only as a silent observer of the proceedings in the political forum he so greatly loved. For a few years after his retirement he was consulted on government and party questions, particularly at the time of Eden's resignation in the aftermath of the tragicomic Suez episode, but on many of the issues confronting Britain by the later 1950s, Churchill had little to offer. A revered figure after his retirement, he was never an active elder statesman, although a final autumnal literary endeavor still remained for him to carry to completion.

His principal activity in his first retirement years was bringing out the *History of the English-Speaking Peoples*. Virtually complete in 1939, it had waited sixteen years for his final polishing and editing, which was all Churchill had energy or inclination to do by the time he returned to work upon it, despite the reams of advice given by the many distinguished historians consulted. In the development of Churchill's ideas, the four volumes of the *English-Speaking Peoples* belong to the 1930s, when Churchill was rehearsing, first to himself and then to ever larger audiences, the roots of British greatness and the values that it was so urgent to defend against Hitler. As history it is old-fashioned and reveals Churchill's complete disinterest in economic, social, cultural, and intellectual history, in everything, in fact, but war, politics, and overseas expansion. But almost no one reads it as history, only as one great Englishman's vision of the nation he served. Perhaps its great success as a publishing venture had to do with Churchill's archaic but clear view of history, so forcefully articulated at a time when academic history was withdrawing more and more into itself, breaking into arcane specialties and ceasing to provide society with a coherent picture of the past and its meaning.

By the time the last volume of the *English-Speaking Peoples* came out, the shadows were closing in around Churchill. His physical vitality and mental acuteness were fading, and he became a remote, almost totemic, figure seen only occasionally in public, carefully escorted and shepherded. A mood of deep depression often settled on him, which he could no longer dissipate or hold at bay with political, artistic, or literary activity. In the grip of one such mood he told his cousin Clare Sheridan that his life and work had "all been for nothing. . . . The Empire I believed in has gone."[18] By any measure but his own an almost grotesque misevaluation of his accomplishments, it nevertheless stands as the last in a lengthy catalogue of statements declaring his devotion to British world power, going back to the aftermath of World War I when the erosion of that power first became visible. Old age and depression may have wrung from him this final pessimistic assessment of his life, but it was not merely years and illness speaking. By his own standards, a retrospective on his sixty years of public life could not but be touched with melancholy. He had sought to preserve Britain as a great power, and there was no disguising the gap between intention and accomplishment.

Notes

1. Charles, Lord Moran, *Churchill: The Struggle for Survival, 1940–1965* (Boston, 1966), 312–13, 317.

2. Diary entry, 26 January 1949, in Nigel Nicolson, ed., *The Diaries and Letters of Harold Nicolson*, vol. 3, *The Later Years, 1945–1962* (New York, 1968), 163–64.

3. *TT*, 631–32.

4. Diary entry, 28 November 1954, quoted in Moran, *Churchill*, 649.

5. J. H. Plumb, "The Historian," in A. J. P. Taylor et al., *Churchill Revised* (New York, 1969), 166.

6. Lieutenant General Sir Ian Jacob is the source of this figure.

7. Moran, *Churchill*, 358. It is fairly obvious from the context that this assessment, which follows a diary entry for 25 August 1949, represents subsequent reflection on Moran's part. One of the problems with Moran's book as a source is that diary entry and later thoughts are not always clearly distinguished.

8. R. A. Butler, *The Art of the Possible: The Memoirs of Lord Butler* (London, 1971), 133.

9. Ibid., 145.

10. *CCS*, 7:7289.

11. Ibid., 7:7296.

12. Ibid., 7:7301–02.

13. Ibid., 7:7293.

14. All the quotations in this paragraph are taken from two papers by the Steering Group, assembled to prepare background papers for talks between the president and the prime minister. Copies of the papers dated 21 and 28 December 1951 are in the Harry S Truman Library, Independence, Missouri.

15. Diary entry, 7 January 1952, quoted in Moran, *Churchill*, 381.

16. John R. Colville, *The Churchillians* (London, 1981), 102–03.

17. All quotations in this paragraph are from *CCS*, 8:8625–33.

18. Anita Leslie, *Clare Sheridan* (New York, 1977), 304–05.

Epilogue
London, 25 January 1965

It was a grey, wintry, January Saturday when the gun carriage, drawn by men of the Royal Navy, bore Churchill's coffin through the streets of London. He had died on 21 January 1965, seventy years to the day after his father's death. His body lay in state for three days in Westminster Hall, while over 320,000 people filed by. Now it was passing up Whitehall, along the Strand, and finally up Ludgate Hill to Wren's mighty St. Paul's, whose dome, towering over smoke and flame, had been the visual counterpart to Churchill's defiant rhetoric in 1940. Men of every British regiment lined the streets, the guns of the Royal Horse Artillery thudded in salute from St. James's Park, and the galaxy of notabilities who attended the service at St. Paul's was headed by the queen, breaking precedent to attend the funeral of a subject. Churchill's Anglo-American heritage was stressed by the selection of hymns. "The Battle Hymn of the Republic," its martial and moral certainties so congenial to the spirit in which Churchill had met his destiny in 1940, reverberated around Wren's great dome. Afterward the coffin traveled from the Tower upriver to Waterloo Station as Royal Air Force jet fighters, lineal descendants of the Few of 1940, roared overhead. Then came the final train journey to tiny, rural Bladon churchyard and burial near his parents in the shadow of his birthplace, Blenheim Palace.

The crowds that filed past his coffin and lined the streets were predominantly the war generation, itself now entering middle age and moved by recollections of the most dramatic years of their lives. The young were there but mostly out of curiosity. In the England of the Beatles, Churchill already seemed to belong to a very remote past. What did his countrymen make of Churchill as they bade him farewell?

The assessments that accompanied the impressive state funeral concentrated on the great days of 1940, saying little of the years that followed.* Those spring and summer months were already the stuff of legend, and at its heart stood the figure of Churchill. By the time of his death it was only just beginning to be apparent to what extent the victorious war, presided over by Churchill, had been a major ingredient in the decline of British power he later so bitterly lamented. Could he have fought a different war? If he had, he would not have been the same man whose personality and achievements had brought him to Ten Downing Street in May 1940. Perhaps on a cold and narrow calculation of Britain's interests as a world power he might have tried to fight a different war, but cold calculation of that sort was alien to the romantic in him.** One usually sceptical British historian, writing at the time of his death, said of Churchill's first statement as prime minister, with its ringing vow to win total victory: "This was probably the will of the British people."[1] If this assessment is correct, then the central irony of Churchill's career, in which maintenance of British power is so evident a theme, is that it reached its climax at the moment when Britain's situation demanded measures that could only hasten the end of that power.

Does this mean that Churchill's career must be assessed as a failure? He himself, in his darker moments, thought so. But world power was not the only value that animated him. As he told the Conservative party meeting that accepted him as leader in 1940, his life was devoted to two principles: the defense of Britain's empire and its institutions. The values he believed resided in those institutions were as crucial to him as was India. He passionately believed in "decency" in public life and policy, even if his definition of the term had a distinctly Victorian tinge, emphasizing as it did political, not social, democracy. He argued in the 1930s that Britain's history had produced a considerable measure of decency, and that it might be necessary to fight to preserve a world in which such a standard

---

*Yet to many observers Churchill's funeral was obviously a memorial not only to a man but also to an era. It is hard to avoid the conclusion that, even if it were not verbalized, the end of Churchill's life marked for many of his countrymen a full stop to a long chapter in their national experience.

**Should Churchill have tried to fight a different war? This was one of the issues, perhaps the central one, in the tense war cabinet discussions of 26–28 May 1940, described in the Prologue. Halifax and Chamberlain were arguing to limit Britain's losses because only some limits to the conflict would ensure Britain's survival as a great power. Churchill rejected this strategy because he did not believe compromise with Hitler was compatible with Britain's fundamental values. In this sense, he was doubtless right, although pure self-interest might have indicated the wisdom in the Baldwin-Chamberlain-Halifax line.

was possible. It is this Churchill upon whom the legend is based. The tireless, unflinching defender of national freedom and parliamentary democracy is the Churchill who will be remembered.

Note

1. A. J. P. Taylor, *English History, 1914–1915* (New York, 1965), 475.

Note on Further Reading

This is not a bibliography of books on Churchill, which in itself would require a volume of this size. It is intended only as a guide to some of the more important works on various aspects of his career discussed in the text. These sources have bibliographies of their own which will lead readers further in almost any direction they wish to go.

Chapter One
The Long Preparation

To put Churchill in proper context it is necessary to have a general picture of British history during his lifetime. *The British Revolution: British Politics 1880–1939*, 2 vols., by Robert Rhodes James (London, 1976–77) is a good beginning. *English History, 1914–1945* (New York, 1965) by A. J. P. Taylor is written with gusto and shrewdness, unmarred by excessive scholarly impartiality. There is nothing of comparable quality for the post-1945 years, but *Britain in Transition: The Twentieth Century* by Alfred Havighurst (Chicago, 1979) provides the basic information.

Biographies of Churchill are numerous but surprisingly dull. The official biography, begun by Winston's son Randolph and continued after his death by Martin Gilbert, is very thorough but has become more ponderous and less analytical with each volume. *Winston Churchill* by Henry Pelling (New York, 1974) is a clear, competent, single-volume account. There have been several noteworthy attempts at assessing various aspects of both Churchill and his career. *Churchill: A Study in Failure, 1900–1939* by Robert Rhodes James (New York, 1970) argues that until the outbreak of the Second World War the "brilliant failure" label had more than a little validity. *Churchill Revised* by A. J. P. Taylor et al. (New York, 1969) is a collection of essays, two of which should be read: Anthony Storr on Churchill's psychology and J. H. Plumb on Churchill's approach to history.

Free from the constraints of his role as official biographer, Martin Gilbert has analyzed *Churchill's Political Philosophy* (New York, 1981). Churchill wrote little on his political career until his arrival at the Admiralty in 1911, and historians have followed his example. The sole exception, *Churchill and Elgin at the Colonial Office, 1905–1908* by Ronald Hyam (New York, 1968), is a careful study, but Churchill as a social reformer at the Board of Trade and a "law and order" home secretary await detailed scrutiny. Churchill began the first volume of *The World Crisis* (New York, 1923) with his installation as first lord and this, along with the second volume (New York, 1924), carry the story up to his resignation from the government in December 1915. Both are powerfully argued, more so than any of the volumes of *The Second World War*, but both are also very partial. They have been the subject of a careful and enlightening analysis by Robin Prior, *Churchill's World Crisis as History* (London, 1983).

From the Dreadnought to Scapa Flow, vol. 1, *The Road to War, 1904–1914* by Arthur J. Marder (New York, 1961) has the most careful assessment of Churchill's prewar contribution to the Royal Navy's readiness in 1914. Marder continued his meticulous examination in vol. 2, *The War Years: To the Eve of Jutland, 1914–1916* (New York, 1965). The third volume of the official biography, by Martin Gilbert, is also essential reading. There is a vast amount of literature on the Gallipoli operation itself, most of it less important to assessing Churchill's role than the studies of planning and decision in London by Marder and Gilbert.

Churchill's loss of office in May 1915 must be seen against the backdrop of politics in wartime. A brilliant one-volume account by a key figure, Lord Beaverbrook, is *Politicians and the War 1914–1916* (London, 1960), which has recently been supplemented and corrected by Cameron Hazelhurst, *Politicians at War* (New York, 1971). Churchill covered the balance of the war, during which he was an outsider, in volumes three and four of *The World Crisis* (New York, 1927). He wrote nothing about his time as a battalion commander in the trenches, but the subject is thoroughly covered in the third volume of the official biography.

Churchill's treatment of his four years in Lloyd George's post-war coalition is a curious book: *The World Crisis*, vol. 5, *The Aftermath* (New York, 1929). In it he discusses Russia, Ireland, and the Greco-Turkish war, as well as the framing of the Versailles treaty, but says nothing about the settlement of the Middle East and little about domestic politics. To put his activities there in perspective it is necessary to look at Martin Gilbert's fourth volume in the official biography and John Darwin's *Britain, Egypt and the Middle East: Imperial Policy in the Aftermath of War 1918–22* (London, 1981). The background is provided by Elie Kedourie, *England and the Middle East: The Destruction of the Ottoman Empire, 1914–21* (Totowa, NJ, 1977) and, in more detail, by Briton Cooper Busch, *Britain, India, and the Arabs, 1914–1921* (Berkeley, 1971).

An essential commentary on Churchill's rather evasive account of the Anglo-Irish war is Charles Townshend, *The British Campaign in Ireland 1919–1921* (New York, 1975). While Churchill never sought to conceal his role in the Allied intervention in Russia, Richard Ullman's three-volume *Anglo-Russian Relations, 1917–1921* (Princeton, NJ, 1961–72) makes it clear that, as in the case of the Dardanelles, the evolution of policy was a tangled and muddled affair in which Churchill was one influence among many and by no means always the key figure.

The domestic political background which, as usual, Churchill deals with sketchily is in Maurice Cowling, *The Impact of Labour, 1920–1924: The Beginning of Modern British Politics* (New York, 1971); and Kenneth O. Morgan, *Consensus and Disunity: The Lloyd George Coalition Government, 1918–1922* (New York, 1979). Beaverbrook, in his last book, *The Decline and Fall of Lloyd George* (New York, 1963), gave his own special perspective.

With the fall of the coalition we come to the years covered, with varying thoroughness and accuracy, in *The Gathering Storm* (Boston, 1948). Martin Gilbert's fifth volume in the official biography fully details precisely those areas—his years as Baldwin's chancellor and the campaign against the India Bill—Churchill skipped lightly over. There is a good assessment of the India controversy, in the context of Conservative politics, by Gillian Peele, "Revolt over India," in Chris Cook and Gillian Peele, eds., *The Politics of Reappraisal 1918–1939* (London, 1975). *Winston S. Churchill: His Complete Speeches, 1897–1963*, 8 vols., edited by Robert Rhodes James (New York, 1974) is also invaluable in recreating the man contemporaries saw, heard, and long distrusted.

The Gathering Storm concentrates on diplomacy and rearmament, recently two areas of intense scholarly activity. *Naval Policy*

Between the Wars by S. W. Roskill, 2 vols. (London, 1968–76); *British Air Policy Between the Wars 1918–1939* by H. Montgomery Hyde (London, 1976); and Brian Bond, *British Military Policy Between the Two World Wars* (New York, 1980) all demonstrate the flawed weapons that Britain wielded and the multiple pressures that until the late 1930s made it difficult to repair the weaknesses. N. H. Gibbs, *Grand Strategy*, vol. 1, *Rearmament Policy* (London, 1976), the last volume in the official series on British strategy during the Second World War, charts the slow and halting process of rearmament and the considerable degree of strategic confusion that accompanied it. Correlli Barnett, *The Collapse of British Power* (London, 1972) offers a provocative interpretation of the interwar years. The evidence marshaled by these authors demonstrates how much more difficult it would have been for the British to assert themselves against Germany than Churchill's indictment implies.

Churchill's version of what happened implanted itself so firmly that, when A. J. P. Taylor published his controversial *The Origins of the Second World War* (New York, 1962), Churchill's orthodoxy had to provide the starting point for his exercise in revisionism. While Churchill certainly blamed the war on Hitler, he did not do so as exclusively as Taylor claimed. *The Gathering Storm* is a sustained indictment of Baldwin and Chamberlain for failing to take forestalling action. Churchill tended to ignore many of the practical and political problems that stood in the way of rapid rearmament and an aggressive foreign policy, but he saw quite clearly that a key problem lay in the attitudes of Baldwin and, particularly, Chamberlain.

Much post-Taylor writing makes the same point. Christopher Thorne, *The Approach of War, 1938–39* (New York, 1968); Keith Middlemas, *The Strategy of Appeasement: The British Government and Germany, 1937–39* (Chicago, 1972); and Telford Taylor's monumental *Munich: The Price of Peace* (New York, 1979) emphasize the crucial role Chamberlain played in shaping British diplomatic and rearmament strategy. That Chamberlain's policy had domestic political goals as well is stressed in Maurice Cowling, *The Impact of Hitler: British Politics and British Policy, 1933–1940* (New York, 1975), a far more important corrective to *The Gathering Storm* than Taylor's. Neville Thompson, *The Anti-Appeasers: Conservative Opposition to Appeasement in the 1930's* (New York, 1971), is a useful reminder that none of Chamberlain's foes were as completely consistent as they subsequently claimed. It was the general perception that he had been opposed to appeasement, however, that put Churchill back in office and on the way to the premiership.

There are three important studies of Churchill during the "twilight war." Arthur J. Marder, "'Winston Is Back': Churchill at the Admiralty 1939–40," in Marder, *From the Dardanelles to Oran: Studies of the Royal Navy in War and Peace 1915–1940* (London, 1974); and Patrick Cosgrave, *Churchill at War*, vol. 1, *Alone 1939–1940* (London, 1974) both examine the minister and strategist. Paul Addison, *The Road to 1945: British Politics and the Second World War* (London, 1975) is an excellent account of the politics of the "phoney war," the emergence of Churchill as a consensus national leader, and the final crisis of May 1940.

Chapter Two
We Shall Never Surrender

Churchill's own six-volume memoir-history, *The Second World War* (Boston 1948–53), is obviously the primary source here, together with *Winston S. Churchill: His Complete Speeches, 1897–1963* edited by Robert Rhodes James (New York, 1974). Once again, however, it is necessary to look elsewhere for wartime politics; for example, to Paul Addison's study and Angus Calder, *The People's War: Britain, 1939–1945* (New York, 1969). Writing from a determinedly left-wing standpoint, Calder's ambivalence toward Churchill is a reflection of the uneasy wartime alliance that made Churchill a national leader while allowing Labour a preponderant voice in domestic affairs.

Churchill's administrative style is best examined in John Wheeler-Bennett, ed., *Action this Day: Working with Churchill* (New York, 1969), a collection of essays by six members of his wartime staff. Although written avowedly to dispute Lord Moran's *Churchill: The Struggle for Survival, 1940–1965* (Boston, 1966) in which Churchill's long-time physician (1941–65) portrays the prime minister as ailing, querulous, and often uncertain, these essays are nonetheless invaluable as a collective portrait of Churchill at work. Two additional books by one of the contributors, Sir John Colville, a former private secretary who has made himself one of the principal custodians of the Churchill legend, add a great many vignettes and anecdotes: *Footprints in Time* (London, 1976) and *The Churchillians* (New York, 1981).

Churchill's personal chief of staff, Sir Hastings Ismay, published an account, *The Memoirs of General Lord Ismay* (New York, 1960), which explains both Churchill's methods of work and even more the tact and discretion that made Ismay so successful.

Churchill's own account focuses on strategy and alliance politics. Patrick Cosgrave's study, which only goes up to December 1940, is a useful commentary on *Their Finest Hour*. His study is based on British archives but not on Churchill's own papers, which remain closed pending Martin Gilbert's completion of the official biography. *Grand Strategy*, vol. 2, *September 1939–June 1941* by J. R. M. Butler (London, 1957) is a bland and complacent official history that adds little to Churchill's own account. The two volumes published to date of the three-volume *British Intelligence in the Second World War: Its Influence on Strategy and Operations* by F. H. Hinsley et al. (London, 1979, 1981), despite their determinedly pedestrian style, are an indispensable complement and corrective not only to Churchill's own account but also to earlier official histories and the secondary works derived from them. Much more readable surveys are Ronald Lewin's *Ultra Goes to War* (New York, 1978); and Peter Calvocoressi's *Top Secret Ultra* (New York, 1980).

Assignment to Catastrophe, 2 vols. (London, 1954) by Sir Edward Spears, Churchill's liaison officer with Paul Reynaud, provides a vivid eyewitness account of the prime minister in action during the Battle of France. Arthur Marder, "Oran, 3 July 1940: Mistaken Judgement, Tragic Misunderstanding or Cruel Necessity?" in *From the Dardanelles to Oran* is the best account of the preemptive strike against the French fleet. Churchill does not discuss the strategic reappraisal that followed the fall of France, although Butler does. The best guide to the controversial bombing offensive is the remarkably frank official history by Charles Webster and Noble Frankland, *The Strategic Air Offensive Against Germany*, 4 vols. (London, 1961). There is also a shorter, more graphic narrative by Max Hastings, *Bomber Command* (London, 1979).

The European resistance and Britain's connection with it have been described as a "Serbonian bog," in which presumably unwary historians sink without a trace. A good starting point for this aspect of British strategy, which Churchill chose to say virtually nothing about in his memoirs, is David Stafford, *Britain and the European Resistance, 1940–1945: A Survey of the Special Operations Executive, with Documents* (London, 1980). A comparison with Henri Michel, *The Shadow War: European Resistance, 1939–1945* (New York, 1972) shows how different the resistance looks when viewed from occupied Europe rather than London.

Churchill's American policy can best be evaluated by comparing what he wrote with the detailed account of Anglo-American relations in 1940 contained in E. L. Woodward, *British Foreign Policy in the Second World War*, volume 1 (London, 1970) as well as with a recent American version of the same events in Robert Dallek, *Franklin D. Roosevelt and American Foreign Policy, 1932–1945* (New York, 1979). Pending a full edition of the Churchill-Roosevelt correspondence, the selection by Francis Loewenheim and Harold D. Langley, eds., *Roosevelt and Churchill: Their Secret Wartime Correspondence* (New York, 1975) is essential.

The central position on the Mediterranean, both in Churchill's wartime strategy and in postwar controversy, has been reflected in the amount of attention devoted to the question by historians. L. R. Pratt, *East of Malta, West of Suez: Britain's Mediterranean Crisis, 1936–1939* (New York, 1975) is a good survey of the origins of British wartime policy in this area. Michael Howard, *The Mediterranean Strategy in the Second World War* (New York, 1968) picks up the story in 1939 and covers the entire conflict, stressing Anglo-American arguments after 1941.

There is no comparable authoritative survey of British imperial policy in the Middle East, although an older account by George E. Kirk, *The Middle East in the War* (New York, 1952) still has considerable value. There are, however, two good surveys of the Palestine problem during the war. Michael Cohen, *Palestine: Retreat from the Mandate* (London, 1978) is a scholarly monograph, while Nicholas Bethell, *The Palestine Triangle: The Struggle for the Holy Land, 1935–48* (New York, 1979) is a more popular account. Both demonstrate how much out of joint with official thinking Churchill's pro-Zionist attitudes were. To assess the Wavell era in the Middle East, Churchill's policies, as well as General Sir Archibald Wavell's, have to be reexamined against the intelligence background provided by Ultra. Ronald Lewin has done this in *The Chief: Field Marshal Lord Wavell, Commander-in-Chief and Viceroy, 1939–1947* (New York, 1980), a study informed by sympathy for all the principals.

Churchill's oft-repeated criticism of the tactical handling of British troops is best assessed against both the background of prewar British military thought and detailed studies of the battles in the western desert. Barrie Pitt, *The Crucible of War: Western Desert 1941* (London, 1980) is a good introduction to the latter.

The crucial Balkan campaign of 1941 is examined by Charles Cruickshank, *Greece 1940–41* (London, 1976); and Martin van Creveld, *Hitler's Strategy, 1940–41: The Balkan Clue* (London, 1973). Geoffrey Warner, *Iraq and Syria 1941* (London, 1974) is an excellent study of a British crisis that may have been a great lost German opportunity. Another imperial crisis in the making is discussed in Raymond Callahan's *The Worst Disaster: The Fall of Singapore* (Newark, DE, 1977), while Churchill's impact on Indian policy is outlined in R. J. Moore, *Churchill, Cripps and India, 1939–1945* (New York, 1979).

Chapter Three
We Mean To Hold Our Own

Nearly all the books mentioned in the bibliographical note to the preceding chapter continue to illuminate this period. British strategy and Churchill's role in its formation during this period require, however, a careful analysis of the prime minister's relationships with Sir Alan Brooke. Sir Arthur Bryant took bits of Brooke's wartime diaries, added snippets from his postwar second thoughts, embedded the collage in his own florid prose, and produced the first sensational challenge to Churchill's account of events: *The Turn of the Tide* (New York, 1957), which takes the story to September 1943; his *Triumph in the West* (New York, 1959) covers the remainder of the war. The Bryant/Brooke version of the war upset Churchill and infuriated the distinguished American naval historian Samuel Eliot Morison who wrote *Strategy and Compromise* (Boston, 1958) to emphasize that there had been an American contribution to the shaping of alliance strategy. A more balanced view of Brooke's role and contribution is David Fraser, *Alanbrooke* (New York, 1982).

The desert war up to El Alamein has recently been examined in three new accounts: Barrie Pitt's *The Crucible of War: The Year of Alamein* (London, 1982), the second volume of his projected trilogy is, like its predecessor, well written, but for critical analysis the reader must turn to Shelford Bidwell and Dominic Graham, *Fire-Power: British Army Weapons and Theories of War 1904–1945* (London, 1982), a devastatingly critical book of great importance which, among other things, tends to validate Churchill's wartime position that there was a great deal wrong with the way British formations were commanded. Nigel Hamilton's *Monty: The Making of a General, 1887–1942* (New York, 1981), is the first installment of a massive official biography of the British commander whose fortunes came to be so closely intertwined with those of the prime minister. A good dispassionate account of the Sledgehammer controversy and the mounting of Torch is Keith Sainsbury, *The North African Landings 1942* (London, 1976).

On the Anglo-American controversies over the second front, in addition to the works by Howard and Morison already cited, there is a useful article by Richard M. Leighton, "Overlord Revisited," in *The American Historical Review* (July 1963). Australian war correspondent Chester Wilmot's *The Struggle for Europe* (New York, 1952) still has value not only for its clear narrative of the campaign in Northwest Europe from D-day to VE Day but also its argument—expansion of Russian power could have been contained if the Americans had been as prescient as Churchill—coming at the height, or depth, of the Cold War had an influence second only to that of Churchill himself. The latest entry in the second front controversy is John Grigg, *1943: The Victory that Never Was* (New York, 1980), a brilliantly constructed argument for a very shaky case. A succinct treatment of the convoluted Burma campaign and the prime minister's contribution to its unfolding is the present author's *Burma 1942-1945* (London, 1978).

The story of imperial policy during this stage of the war has become clearer with the publication of several important studies: Christopher Thorne's magisterial *Allies of a Kind: The United States, Britain, and the War Against Japan 1941-45* (London, 1978); and William Roger Louis's equally authoritative *Imperialism at Bay: The United States and the Decolonization of the British Empire, 1941-1945* (New York, 1978). Together they illustrate how deftly for a quarter of a century Churchill, by excising a major area of wartime policy from his memoirs, also removed it from the attention of historians.

On India, Moore's study is very summary after 1942, but Gower Rizvi's *Linlithgow and India: A Study of British Policy and the Political Impasse in India 1936-43* (London, 1978) provides important detail. Penderel Moon has edited Wavell's diary as viceroy, in *Wavell: The Viceroy's Journal* (New York, 1973), a crucial document for understanding how truly negative Churchill's Indian policy was. In many ways the best picture of India during Churchill's years of power is found in the four novels that make up Paul Scott's one-volume edition of *Raj Quartet* (New York, 1975).

On the Middle East the works cited in connection with the previous chapter are important for this period as well. Additional light is cast by Bernard Wasserstein, *Britain and the Jews of Europe* (London, 1979), in which Churchill's humanity shines through.

On the two novel approaches to weakening Germany—bombing and subversion—that Churchill consistently supported, coverage is uneven. Hastings is the best guide to the fortunes of Bomber Command in the second half of the war. In the Balkans, however, SOE has been the beneficiary of the unsealing of archives and memories in the last decade and the subject consequently of a number of important books that shed much light on the prime minister's role in this area. Elizabeth Barker, *British Policy in Southeast Europe in the Second World War* (London, 1976) is an important survey. Even more revealing is a collection of papers read at an Oxford seminar and printed, together with the discussion they evoked, in Phyllis Auty and Richard Clogg, eds., *British Policy Towards Wartime Resistance in Yugoslavia and Greece* (London, 1975). C. M. Woodhouse, SOE's principal agent in Greece, has written a careful historical account, *The Struggle for Greece 1941–1949* (London, 1976) and a frank personal memoir, *Something Ventured* (London, 1982). Finally, from another perspective, that of the romantic Left, Basil Davidson, whose wartime SOE service took him to the Balkans and Italy, has published *Special Operations Europe: Scenes from the Anti-Nazi War* (London, 1980). These works, plus the important but tediously presented material in volume three of E. L. Woodward, *British Foreign Policy in the Second World War* (London, 1971), make it abundantly clear that on key issues Churchill's decisions were absolutely crucial.

The question of the origins of the Cold War is as hotly debated as that of the timing of the second front; indeed, the two are commonly linked. Three recent treatments bear upon Churchill's role and act as an important commentary upon and corrective to his memoirs: John Wheeler-Bennett and Anthony Nicolls, *The Semblance of Peace: The Political Settlement After the Second World War* (New York, 1972); Roy Douglas, *From War to Cold War: 1942–1948* (New York, 1981); and Victor Rothwell, *Britain and the Cold War 1941–1947* (London, 1982).

The best accounts of domestic politics during this period continue to be those of Paul Addison and Angus Calder. That close but shrewd observer of the prime minister and the world of politics, Harold Nicolson, is indispensable for an understanding of Britain at war, in *The Diaries and Letters of Harold Nicolson*, vol. 2, *The War Years, 1939–1945*, edited by Nigel Nicolson (New York, 1967).

Chapter Four
Missing the War

After 1945 the student of Churchill's career loses the valuable thread of continuity provided by Churchill's own writings. The *Complete Speeches*, however, provides a considerable insight into his views and preoccupations during his last decade in politics. As Churchill's health erodes, Lord Moran's account becomes a major source, but it has to be read in conjunction with Sir John Colville's books and the symposium edited by John Wheeler-Bennett. Of Churchill's postwar colleagues, only Harold Macmillan's *Tides of Fortune* (London, 1979) is at all illuminating on this stage of Churchill's career. The history of Britain since 1945–and Churchill's place in it—is, in fact, still difficult to bring properly into focus, the stage where historians move from monographs to synthesis not yet having arrived. Alfred Havighurst provides an outline of events, and Arthur Marwick in *British Society Since 1945* (New York, 1982) furnishes an interesting interpretation, to which, incidentally, Churchill is quite peripheral.

The only major study that has addressed this period of Churchill's career is Anthony Seldon's massive *Churchill's Indian Summer: The Conservative Government 1951–1955* (London, 1981). Seldon has worked meticulously but without access to either most official records of the period or the Churchill papers, both of which are still closed. Although the opening of the archives and the completion of Martin Gilbert's official biography will doubtless alter the details, it is unlikely that the general picture of Churchill's last decade in politics will change substantially.

Index